SFP®

SCHIFFER FASHION PRESS

MADE
FOR
Walking

A Modest History of the Fashion Boot

andy
PEAKE

Designed by Danielle D. Farmer
Cover design by Danielle D. Farmer
Data points for infographics used in the book were sourced, compiled, and graphed by the author.
All uncredited images are by the author.

Type set in Bodoni/Goudy Old Style/Wendy LP/Avenir Lt Std

ISBN: 978-0-7643-5499-1
Printed in China

Published by Schiffer Fashion Press
An Imprint of Schiffer Publishing, Ltd.
4880 Lower Valley Road
Atglen, PA 19310
Phone: (610) 593-1777; Fax: (610) 593-2002
E-mail: Info@schifferbooks.com
Web: www.schifferbooks.com

For our complete selection of fine books on this and related subjects, please visit our website at www.schifferbooks.com. You may also write for a free catalog.

Schiffer Publishing's titles are available at special discounts for bulk purchases for sales promotions or premiums. Special editions, including personalized covers, corporate imprints, and excerpts, can be created in large quantities for special needs. For more information, contact the publisher.

We are always looking for people to write books on new and related subjects. If you have an idea for a book, please contact us at proposals@schifferbooks.com.

Other Schiffer and Schiffer Fashion Press Books on Related Subjects:

The Sweater: A History, Jane Merrill, Keren Ben-Horin & Gail DeMeyere, 978-0-7643-5261-4

She's Got Legs: A History of Hemlines and Fashion, Jane Merrill, Keren Ben-Horin, 978-0-7643-4952-2

Classic Beauty: The History of Makeup, 2nd edition, Gabriela Hernandez, 978-0-7643-5300-0

contents

MADE
FOR
Walking

The origins of this book stretch back more than twenty years, to a visit that I made to the Victoria and Albert (V&A) Museum, in London. There I saw, in an exhibit case devoted to footwear, what looked like a typical fashion boot from the 1970s. It was knee-length, with a 2″ heel, and was made from a glossy bronze shade of leather.[1] There was nothing especially remarkable about this boot except for the date on the exhibit label, which I at first believed was a mistake. There was no way that someone was wearing these boots in 1925.

Except that they were, as we'll see in the second chapter of this book. Fashion histories of the 1920s generally ignore the "Russian boot," as this style was known, and fashion historians in general have little to say about boots. "Popular in the sixties" is as much as one can hope for from most accounts of the twentieth century. It was frustration with this absence of information, as much as anything, that started me down the road that eventually led to this book.

Twenty years ago, that was a much harder path to follow. Today, the number of resources available online means that it's possible to work through newspapers and magazines from the past in ways that would have been unimaginable even a few years ago. It was the digitization of one of those resources, the archives of *Vogue*, that prompted me to start a blog called *Made for Walking* in 2013. A lot of the material from that blog has made its way into this book.

In writing this account, I realize how enormously indebted I am to the fashion writers of the past, who carefully recorded their thoughts on the fashion boot for their readership. Wherever possible, I've tried to let their own words tell the story, but in acknowledging the people who have helped with the project I particularly want to thank (in some cases, I fear, posthumously) Alison Adburgham, Raymonde Alexander, Iris Ashley, Mary Ann Crenshaw, Sandy Fawkes, Barbara Griggs, Phyllis Heathcote, Bernadine Morris, Enid Nemy, and Eugenia Sheppard.

A number of people took the time to comment on the blog, and from those comments came some interesting offline discussions that helped shape and inform the development of the book. I'd especially like to thank Bruce for his encyclopedic recall of the appearances of different styles of fashion boot in film and television over the past five decades and Dean for his thoughts on the evolution of the boot in the 1970s.

All histories are dependent on the support of librarians, and I've been fortunate to have been assisted by some great ones. Access to online resources was provided through the Yale University Library system, while Roger Fairman, Research and Development Librarian at the University of Worcester, and Jane Holt of the London College of Fashion helped with obtaining image permissions, as did Joanne Wilkinson of Freeman-Gratton Holdings, Patricia Perez for the V&A, and Robbi Siegel for the Metropolitan Museum of Art. Simon Hendy kindly gave permission to publish photos taken by his father.

Finally, it is the lot of occasional authors that much of their work takes place in time that should be spent with their families. I thank my long-suffering wife and daughter for their patience.

preface

WHY *Boots?*

In April 1967, *Vogue* published an editorial article titled "The Beautiful People in Boots." It was run without a by-line, and read more like a *Who's Who* of late-sixties society than a fashion article. Scattered across the eight pages were photographs of Italian nobility, Hollywood actresses, and Upper East Side royalty, in Paris, London, Rome, New York, and Madrid. The only thing that linked them was their reported enthusiasm for the boots they all wore. So we have Princess Ira Fürstenberg in long silver *fumée* boots, Catherine Deneuve in knee-length boots of brown-and-black stagskin, Leslie Caron in tall, lean butterscotch boots with tiny buckles on top, and Mrs. Francis Farr of New York in 22" Golo boots of the "softest pale-blue leather." *Condessas*, *Principessas*, and the wife of the American ambassador to Spain all feature.[2]

To understand why this piece is important, you need to appreciate that, for all its go-go-booted reputation, most of the everyday fashions of the sixties were pretty staid. In her 1964 style manual for women, French fashion maven Genevieve Antoine Dariaux was splendidly dismissive of boots, describing them as "a superfluous accessory, more at home in a college girl's closet than in the wardrobe of an elegant woman."[3] The *Vogue* piece is a walloping counterpoint to that view. Look, it says, the blue-blooded style mavens of Europe and America have all bought into the boot. Why not you?

The tone verges on the evangelical, and it's worth quoting the introduction in full, because it absolutely sums up what the fashion boot is all about.

chapter
1

There are few items that sit so solidly at the nexus of fashion and fetish as the modern fashion boot.
(Maria Svetlychnaja/Shutterstock.)

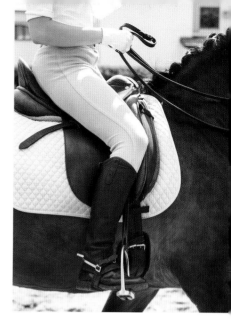

Why boots? Because they give the best proportions in the world. Because, taken top to toe, every woman looks approximately five-hundred times more dashing with boots than without. That's why boots. Why boots now. And why boots for a long, long time to come—every way, every day, every evening, everywhere.[4]

There are very few garments that sit as solidly at the nexus of fashion and fetish as the fashion boot. A woman in boots plays with our traditional ideas of gender, even when the style of boot is unreservedly feminine. Boots also straddle the line between utilitarian and stylish. The great battle of the 1950s and '60s, fought by designers like Beth Levine, was to shift boots into the realm of haute couture. That they succeeded is a measure of the utility of a good pair of boots; that it took so long reflects the tension of that gender paradox. Finally, the emergence of the boot as a fashion item for women is intimately linked with the cultural upheavals of the 1960s and '70s, the so-called youthquake and the upending of the traditional role of a woman as wife and mother. In boots and hot pants a woman could be both objectified and liberated, which was yet another paradox.

Before the early twentieth century, the only high boots worn by women were reserved for riding. They projected legs and hose against mud and water, as well as friction from the horse's flanks, but were impractical for any other purpose. (Katerina Bardyugova/ Shutterstock.)

IN THE BEGINNING

The *Oxford English Dictionary* defines a boot as "a covering for foot and lower part of the leg, usually of leather."[5] The *OED* definition then goes on to clarify that the boot is distinguished from a shoe by extending above the ankle, and that the original 1755 dictionary definition, courtesy of Samuel Johnson,[6] limited its use to horsemen. England's ultimate man of letters was not wrong; for centuries previously, men had been wearing high boots to ride; they protected feet against mud and water, and expensive hose, leggings, or trousers against the friction of the horse's flanks.

But the boot is much older than that—in fact, it is one of the oldest known forms of footwear. In the

Depictions of the Roman goddess Diana, like this statue from Lvov, Ukraine, often show her wearing a high, bootlike sandal, the *campagnus*, which was popular for hunting. (Dimitry Designs/Shutterstock.)

bottes à chaudron

A nineteenth-century engraving of Louis II de Bourbon, prince de Conde (1621-1686). He is shown wearing *bottes à chaudron*, a popular style of boot in the seventeenth century. The boot could be worn over the knee for riding or allowed to settle around the ankles for regular wear. *Chaudron* is French for "cauldron," a reference to the bucketlike appearance of the boot when not extended. (Marzolino/ Shutterstock.)

cave of La Marche, located in the Lussac-les-Châteaux area of western France, alongside depictions of lions and bears that have long vanished from this part of the world, there are painted images of human figures, dating back to 15,000 years before the current era (BCE), some of which are wearing what appear to be boots.[7] Assyrian sculptures dating from the ninth to the seventh centuries BCE depict tall boots worn by horsemen.[8] The ancient Greeks had laced boots called *endromides*,[9] while Roman generals wore the *campagnus*, a boot that exposed the top of the foot, which was trimmed with fur and often decorated with precious stones or pearls.[10] Depictions of the Roman goddess of the hunt, Diana, frequently show her in a short tunic and open-toed boots similar to the *campagnus*.[11]

In the Middle Ages, there were ankle boots, or *estivaux*, that were worn during summer; cloth boots with leather soles, reinforced by a wooden undersole or patten; and heuses, supple high-legged boots of leather that were first seen as early as the ninth century and were originally reserved for noblemen.[12] In the seventeenth century, boot wearing became more widespread—boots could be worn at the French court from 1608 onward, provided that the spur was covered by a piece of cloth to prevent its becoming entangled in women's dresses, and a new style of boot, called *bottes à etonnier* or *bottes à chaudron*, emerged; these could be pulled up over the knee for horseback riding or allowed to fall back around the calf for other occasions. Shorter, lighter boots with a wide cuff, called lazzarines, were very popular during the reign of Louis XIII of France.[13]

But these were boots for men. If you go back more than a couple of hundred years from today, women mostly stayed indoors. If they did go out, wealthy women traveled in carriages, sedan chairs, or other transport. Needing little protection for their feet, they tended to wear delicate shoes or slippers. Poorer women, who might have to work in the fields, would have clogs, rough shoes, or no shoes at all. The change came when wealthy women took up riding for recreational purposes. When they did, they simply co-opted the boots worn by men.

PANTOMIME and PRINCIPAL BOYS

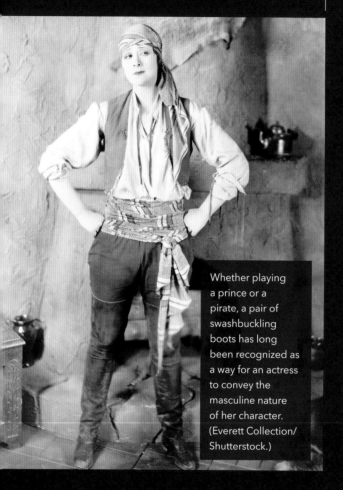

Whether playing a prince or a pirate, a pair of swashbuckling boots has long been recognized as a way for an actress to convey the masculine nature of her character. (Everett Collection/Shutterstock.)

As the unfortunate Joan of Arc could have testified, ultrahigh boots have a long pedigree, going back well into the Middle Ages. As doublet and hose became fashionable wear for men and full plate armor was superseded by lighter, reduced armoring, there was a need for additional protection for the legs of riders. Heavy leather boots that rose to midthigh were the answer.

Riding boots of this style were widespread in the seventeenth and eighteenth centuries and remained in common usage through the late nineteenth century. There's an oft-repeated story (probably apocryphal) that the terms "booty" and "bootlegging" arose from the practice of concealing hip flasks and other valuables in the legs of boots.[15]

Because of these racy historical associations, tall boots came to convey an image of potent, swaggering masculinity, conjuring up images of cavaliers, pirates, or musketeers. A women wearing boots like this was immediately playing fast and loose with gender roles, something both scandalous and a little exciting. Nowhere was this more evident than on the stage.

The years following the Restoration of the English monarchy, in the midseventeenth century, saw the first professional actresses appear in theaters. If this were not sensational enough, audiences were soon thrilled by the increasingly common sight of women wearing male clothes onstage.[16]

The purpose of these "breeches roles" was, undoubtedly, to titillate theatergoers by showing them a lot more of the actress than would normally be the case, a charge made by Elizabeth Howe in her history of the first English actresses.[17] But at the same time these cross-dressing roles subverted conventional gender roles by allowing women to imitate the roistering and sexually aggressive behavior of male Restoration rakes.[18]

The breeches role survives today in the form of the pantomime "principal boy," the term applied to an actress playing the role of the young, male hero of the play. Wearing thigh-high boots was a quick way of emphasizing her masculine character, while showing enough leg to keep adult male members of the audience engaged with the plot of *Cinderella or Dick Whittington*. So it's not surprising that, even today, fashion articles discussing the popularity of over-the-knee boots can rarely

To do so was not without its risks, at least in more superstitious times. One of the charges laid against Joan of Arc at her trial in 1431 was that she wore male dress, "a tunic, hosen, and long boots that went up to the waist."[14] The adoption of masculine dress was considered quite as shocking and subversive to the natural order of things as any accusation of witchcraft or heresy; Joan's long boots were enough to get her burned at the stake.

THE BOOT AS FETISH

There have been other times since the Middle Ages when boots have had what could be described as an image problem. In his landmark sex manual, *The Joy of Sex* (1972), Alex Comfort described boots as a "notorious turn-on, once the badge of the prostitute,[20] now considered straight wear," contrasting this with corsets, which had started out respectable and were now worn solely for pleasure.[21] Boots may have become mainstream fashion in the 1960s, but they retain that edge. Even as recently as the 1990s, when boots returned to mass popularity after a significant break, *The Guardian* was able to publish a piece discussing women's often baffled reactions to the male attention they received when wearing the new breed of tall, elegant boots. For a generation of women used to wearing skintight Lycra and thinking nothing of sunbathing topless, the idea that something as

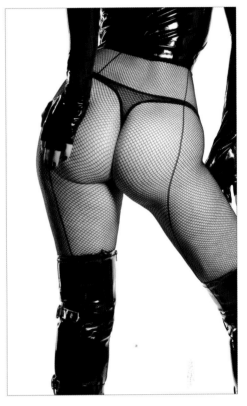

Shiny surfaces on boots or other clothing send out a "super-skin" signal that may be one reason for the enduring fetishistic appeal of women in boots. (Bruno Passigatti/ Shutterstock.)

unrevealing as a knee-length boot should still give so many men an almost illicit thrill was an unexpected source of amusement. "It's like having cleavage for your feet," said one young woman.[22]

There are two schools of thought as to why this should be so, which could be loosely termed "sensory" and "societal." The sensory hypothesis, which was a favorite of Comfort (and others), is that our brains are attuned to react sexually to various cues of shape, texture, and scent that are inherent in the skin of our partners. Boots, especially ones made from natural materials like leather, send out a "super-skin" signal, as Comfort termed it. Boots emphasize the shape of the leg and draw attention to erogenous areas like the ankle, the back of the knee, or (in very tall boots) the thigh. Shiny, polished surfaces and the scent of leather all play a role. Interviewed by *The Guardian* in 1995, Glenn Wilson of London's Institute of Psychiatry put the popularity of boots down to sexual imprinting, which happens around the age of three. "At that age the infant is seeing the mother from the point of view of her legs . . . you don't get many hat fetishists."[23]

The societal hypothesis, which is favored by fashion historians like Valerie Steele,[24] proposes that it's all about turning our conventions of womanhood on their heads. "The symbolic power of boots runs very deep in our culture," Julia Thrift wrote in *The Guardian*. "From Puss-in-Boots, to jack boots, to kinky boots, it is clear that of all footwear, the boot is loaded with connotations which we pick up from a very early age." As Jack Zipes, a professor of German folklore at the University of Minnesota, interviewed by Thrift, pointed out, Puss-in-Boots gains an audience with the king, a crucial part of the fairy tale, only because he has the boots. The cat knows this when he asks for the boots; they will empower him.[25]

Boots are an essentially masculine style of clothing that, as we'll see, were co-opted by designers as a reaction against traditional femininity as exemplified by the "New Look" of the postwar age. The fashion boot sends a mixed signal of strength and sexiness. On a microlevel, it's the same mixed signal that underlies the dominatrix, only translated into day-to-day wear. As far back as the nineteenth century, there was an underground market for bespoke, tailored boots; tightly laced, rising to the thighs, and with heels much higher than conventional boots of the period, these were unmistakably fetish objects. Even when boots for women—riding boots, Russian boots, and the like—began to become mainstream items in the early twentieth century, this underground market persisted. John Willie's *Bizarre* magazine, published from 1946 to 1959,[26] regularly featured these specialist products of shoemakers, at a time when fashion boots for women were on the verge of respectability.

Whether women wearing the sorts of boots that men find sexy are empowered by them, or quite the reverse, was—as *The Guardian* reported in 1995—a matter of debate. Nonetheless, the emergence of a generation of women who see no intrinsic conflict between feminism and glamor has shifted the parameters. Interviewed by the paper, Michelle Olley, features editor of the fetish magazine *Skin 2*, noted that far more single women were now buying clothing that would previously have been regarded as fetishistic—including stiletto-heeled thigh boots—for themselves. "A lot of them are being worn by women who are in control already . . . we had to get to the point where women were more confident and had a sense of their own power."[27]

Popular culture has embraced the idea of the boot as sex object, while for the most part avoiding tarnishing the whole concept with this association. As we'll see, Honor Blackman's adoption of boots and leather in the popular sixties TV show *The Avengers* (1962-64), which looks quite tame today, was seen as extremely risqué for the time; the edginess of the costumes was embraced by the creators of the show. Blackman's character, who used martial arts moves to defeat the bad guys, was a radical departure from the traditional female role on TV, and the boots were portrayed as an integral part of her "tough girl" look.

THE BOOT AS FASHION

The issue of integration is one reason that boots have been able to capitalize on, rather than be overwhelmed by, that sense of edginess. Perhaps more than any other category of accessory, and certainly more than any type of shoe, boots can be an integral part of an outfit rather than simply a complement for one. That expanse of material covering the leg can be used as a canvas by a designer, and some of the most creative designers of the modern era—Yves Saint Laurent, André Courréges, Mary Quant, Pierre Cardin, Karl Lagerfeld, Gianni Versace, Roberto Cavalli, and Alexander McQueen, to name just a few—have recognized and embraced this.

The idea that boots could be an integral part of a woman's outfit is often credited to Beth Levine,[28] and Levine deserves enormous credit for the modern vision of the fashion boot, but from their first appearance in the years before World War I, boots have always been used to draw attention to women's outfits. The brightly colored morocco leathers of Denise Poiret's boots caused a stir in prewar New York,[29] much as the ornate stitching and fur trim of the so-called Russian boots did in the Roaring Twenties. Modern materials like vinyl and plastic gave the boots of the mid- to late sixties a space-age sheen that was in keeping with the technocentric *zeitgeist* of their time, while suede, velvet, and brocade boots brought a whiff of Renaissance glamor to the end of the eighties.

Jennifer Lopez arriving for the Capital Summertime Ball at Wembley Stadium, London, 2011. The boots provide an additional expanse of material that can be used to complement or contrast with the rest of the outfit—in this case matching the snakeskin material of her dress. (Steve Vas/Featureflash Photo Agency/ Shutterstock.)

The effect of a pair of boots on an outfit is not limited to color or pattern. Boots have a profound influence on silhouette. Heavy boots add weight to the lower half of an outfit, working well with fuller skirts. By contrast, lightweight ankle boots or bootees work better with a broad-shouldered outfit, a fact that designers of the 1980s were well aware of. Tight-fitting thigh-length, or even hip-high boots were a key part of the sleek, space-age looks of Cardin in the late 1960s, while the modern trend known as "lampshading" pairs a voluminous, loose-fitting sweater with tall, slender boots (see Chapter 10).

And it's not just about the look, either. Boots, as Rachelle Bergstein notes in her 2012 history of twentieth-century feminine footwear, *Women from the Ankle Down*,[30] are closely associated with a woman's inherent capability. If high heels are the mark of the *femme fatale*, who uses her feminine wiles to get what she wants,[31] then boots are the badge of the Valkyrie or the Amazon. Boots, in Bergstein's view, symbolize the intersection of masculine strength and feminine compassion[32] and of physical strength and moral courage, as well as the ability to rise to a challenge and look good doing it. Small wonder that from Wonder Woman to Supergirl, or from Batgirl to Black Widow, boots have been the badge of the female superhero (see sidebar). They are also, in their own way, associated with the emerging freedom of women during the sixties. "Boots moved into prominence the same time The Pill did," Beth Levine wrote. "Both were symbols of a woman's new freedom and emancipation."[33]

Despite all this, for the most part fashion histories spend little time on the boot. Fashion historians have a limited amount of source material to draw on. Most of it reflects the dress tastes of the wealthy and powerful, because they are the people who make history. And there is a compelling need to generalize: "In this decade, people mostly wore these types of clothes." The history of the boot is rooted in a mass of misconceptions and oversimplifications. As we'll see in the next chapter, there is a spectacular history of fashion boots in the 1920s that is mostly ignored by costume histories because—being largely populist—it doesn't feature in the major fashion journals of the time. You can track it only via newspapers and the trade reports of that time.

Later decades can be just as confusing. The conventional view of the 1960s as an *Austin Powers* era of miniskirted dolly birds in go-go boots doesn't actually match up with the reality. As Dominic Sandbrook points out in *White Heat*, his excellent history of 1960s Britain, if you were commuting on the bus or tube in 1966 most of your fellow passengers would be quite soberly dressed, in clothes that would not have looked out of place ten years earlier.[41] There's also ample evidence that despite the plethora of boots in late-sixties and early-seventies editions of *Vogue*, they were regarded with a certain amount of suspicion by many people. In a *New York Times* report from 1968, 75 percent of office managers surveyed said they wouldn't want their female employees wearing boots to work.[42]

THE POPULAR BOOT

So how does a history like this one track the popularity of the boot? Modern-day measures of interest are relatively easy to come by. For example, if you use the online service called Google Trends, which tracks the number of times a particular word or expression is searched for over time, you find that, unsurprisingly, searches for the word "boots" follow a regular cyclical pattern, peaking each year in the fall and winter.[43]

But searching for the specific expression "over-the-knee boot" reveals an interesting variation on this: a dramatic surge in interest, beginning suddenly in 2009, cresting dramatically in 2011, before dropping to lower but still impressive levels in 2012. This public interest was driven by media coverage, which in turn was driven by the dramatic resurgence of very tall boot styles on the catwalk in the latter

From the very moment of her birth, in 1941, Wonder Woman wore boots. At a time when public concern over the celebration of violence, and especially sexualized violence, in comic books was on the rise, the launch of a female superhero was the tactic devised by her creator, William Moulton Marston, to fend off the "comics' worst offense . . . their blood-curdling masculinity." With the backstory of her Amazonian past, where women were kept in chains by men until they broke free and escaped, Marston was creating a parable of the growing power of women—one which, in the case of the Amazons, was both physical and mental. The fact that she was fighting feminism in a golden tiara, red bustier, blue underpants, and knee-high, red leather boots was seen as liberating rather than exploitative—even if, in the words of Jill Lepore, the David Woods Kemper '41 Professor of American History at Harvard University, she was "a little slinky; she was very kinky."[34]

Boots imply power, so it's perhaps not surprising that booted heroines abound in comic books, from Batgirl and the Black Cat to Supergirl and Wonder Woman and including film outings for characters like *Barbarella* (1968), *Catwoman* (1992), and even Pamela Anderson's execrable version of *Barb Wire* (1996). As Lepore noted, there is certainly an element of kink in this, as will be obvious to anyone who has seen Michelle Pfeiffer's incarnation of Catwoman straddling Batman or Ann Hathaway's more recent interpretation pinning a bad guy's hand to the wall with the dagger-like, weaponized heel[35] of her thigh

more serious debate has arisen about the role of superheroines, especially given the rapidly increasing number of young girls and women who are fans of comic books. The appearance of the earlier generation of female characters, both heroes and villains, was intended to appeal to a male readership; this has raised well-founded concerns that their costumes are intended to titillate and objectify. Today, women readers are looking to emphasize other aspects of the characters—strength, courage, intelligence—and costumes are being modified to tone down some of the more obviously sexual connotations.[38]

Not that this means the end of the boot as an element of our heroines' costumes. As already noted, the paradox of the fashion boot is its capacity to both objectify and empower the woman who wears it. One of the newer generations of fantasy female heroines is Yara Greyjoy, a sexually fluid pirate captain from the award-winning HBO series *Game of Thrones*. Greyjoy captains a fleet of ships, leads her men in battle, and wears a battered leather outfit of breastplate, coat, and breeches that is suited to weathering a

years of the first decade of the Millennium, a phenomenon that we will return to in the last chapter of this volume.

Thinking in terms of numbers has advantages, even in a study of fashion history. Quantifying an issue can provide support for a qualitative opinion or help reveal patterns that you might otherwise miss. Currently Google Trends can take you back only about ten years, but worldwide there is a rapidly growing digital archive of publications, from fashion journals like *Vogue* and *L'Officiel* through weekly magazines like *Australian Women's Weekly*, and daily newspapers such as the *New York Times*, *Washington Post*, *Guardian*, *Daily Mail*, and *Toronto Star*, to name just a few. And increasingly, these archival services come with tools for search and analysis.[44]

If you assume that the number of times the word "boot" (or its non-English-language equivalents) appears in press is a measure of popular interest,[45] then searching for that term across these publications reveals a pattern that is remarkably consistent. A dramatic peak in references to boots spans the late 1960s and early 1970s, which in turn forms part of one of two extended periods of frequent references—the first from the early sixties to the early seventies, the second from the mid-nineties through today. There are also significant troughs around 1973-74, 1979-80, and 1984-87, when references to boots are far less common. In subsequent chapters we'll delve into exactly what these articles are saying and what they tell us about the history of the fashion boot.

THE SEAMIER SIDE of BOOTS

and WHAT WE CAN LEARN FROM IT

Fashion boots clearly have both a fetishistic aspect and an association with the darker side of sexuality. From images of booted prostitutes in Weimar-era Germany[46] to Anaïs Nin's literary depictions of French demimondaines in 1930s Paris[47] to the fetish photography of the 1940s and '50s, cinematic depictions of sex workers in movies like *Klute* (1972), *Pretty Woman* (1990), *Showgirls* (1995), and *Striptease* (1996), and today's ubiquitous pinup and pornographic imagery, boots have a long and undistinguished history as an emblem of commercial sex that has colored—and in some cases overshadowed—their status as a pure fashion item.

When I first started planning this book I was reluctant to delve too deeply into what seemed, at best, a distraction. But there was one obvious crossover with mainstream fashion history, and that was the frequency with which boots appear in what are euphemistically known as "men's magazines" and the extent to which this might mirror the patterns seen in fashion magazines and newspapers. Going back to the postwar years, there have always been publications like John Willie's *Bizarre* that have focused on boots as a fetish object;[48] these were replaced in the 1960s by a stable of limited-circulation publications, many of which

■ CONTINUED ON PAGE 18

Given their associations, it's not surprising that boots frequently appear as costume elements for pinup photography. (Syda Productions/ Shutterstock.)

were produced by a British company, Town and County Publications,[49] that catered to those with interests in stockings, high heels, and boots.

These sorts of publications are not really comparable to mainstream news or fashion magazines, because their content is necessarily slanted toward those who already have a fetish. What is more interesting is the frequency with which boots turn up in pictorials where there is no particular reason, *per se,* for them to be there. To study this, I turned to probably the two best-known magazines in this genre, *Playboy and Penthouse.* For various practical reasons, I limited myself to the years 1970-97. Also, rather than try to find every pictorial from the magazines, I focused on the models who were the centerfolds for each issue: "Playmates" *(Playboy)* or "Pets" *(Penthouse)* of the Month. I dutifully waded through 566 *photosets* (256 *Penthouse, 310 Playboy*).[50]

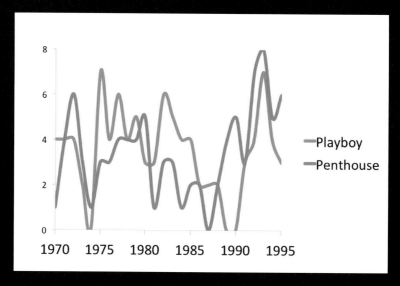

The number of booted centerfold pinups that appear in the magazines *Penthouse* and *Playboy* during the years 1970 to 2006.

The end results were quite surprising. In both *Playboy* and *Penthouse,* the occurrences of boots mirror those seen in the fashion magazines *Vogue* and *L'Officiel.* A peak at the very beginning of the 1970s is followed by a steep drop in 1972-74, followed by a second peak in the mid- to late '70s; then a drop through the '80s and a steep climb back to even greater heights in the '90s. There are some slight differences; *Playboy* seems to sustain its interest in booted pinups well into the 1980s, for example. But in general, if the magazines are reflective of the tastes of their male readership, then those tastes are reflective of fashion in general.

Of course, there are other reasons that sex workers wear boots. In her 1993 autobiography *Try Everything Once Except Incest and Morris Dancing, the former stripper and pinup model* Linzi Drew discusses a little-known condition called "stripper's kneecap"—namely, the blackened knees that result from "floorwork" during the act. Afflicted by this at the beginning of her career, during the late seventies, Drew took to performing in thigh-length boots.[51] Knees saved, problem solved.

The Evolving Boot

People often loosely talk about things "evolving," as a shorthand for change. Fashion is no exception. But can an inanimate object like a boot really evolve in the same way that a species of animal or plant evolves, changing over time in response to external factors? The answer is a qualified "yes." People have mapped evolutionary progressions in a number of nonorganic objects, including machine parts and musical instruments.[52]

Of course, in biological entities like animals, things such as eye color and hair color are controlled by genes, sequences of DNA that are passed down from ancestor to descendant. But there is an argument that equivalent, nonbiological agents control how ideas, including fashion, spread through society. These agents are called memes.

Today, the term "meme" tends to be attached to things like a humorous image, a video, or a piece of text that is copied and spread rapidly by Internet users.[53] But it has a more serious meaning, which was first articulated as a concept by the evolutionary biologist Richard Dawkins in his 1976 masterwork, *The Selfish Gene*[54]: an idea, behavior, or style that spreads from person to person within a culture.[55]

Mapping the occurrence of features associated with particular genes—or characters, as biologists call them—across different species is one way of charting the history of evolution (see sidebar for an example of this). The relationships between the species can be represented as an evolutionary "tree"—a diagram rather like a family tree that shows which species share a common ancestor. As it turns out, boots also have characters; platform soles, stacked heels, fitted legs, and shaft height are all examples of these. The existence of memes is what lets us use these characters to build meaningful evolutionary trees of inanimate objects like women's fashion boots.

Instead of showing how the popularity of boots changes over time, mapping characters shows how the styles of the boots themselves change, and how those changes are related to each other. The result, if you do this, is a "family tree" of boots.

The advantage of the tree is that it lays bare some of the critical moments in the history of the boot: the point when they were first recognized as shoes, the fundamental split between casual and dress boots that took place in the 1970s, and the way in which apparently similar styles, such as the over-the-knee boots of the 1960s, 1970s, 1980s, and 2000s, actually emerged from very different design ancestors. All of these events are explored in more detail in subsequent chapters.

☐ "FAMILY TREE" OF BOOTS, SHOWN ON FOLLOWING PAGE

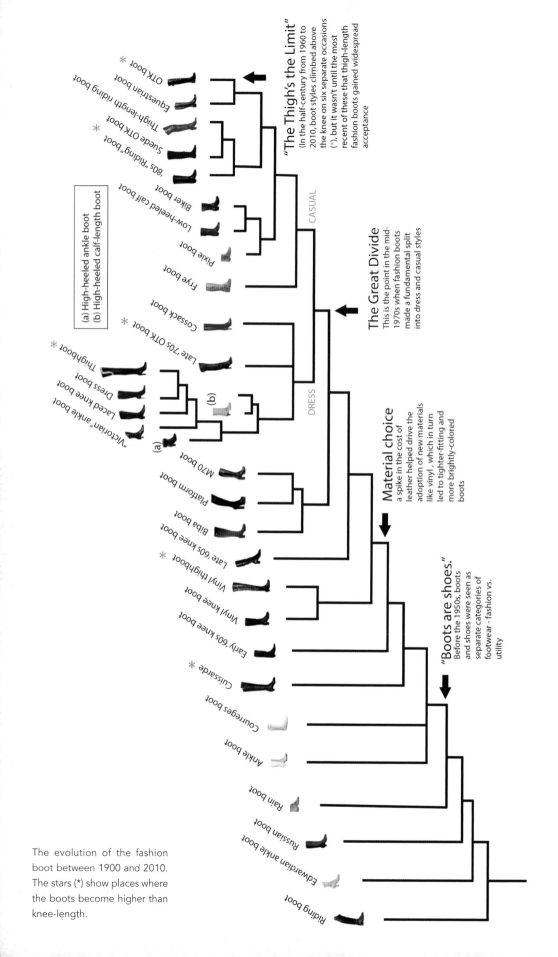

"The Thigh's the Limit"
(In the half-century from 1960 to 2010, boot styles climbed above the knee on six separate occasions (*), but it wasn't until the most recent of these that thigh-length fashion boots gained widespread acceptance

OTK boot *
Equestrian boot
Thigh-length riding boot
Suede OTK boot *
'80s "Riding" boot
Biker boot
Low-heeled calf boot
Pixie boot
Frye boot
Cossack boot
Late '70s OTK boot *
Thighboot *
Dress boot
Laced knee boot
"Victorian" ankle boot
M70 boot
Platform boot
Biba boot
Late '60s knee boot
Vinyl thighboot *
Vinyl knee boot
Early '60s knee boot
Cuissarde *
Courrèges boot
Ankle boot
Rain boot
Russian boot
Edwardian ankle boot
Riding boot

(a) High-heeled ankle boot
(b) High-heeled calf-length boot

CASUAL

DRESS

(a)

(b)

The Great Divide
This is the point in the mid-1970s when fashion boots made a fundamental split into dress and casual styles

Material choice
a spike in the cost of leather helped drive the adoption of new materials like vinyl, which in turn led to tighter-fitting and more brightly-colored boots

"Boots are shoes."
Before the 1950s, boots and shoes were seen as separate categories of footwear - fashion vs. utility

The evolution of the fashion boot between 1900 and 2010. The stars (*) show places where the boots become higher than knee-length.

Let's imagine that we have three unusual people called Sara, Sue, and Sam. All three of them have red eyes, but Sue and Sam also have blue hair.

Observing the distribution of these two characters lets us make some statements about how the three girls might be related. They all have red eyes, but the fact that only Sue and Sam have blue hair suggests that they might be more closely related to each other than they are to Sara. We can illustrate this by drawing a tree.

Evolutionary biologists take this one stage further. They would say that this distribution came about because Sue and Sam share a common ancestor who also had blue hair. Sara does not share this common ancestor, but at some point she, Sue, and Sam did have a common ancestor with red eyes.

Simple, right? Well not entirely. By now you may have started to think there are other scenarios that could explain this distribution of characters. For example, Sara, Sue, and Sam could share a common ancestor with red eyes *and* blue hair, and then Sara's ancestors could have developed a different hair color at some time. In this case, Sara could be more closely related to either Sue or Sam than Sue and Sam are related to each other, or our original tree could still be true. There would be no way to distinguish between these options.

HOW TO *Grow* A TREE

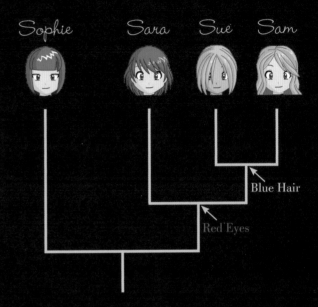

How evolutionary tree diagrams are built. Sue and Sam are more closely related to each other than they are to Sara and Sophie, as shown by their sharing blue hair. Sara is more closely related to the two blue-haired girls than she is to Sophie, because all three girls share red eyes. The same process can be used for characteristics of boots, such as heel height, leg length, or the shape of the toe.

Biologists get around this in various ways. An obvious solution is to use more than one character. That might allow us to differentiate between three equally likely options like the situation just described. Or we could go to another person, more distantly related than the three people we're interested in, and see if they have blue hair; this would tell us whether it was more likely that Sara's ancestors had lost their blue hair or had never had blue hair in the first place. In this example, our more distant relative, Sophie, has brown hair and brown eyes. So our original tree is most likely to be correct.

And, as it happens, you can do the same thing with boots. Instead of red hair or blue eyes, imagine that we're talking about high heels, a fitted leg, or a round toe. In this case, it's not genes that are the mechanism of transfer, but memes–those ideas and styles that spread from person to person, by communication and imitation.

A Unifying Theory of the Boot

Everyone likes a unifying theory—evolution by means of natural selection, or relativity, or quantum field theory. There's something very satisfying about wrapping up a bunch of observations under the umbrella of a simple and elegant theoretical framework.

The development of the fashion boot took a historically masculine item of footwear—and quite an aggressively masculine one, at that—and co-opted it as a high-fashion item for women. The fashion boot has carried that male heritage with it for well over fifty years—longer, if you include the Russian boots of the 1920s.

At the same time, the boot has certain characteristics that make it well suited to women's fashion. It can emphasize certain aspects—the length and shape of the legs, for example—while covering other, less desirable features (such as excessive exposure of skin or unfortunate ankles). It can be used to heighten a slim-line clothing silhouette or to supply weight and balance to fuller fabrics. And it provides a blank canvas on which designers can play with color, texture, and pattern.

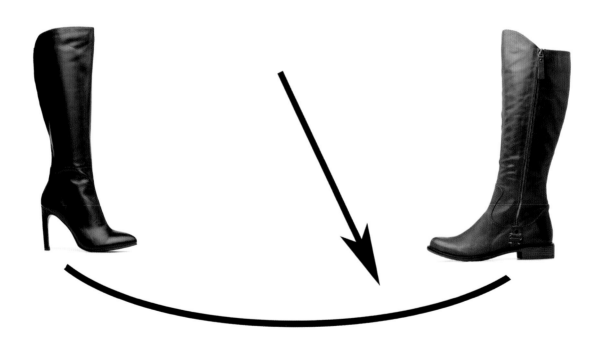

Changes in the popularity of women's fashion boots over time can be visualized as a pendulum that swings between "feminine" and "masculine" extremes.

These dual aspects of the boot—masculine or feminine, practical or fashionable, the pantomime principal boy or the sex kitten—form two extremes, and prevailing fashion swings like a pendulum from one to the other and back again. At one end is the "male" boot—sturdy, low-heeled, straight-legged, loose-fitting. At the other end is its "female" counterpart—lightweight, high-heeled, close-fitting.

This is not to say that the prevailing taste is always one way or another. The styles can coexist, even within the same wardrobe. But it does affect how the boot is fitted into an outfit, whether on the runway or in real life. As we'll see in a future chapter, this was the breakthrough that Beth Levine made in the mid-1950s, when she recognized that boots could be designed as part of an outfit rather than something that was added to cope with specific circumstances (rain, snow, etc.). So the feminine boot is paired with skirts and dresses, in the office or for a night on the town; the masculine boot with pants or leggings, for taking the kids to school or for a weekend in the country.

As we'll discover, when the fashion boot first achieved widespread appeal, in the early 1960s, it was unashamedly masculine. But as the decade wore on, new materials enabled a closer fit and brighter colors; boots became associated with the miniskirt, the body-hugging silhouettes of space-age designs, and later with hot pants and Victorian retro fashions.

The pendulum had swung toward femininity, and it stayed there through the first half of the seventies. But later in the decade, it began to swing back. Even before the start of the sixties, heels had become heavier, as the kitten heels of the sixties gave way to stacked heels. Then, by the late seventies, the close-fitting boot morphed into a looser, straighter leg. Heel height dropped, and by the middle of the 1980s the boot was once again loose-fitting and low-heeled. Masculinity had prevailed.

This remained the situation until the middle part of the nineties, when the pendulum swung back again. The boots of the Millennium years were some of the most aggressively feminine yet seen—spike-heeled, pointy-toed, and glove-tight. Leggings and heavy, woolen tights were ditched in favor of bare legs and higher hemlines. But by the second half of the following decade, pants were being tucked into boots, and with that came straighter, roomier shafts, lower heels, and a rediscovered enthusiasm for rugged boots like those from the American company Frye. And that takes us to the present day.

Certainly, there were high-heeled boots in the eighties, and low-heeled boots in the seventies, and all styles coexist today, but the key issue is one of balance. There are plenty of high-heeled boots around today, but they are greatly outnumbered by low-heeled styles. And sometimes one type of boot may show primarily feminine tendencies, as with the faux-Victorian ankle boots of the late eighties and early nineties, but the balance across all styles of boots can still be predominantly masculine, as it was in the eighties.

You may also be wondering how this relatively simple model relates to the complex tree of interrelationships between different boot styles that we just looked at. The best way of explaining this is to say that the tree is the "how," while the pendulum is the "why." The tree shows how the back-and-forth swings of fashion cause boot styles to change over time. Together, the pendulum and the tree chart the history of the boot that we're about to explore.

WHAT *is a* FASHION BOOT?

A fashion boot is a boot worn primarily for reasons of style or fashion. This is an important distinction. There are many styles of boot—hiking boots, riding boots, and rain boots, to name just a few—and many of them are quite fashionable. But that doesn't make them fashion boots.

Take, for example, the rain boots shown here. They are not at all like a classic Wellington boot. They have a high heel and a decorative feature at the top of the shaft that mimics the strap-and-buckle accent seen on many contemporary fashion boots. But their main function is as waterproof rainwear. It's hard to imagine them being worn for any other reason.

This is an important distinction, because it references a battle that marked the very earliest emergence of modern fashion boots in the 1950s. At the time, footwear manufacturers drew a very firm line between "shoes," which could be fashionable, and "boots," which had a purpose, usually protective. The major breakthrough, as we'll see, was when designers like Beth Levine managed to persuade manufacturers that there were occasions when boots could be shoes.

This rain boot shares a number of features with fashion boots, including a high heel and various decorative aspects. At the same time, it is clearly utilitarian in a way that fashion boots are not.

MADAM POIRET'S *Boots*

Paul Poiret, c. 1913. A visionary designer, Poiret was famed for liberating women from the restrictive fashions of the Victorian era. (Library of Congress, Prints & Photographs Division, LC-USZ62-100840.)

The history of the modern fashion boot really begins with a man named Paul Poiret. Despite his importance to this story, you could argue that the boot was one of the least of Poiret's accomplishments, because he is perhaps the most remarkable man in the history of Western fashion. Poiret was the critical figure in the transformation of women's clothing from the starched, buttoned-up styles of the Victorian and Edwardian eras to the much less restrictive styles of the twentieth century and today. It is because of Poiret, among others, that today's women are no longer required to truss themselves up in corsets. They have a lot to thank him for.

Poiret was born in Paris in 1879, the son of a cloth merchant.[56] Apprenticed to an umbrella maker as a child, he collected leftover scraps of silk from the umbrellas and used them to create outfits of his own design for a doll that his sister had given him. As a young man, he sold sketches of his outfits to some of

chapter
2

A Russian boot, c. 1925. Note the hourglass-shaped Louis heel and decorative stitching. (With kind permission of the University of the Arts London, London College of Fashion Archives.)

the leading couturiers of the day, and by the turn of the century he had landed himself a position as a dress designer for one of the major fashion houses in Paris. Unfortunately, the modernity of his designs, which were loose-fitting patterns created specifically for a slim, uncorseted figure, won him few admirers among their staid clientele,[57] and by 1903 he had set up in business for himself.

In 1905, Poiret married Denise Boulet. She came from the provinces and was, by the standards of the time, unfashionably tall and slender. Poiret's friends were horrified. "All those who have admired her since I made her my wife would certainly not have chosen her in the state in which I found her," Poiret wrote a quarter century after they met. "But I had a designer's eye, and I saw her hidden graces. . . . She was to become one of the queens of Paris."[58] Denise Poiret was her husband's muse, mannequin, and the mother of their five children. She was prepared to wear his most outrageous fashions; he dressed her up as a slave girl in a lampshade tunic, harem pants, and a turban for one ball in 1912, and as the Queen of Sheba in an outfit that exposed her leg from ankle to hip. Even in Belle Époque Paris, she was considered shocking.

In 1911, Poiret made a trip to Russia, his first international tour. He stayed in Moscow and Saint Petersburg, and his fashion shows were a huge success in both cities, attracting the local nobility and patrons of the arts. Russia made a great impression on Poiret, and, inspired by what he saw there, he created several collections with names like Samovar and Petrushka. In 1913, when the couple made a visit to America, Denise wore one of Paul's Russian-themed garments, named Moscovite,[59] which is where the Poirets' story merges with ours.

There is a single contemporary photograph of Denise Poiret wearing the Moscovite outfit. She stands in a door frame, leaning on the jamb with one hand while, rather coyly, using the other to lift the hem of her long skirt to midcalf, revealing a pair of loose-fitting leather boots. The boots were not incidental to the outfit. They were a key element of it, designed by Poiret as part of its overall Russian look. He was mimicking the *valenki*, a flat-heeled, wide-topped, knee-length boot that was widely worn in Russia. And he caused a sensation, in New York and in Paris.

Denise Poiret, 1913. This outfit, known as "Moscovite," was designed by Poiret to reflect the peasant clothing that he saw on his visit to Russia. The tall boots, revealed by Denise's lifting of her skirt hem, were an integral part of the outfit. (Library of Congress, Prints & Photographs Division, LC-USZ62-56754.)

BOOTS OF MOROCCO LEATHER

To understand why Denise Poiret's boots generated such a stir, we have to take a step back and look at what most women were wearing on their feet at the turn of the twentieth century—the prehistory of the fashion boot, if you like. Boots for women were not uncommon; in fact, it was quite the opposite. The nineteenth century had seen a massive growth in urbanization. In England, for example, the proportion of the population living in cities rocketed from 17 percent in 1801 to 72 percent in 1891.[60] These new metropolitan areas, with their dense populations of humans and draft animals, coal smoke and garbage, presented new challenges underfoot for anyone venturing out into the streets.

A pair of women's button boots, typical of the early twentieth century. Restrictive and quite fiddly to put on and remove, it was these sorts of boots that Paul Poiret sought to replace with his easy-on, easy-off, Russian-style design. (Eurobanks/ Shutterstock.)

Over the course of the nineteenth century, more and more of those people were women. An increasing number of women in Western countries were taking jobs in factories; working as hawkers of produce, flowers, and other market goods; and doing piecework such as weaving, embroidery, and winding wool or silk.[61] For these people, sturdy, protective footwear was a must. As a result, there was a tremendous growth in the popularity of boots for women. For the most part, these were ankle or calf length, tight-fitting, and secured by laces or tiny buttons. Their appeal was not limited to the working classes, and from the 1860s onward boots were by far the most common style of footwear worn outside the home.[62]

They were also tight, restrictive, and fiddly to put on and take off, not unlike the corsets, bodices, and other restrictive clothing that were the targets of Poiret's new designs. So Denise Poiret's boots—made from soft leather, comfortable, and easy to pull on and off—can be seen as an element of Paul Poiret's wider fashion philosophy. They are part of the same movement that led to the turbans, harem pants, and flapper dresses that were to come into fashion in the 1920s.

Even viewed from a distance of over a hundred years, the Poiret boot is a remarkably modern design, not dissimilar to boots that are worn by women today. It is a simple, pull-on design in a soft, wrinkled morocco leather, low-heeled and square-toed, which rises almost to the knee. Poiret commissioned the boots from La Maison Favereau, a well-known Parisian *bottier* in the rue de la Boétie, and they were durable enough for Denise to continue wearing them for decades afterward, often scrunched down around her ankles.[63] She had pairs in red, white, green, and yellow, which must have made for a dramatic flash of color when she raised her skirts to cross the street or get in and out of a car or carriage.

The new boots garnered not just attention but also approbation, and not necessarily for reasons of style alone. The second decade of the twentieth century saw a slow but steady rise in the hemline of skirts; this raised the shocking possibility that a woman might expose not just her ankles but even portions of her calves as she walked around the city. As the *New York Times* reported, approvingly, in 1915, Mme. Poiret's boots were the ideal antidote to such offenses against decency. Two years after her initial visit, what the *Times* called "Russian boots" were becoming an outré statement by some cutting-edge fashionable women.[64]

Rising hemlines ought to have been just the thing to show off those brightly colored boots, but, as it happened, the fates were against the Poirets. Across the ocean, in Europe, war was raging. In 1917, the British government introduced new regulations to manage the demand for leather, which was now urgently required for military uses. Henceforth, no boot could be taller than 8″. Inevitably, a less-than-stylish break appeared between boot top and skirt hem, and by 1918, when skirts were 8 to 10″ off the ground, boots could rise no higher.[65]

For Paul Poiret, the war brought its own problems. He joined the French army early on, and by the time he demobilized, in 1919, other designers, such as Coco Chanel, had overtaken him, and his business was on the verge of bankruptcy. He struggled on for another decade, but in 1929 he finally closed his business and left the fashion world for good. By the time he died, in 1944, he was largely forgotten.[66] But if Poiret's star was fading by the beginning of the 1920s, the fashion world had not yet done with the Russian boot.

RETURN OF THE BOOT

In the summer of 1909, Paris was entranced by a new artistic sensation, the Ballets Russes. Conceived by the impresario Sergei Diaghilev, the Ballets Russes reinvigorated the art of performing dance and introduced European and American audiences to tales, music, and design motifs drawn from Russian folklore. It was massively influential, not just in the realms of dance and music, but also from a design perspective, and especially because of its costumes. As the Ballets Russes toured a series of European cities over the next decade, designers like Paul Poiret began to incorporate some of the elements of the ballet costumes into fashion, including turbans and harem pants.[67]

Those of a creative bent had been looking to the Orient for inspiration as far back as the Renaissance.[68] Over time, ideas about what exactly constituted "the Orient" changed; while China and Japan were clearly "oriental," the fashion and design movement of "orientalism" often encompassed Middle Eastern and even North African elements.

What united them was the concept of a richer, freer, and more sensuous life—the sort of freedom that Paul Poiret was looking for in the clothing he designed for early-twentieth-century women. Russia was a subject of particular fascination, because it was both European and Asian. So Russian-themed clothing became popular, merging elements like fur trims, elaborate brocade and stitching, and gold detailing into clothes that could be exotic and practical at the same time.

There were other reasons that Russia was on people's minds. The upheavals of the February and October Revolutions of 1917 and the appalling chaos of the Civil War that followed—which did not end until 1923—created a vast diaspora of mostly middle- and upper-class Russians. These refugees from Bolshevism settled around the world; thriving Russian émigré communities sprang up in cities as disparate as Paris, Berlin, and Shanghai. Those with access to money prospered, but many suffered appalling privations; in Shanghai, for example, Russian women opened dress stores and beauty parlors and taught music to children; at night, others played in nightclub orchestras or acted as hostesses, cabaret dancers, and performers; sometimes they worked in opium dens or as prostitutes. The other expatriate communities in China, motivated by the horror of seeing fellow Europeans reduced to penury in the face of "the natives," regarded them with suspicion and often outright hostility. At the same time, they were the objects of fascination—exotic, glamorous, romantic, and sometimes wild.[69]

The 1920s also saw a considerable shift in the role of women in Western society. The suffrage movement had become unstoppable, with women in a number of countries, including Denmark (1915), Britain (1918), Austria (1919), and the United States (1921), gaining the right to vote. In the aftermath of World War I, when many women had taken the place of men who had been called up for war, women continued to enter the workplace in even greater numbers. Clothing fashions changed with women's changing roles in society, particularly where younger women were concerned. The confining corset was discarded, and for the first time in hundreds of years women's legs were seen, with hemlines rising to the knee and dresses becoming more fitted. The new fashions put an emphasis on a more boyish figure, with flattened breasts and hips and shorter hairstyles.

So it's perhaps not surprising that the twenties saw a huge resurgence in the popularity of fashion boots, a form of clothing that, as we've already seen, challenges established gender roles while at the same time providing the whiff of exoticism sought by the fashionable orientalists. They were available in a variety of styles, calf- or knee-length, with a Cuban or a Louis heel,[70] which could be pulled-on or zip-fastened for a closer fit. Worn with calf-length and, ultimately, knee-length skirts, they often featured decorative accents such as elaborate stitching or fur trim.[71] The plain brown willow calf was declared by those in the know to be the most popular, but there were also examples in black patent, tan, glacé, and colored kid.[72]

There exists, in the archive collections of the British Pathé newsreel company, a two-minute film that offers silent testimony to the range of boot styles available in the 1920s. Titled *Boots, Boots, Boots—Latest Russian Styles for Eve*, it begins with a shot of six women in typical winter clothes of the late 1920s—knee-length skirts, tweeds, fur stoles, cloche hats—strolling arm in arm toward the viewer. In close-up the camera pans across their booted legs (with a couple of pairs of knee-length spats for good measure), showing a range of styles that would not have looked out of place fifty years later. Subsequent shots show a variety of design features, including inlaid details, ruched leather, fur trims, and a front zipper. "Ever after novelty, fashion is searching the world for variety of material and shape," a title card helpfully explains. "And wouldn't Adam like these time-savers?" another adds, perhaps a tad suggestively, as one of the models perches on a rock and slowly unzips her boot.[73]

By the mid-1920s, British shoe manufacturers were reporting record orders for high-legged women's boots, and they were so popular that they were being blamed for causing women to catch colds, have accidents in the street, and even injure themselves (see sidebar). Initially popular in Britain, the new boot style quickly spread to Paris,[74] while English women in

An early-twentieth-century woman's riding boot. Looser-fitting than later styles of riding boots, its relationship to the Russian boot is clear to see. (With kind permission of the University of the Arts London, London College of Fashion Archives.)

India complained that Russian boots were not yet available in the stores in Bombay.[75] In America, the arrival on the Leyland Line steamer *Winifredian* of the young Misses Brinkler, Dorothy and Gladys, from London made front-page news in the *Boston Daily Globe*. Pictured standing arm in arm on deck, the sisters were clad in matching, fur-trimmed Cossack-style coats, the flared hems of which just skimmed the tops of their tall leather boots, "now the fashion in London," the paper announced in December 1925.[76]

Another measure of the impact of the Russian boot is the number of times it turns up as the subject of cartoons in the London journal *Punch*. As a writer for the *Times of India* commented, "From *Punch*, which is always admitted to be a better guide to the real mode than any of the fashion-books, it is obvious that these boots are really being worn. There is a joke on the subject every week, and the other papers follow suit."[77] In 1922, the artist E. H. Shepard, better known as the original illustrator of A. A. Milne's *Winnie the Pooh*, produced a full-page cartoon in which the appearance of a young woman wearing "an ultra muscovite confection" of furs, brocade, and decorated knee-length boots causes chaos in a busy London thoroughfare.[78] Other contemporary cartoons satirize women wearing boots that look like a guardsman's[79] or who have adopted Russian manners to go with their boots ("Two small vodkas, comrade," says one of a pair of booted flappers to a waiter in a café[80]).

While *Punch* was chuckling indulgently at the frivolity of feminine fashions, there were others who perceived something of more fundamental significance in the newfound

Modern Girl (living up to her Russian boots). "Two small vodkas, comrade."

Russian boots proved to be a rich source of humor for the London magazine *Punch*. In this cartoon, from 1925, two young women have embraced more than just the fashions of Russia. (Reproduced with permission of Punch Ltd., www.punch.co.uk.)

MANNERS AND MODES.
What our Life-Guards may have to put up with.

In this 1926 cartoon from *Punch*, it is suggested that women's boots may climb high enough to rival those of the famed Life Guards regiment of the British Household Cavalry. (Reproduced with permission of Punch Ltd., www.punch.co.uk.)

THE *Notorious* RUSSIAN BOOT

In the spring of 1928, a most unfortunate fate befell Miss Nila Bradley, a young woman from the English fishing port of Grimsby. While removing her fashionable Russian boots, she crossed her left leg over her right knee and gave a vigorous tug, which resulted in her breaking her left thigh. According to the *Times of India*, which reported this tale of woe from the motherland, Miss Bradley was rushed to the hospital.[81]

One thing the Russian boot did not lack was press coverage. Some of it verged on the alarmist. "Russian boots endanger the health of English women," the *New York Herald* trumpeted in 1926, but this turned out to be a case of bait and switch; it was not the boots themselves that were keeping London doctors busy, but the tendency of women to wear the knee-length leather or patent footwear in the mornings, only to discard it in favor of slippers for afternoon teas and evening parties. "Boots are like woolen underwear, doctors advise. Once they are put on, they must be kept on."[82]

Most of the news stories, however, were of the humorous variety. "Russian Boots Trap Girl," the *New York Times* reported on November 27, 1925; an unnamed girl[83] alighting from a bus in a busy London street had gotten her "dainty Muscovite heel" stuck in a grating. Stamping her other foot to try to free it had resulted in both heels becoming trapped. A crowd gathered, and eventually a plumber tried to free her, only to lift her bodily out of her boots, whereupon she fled the scene in her stockinged feet. The *Times* noted that such incidents seemed unlikely to have an effect on the fashion for boots, "which so far represents the only victory that Sovietism has won in England."[84]

popularity of tall boots for women. Could it be, the *Los Angeles Times* mused in December 1927, that this new footwear was a sign of women's transition from the "leisure class" to the world of business?[85] Professor Robert P. Utter from the University of California, the paper reported, saw in the emergence of the Russian boot a sign of women achieving a transition that men had made more than a hundred years earlier. With the birth of the Industrial Revolution, the fashionable dandies of the late eighteenth and early nineteenth centuries had developed an interest in business. The dictates of contemporary fashion meant that they had to dress in expensive fabrics, but work meant leaving the house and braving the elements. So they added knee-length boots to protect their expensive clothing. Utter recognized the same phenomenon in women of the 1920s; they were engaging in business, but fashion dictated that they still wear fragile dresses, silk stockings, and heeled shoes. Long knee boots served the same purpose as they did for the men of earlier decades: to protect delicate and impractical silk hosiery. Utter could not have known it, but he was foreshadowing Beth Levine's comments about boots and

Miss Hattie Klawans, a clerk in the office of the Prohibition czar Lincoln Andrew, wearing a pair of Russian boots. In the United States, the boots were associated with the sort of girls who liked to frequent speakeasies. Their presence in the office of the man responsible for enforcing Prohibition is quite ironic. (Library of Congress, Prints & Photographs Division, LC-USZ62-97065.)

the changing role of women in society, made nearly a half century later.

The boots had another, less salubrious reputation in Prohibition-era America, being seen as the sort of racy footwear worn by girls who frequented saloon bars and speakeasies.[86] It's interesting that two of the rare contemporary images of Russian boots relate to alcohol: a woman hiding a flask in one of her calf-length boots, taken in 1922,[87] and a picture of Miss Hattie Klawans, a clerk in the office of the Prohibition czar, perched on a desk while wearing her new Russian boots.[88]

And yet, despite this popularity—despite bolstering the transition of women from the leisure class and amusing the readership of *Punch*—the Russian boot had disappeared by the beginning of the 1930s and is more or less forgotten today; most fashion histories of the 1920s fail to mention it at all. When you look at Russian boots—there are pairs in the online collections of the Victoria and Albert Museum, the Metropolitan Museum of Art, and the London College of Fashion (the latter pictured in this chapter), they seem

RUSSIAN BOOT 1925

Russian boots were incredibly popular during the 1920s, but, perhaps because of the poor quality of many pairs, very few have survived to the present day and most of these are in museum collections. This particular example,

from 1925, is in the Cordwainer's College collection of the London College of Fashion. Given that it's more than ninety years old, the first thing that strikes you about this boot is how modern it looks. The only anachronistic feature is the hourglass-shaped Louis heel, which would be rare on a present-day fashion boot. Otherwise, the straight-legged, pull-on style would not have looked out of place on a woman from the 1970s. Even the scalloped band of stitching around the top of the shaft is a motif that was repeated in the era of the "Cossack boot," as the late-seventies designs were called.

This boot (also illustrated at the beginning of this chapter) is relatively plain compared to some of its contemporaries, which featured much more elaborate stitching, inserts of different material (such as patent leather or canvas), and fur trimmings.

absurdly modern. A white pair in the Met's collections, which was designed by Poiret, could have stepped out of London's swinging Carnaby Street boutiques, c. 1966; in fact, they date back to 1920. So why were fashion boots so successful in the 1960s and yet so short-lived in the twenties?

DECLINE AND FALL

The night of November 9, 1925, was the coldest that the London suburbs had seen for six years, and the next morning Londoners awoke to find snow on their doorsteps. By the afternoon it had dissolved into mud, and women were besieging shoe stores in search of high Russian boots to protect their thin silk stockings.[89] Reporting later that month, the *New York Times* remarked that the boots provided a useful means "of reconciling the high skirts of the day with the low temperatures of the season."[90] The combination of knee-length skirts and clothes made to be put on quickly boded well for a longer run of popularity for tall boots than had previously been the case. But the ability to pull the boot on and off quickly required a loose-fitting leg, which—in the opinion of the *Manchester Guardian*—was a great deal less attractive than the fitted ankle and long, clean lines permitted by lace-up designs. "A ready-made example on the short, fat woman is really ugly and draws unnecessary attention to her proportions," the paper declared, a little unkindly.[91]

By the end of 1925, London modistes were declaring the Russian boot doomed because "there is not a chance of the idea being taken up by Royalty and the 'best people' generally." The boot had been popular in the rain and mud of the wet autumn of 1925, but "no member of the King's household ever walks in damp and muddy streets."[92] The French, too, had always been a bit lukewarm about Russian boots. "We have feet and ankles, and some of us have legs, so why should we cover up what no one is displeased to see?" was the view expressed in a *China Press* article of February 1926.[93] Russian-booted Englishwomen visiting the city

A 1928 catalog page from the British mail-order company Kays shows both a Russian boot and its contemporary lace-up rival, the "rinker" boot. The latter, as the catalog states, offers both a more shapely fit and better protection against the elements. (University of Worcester.)

were an object of sympathy from the natives, the paper reported. By May of that year, Parisiennes had come around to the idea of wearing boots, albeit not Russian ones. Instead, these were relatively delicate confections of satin, glazed kid, or moire, which even came in gem-studded versions that could be worn out in the evenings. They were, in the words of the *New York Herald*, "essentially Parisian."[94]

British manufacturers also experimented with alternative designs. By July 1926, similar boots were being shown in London, with the stated aim of replacing the Russian boot. They were 14 to 16" in height and came in a variety of highly decorated styles, including a gray glacé kid pair and another in a combination of python skin and patent leather.[95] But the Russian boot was a big money spinner for the British shoe industry, and they weren't about to give it up without a fight.[96]

In September 1926, a major exhibition of Russian boot styles was held at the Birmingham Chamber of Commerce. The new season's boots were generally higher on the leg and more stoutly soled than in previous years, being designed both to protect

"The main streets of Petrograd and New York have much in common. Russian music, and dancing, Russian plays and costumes, and some boots," the *Boot and Shoe Recorder* reported in May 1922.[100] However, this was not to say that the *Recorder* approved. "The Russian boot stands for utility, not for beauty," the paper cautioned. "It cannot be said to be a fitting and beautiful part of the costume of the American girl, whose skirts are short and whose feet in Russian boots are far from petite."

If Russian boots had proved to be enormously popular in Britain, their reception elsewhere was not so ecstatic. This was particularly so across the Atlantic, where the *Boot and Shoe Recorder* used the relatively newfangled mechanism of the telegraph to survey shoe retailers across the nation. The results were not encouraging.

> "In my opinion . . . the Russian boot fits too few women and looks too clumsy to make it popular." R. C. Cummings, New York.

> "Have had Russian boots for the past three months but have only sold a few pairs." H. E. Fontius, Denver.

> "Not very practical for our climate in either winter or summer . . . are not wanted by refined clientele. Have seen only one pair on the street. Too extreme to be popular." Rosenthal's Inc., San Francisco.

> "The freak dresser is the class of trade that will wear them." E.E.E. Shoe Company, Memphis.

> "Expect slight demand in September for cheap quality boots. Better dressers won't wear them." Walk-Over Shoe Store, Milwaukee.

> "Saw one chorus girl wearing Russian boots and one pair on display in a shop window. . . . A few pairs may be sold to sporty flappers." Roy S. Whitmore, Providence, RI.

> "Russian boots were a popular fad, but will probably not repeat. . . . We had a limited quantity, which we sold out. Could have used more." A. Wachenheim, New Orleans.

> "Thus far have seen only one pair of Russian boots in this city. Personally think they are anything but trim-looking. Cannot see any demand in sight." Anon., New Haven.

> "I would not advise any retailer to carry Russian boots, unless he were an enemy of mine." Arthur Weiss, New York.

The *Recorder* speculated that perhaps a fitted boot, like those worn by English cavalry officers, might have something to be said for it, but such boots required a valet to pull them on and off. By contrast, "the average American woman considers her footwear the last incident of the day's costume and wants her boots to fit in a jiffy."

the feet better and to overcome the complaints about proportion and fit that had plagued earlier versions. Decorations included alternations of color in the uppers, brogue-style stitching on plain tops or collars, a "zigzag Cubist design in black, brown, and champagne," and edgings of fur and astrakhan. New developments included "dress boots," which attached a close-fitting, waterproof stockinette upper to the shoe to give the appearance of seamless gaiters, and the "Lithuanian boot," which employed "a permanent elongated bellows wrinkle" to give the style a slender aspect.[97] No less a personage than the chief medical officer for Birmingham, Sir John Robertson, was on hand to warn salesmen of the importance of making sure that the new boots were well fitted and not of shoddy workmanship.

But the boot makers' most formidable weapon came in the form of Lucy Christina, Lady Duff Cooper. "Lucile," as she was known professionally, was one of the leading fashion designers of the time, a widely recognized innovator in couture, and a woman who—like Paul Poiret—had devoted her efforts as a designer to freeing women from restrictive dresses and corsets.[98] She was also an innovator in public relations for the fashion industry, and she knew how to work a crowd. To the delight of the assembled cobblers, she launched into a barnstorming speech in defense of the maligned Russian boot. She praised the boot makers of England for finally backing her in her role as the "mother of the Russian boot" in their country. These boots were about utility first; by wearing them, women would avoid getting their stockings muddy and be healthier, too, avoiding the chills and pneumonia that might result from wet feet. To laughter, she remarked that plenty of girls liked to show a little bare leg above the boot. The boots were attractive, she remarked to more laughter, but she guessed that some followers were more attracted by that flash of bare leg. And if they sagged at the ankle, so what? That was the intention, and the more the boot sags around the ankle, "the daintier you are."[99]

One suspects that there may have been a note of desperation in that laughter, because the troubles with the Russian boot went deeper than its baggy ankles. At the National Association of Shoe Retailers meeting, held in Birmingham earlier that year, the falling quality of the boots was a subject of concern. One delegate angrily denounced some boots as being "the biggest rubbish on the market and a disgrace to the boot trade." The soles were barely fit for wearing around the house and the behavior of some manufacturers, who "ought never to have dreamed about making Russian boots," was jeopardizing the future of a style that was "exceedingly useful." And profitable, too, with another delegate from Manchester reporting massive sales in Lancashire for just the first two months of that year.[101]

The problem of quality was a serious one, related to the cost of the leather used. A pair of Russian boots required between ten and twelve square feet of hide to make, compared with around three square feet for a pair of shoes. The growth in popularity of the boots meant that suppliers suddenly found an outlet for larger hides, which lacked the fine grain of smaller skins and were also less water resistant. So the boots were cheaper but of poorer quality and lacked the waterproof properties that were one of their main selling points. This was not always evident to the buyer; as the *Manchester Guardian* pointed out in 1926, a woman might not see much difference between a cheap pair of Russian boots and one costing five to ten shillings more, but that difference was significant. "Like all classes of 'cheap' footwear," the *Guardian* concluded, "the boot is far and away from being cheap."[102]

Within a few weeks of the Birmingham show, it was clear that the decline of the boot was going to be hard to stop. The *Hartford Courant* reported in October 1926 that, while autumn rains had caused a few Russian boots to be seen on the streets in London, they were not in the shops and seemed unlikely to be as popular as the previous winter.[103] By the fall of 1927, the fashion industry declared Russian boots to be "as dead as Tutankhamen."[104, 105]

A Chapter Ends

Shoe manufacturers began to cast around for a potential replacement. Lace-up boots provided a better fit around the ankle, but the major stumbling block was the time it took to put them on. In 1927, the manager of a London shoe store used a stopwatch to show that it typically took a woman six and a half minutes to lace herself into one of the new-style tall, lace-up boots. He calculated that women would pay for the well-shaped ankle the boots allowed by spending a cumulative total of four to five days each winter just putting them on, "not counting the time of unlacing them."[106]

Also, the world was changing. The internal combustion engine was beginning its long rise to domination over horsepower. Streets were being paved, mud and animal dung was retreating to the fields, and women wanted to wear delicate little shoes when they went out, rather than restrictive boots. If you needed to walk in the rain, rubber rain boots or galoshes were a better option. And so, eventually, fashion turned back to a boot that was eminently practical. For the woman reluctant to discard her boots for reasons of fashion, the *Guardian* recommended a pair of Wellingtons for bad days, "as these are now available in brown as well as black with Louis heels, and also cut to shape and stiffened until they resemble a smart riding boot."[107]

By the beginning of the 1930s, the Russian boot had more or less disappeared from the scene. In part it failed because of poor business practice and, while it garnered global attention, it never achieved global popularity. But there were darker forces of elitism and snobbery at play. Mass popularity was seen as a barrier to chic women adopting boots as a fashion item.[108] None of the high-fashion modistes of the time wanted to be seen wearing the same boots as the shopgirls and factory workers. The popular press may have been full of Russian boots, but they barely rated a mention in the pages of *Vogue*. It's a popular cliché that history is written by the winners, but in fashion it sometimes seems that history is written only for the one percent.[109]

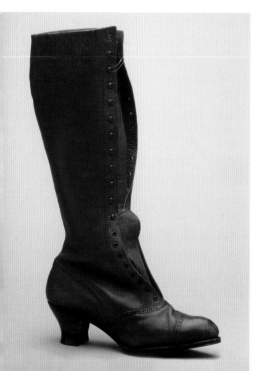

As the Russian boot began to decline in popularity, manufacturers cast about for a replacement. The lace-up knee boot, or "rinker," offered a closer and more flattering fit than the loose-fitting Russian style, but ultimately the time required to lace and unlace the high-legged design made it impractical for most daily wear. (With kind permission of the University of the Arts London, London College of Fashion Archives.)

MRS. LEVINE'S *Inspiration*

As she walked around the streets of Manhattan, Beth Levine had become used to the calls from passing drivers, invariably male. It was always along the same lines: they would lean out of their cars and shout something like

"Hey, where's your horse?"

The attention was not surprising, because the sight of a woman in the heart of the city wearing a skirt or a dress with knee-length boots was an unusual one for the late 1950s. But Levine didn't mind. She saw it as a tribute to the boots she loved to design and wear.[110] She was no stranger to skepticism, amusement, or in some cases outright ridicule. Levine had spent the previous five years on a quest to redefine the utilitarian boot as a fashionable shoe. It was proving to be an uphill struggle. The years since the disappearance of the Russian boot in the early 1930s had not been kind to the idea of a fashionable boot for women. After a brief flirtation with stylish designs, the shoe industry had concluded that the role of the boot was overwhelmingly one of protection. This was something that the rubber rain boot did much better than the leather Russian boot.

There were some short-lived attempts to revive the idea of a fashion boot. At the end of the 1930s there was a brief flurry of interest in fashionable ankle boots for women, associated with clothing that paid homage to the so-called Romantic era. They were not worn very widely, but a number of designers included them in their collections. One of the most notable examples was André Perugia, who came up with leather button boots in black or

chapter
3

Beth Levine, photographed in 1974, shortly before she and her husband wound up their company, Herbert Levine Inc. She's wearing boots, of course. (New York Post Archives/Getty Images.)

In the 1930s and '40s, there was a short-lived period of popularity for ankle boots like this 1939 pair by André Perugia. (Image copyright © The Metropolitan Museum of Art. Image source: Art Resource, NY.)

cream, examples of which can be found in the collection of the Metropolitan Museum of Art in New York.[111] But these were a rarity. For the most part, the women's boot styles of the 1940s and '50s tended to be trim, ankle-length rain boots.

That had not always been the case. If you want to get a sense of what the earlier generation of rain boots for women looked like, mail-order catalogs provide a useful window. The autumn/winter Kays catalog of 1928 shows a couple of styles of Russian boot. But by 1933, the Russian boots were gone. Instead we have two pages of rain boots.[112] Some of these are typical Wellington boots. But the catalog also featured "stylish" models "for city wear . . . extra-high shaped leg, close fitting, 1.5" Cuban heels." The leg height is 16.5", which takes them right to the knee. And they are specifically described as "practical high-leg *fashion boots*" (my emphasis); a similar pair came in two-tone rubber.

So while they may be absent from the high-end fashion press, mail order gives us a different picture. There were still knee-length fashion boots on sale in 1933. But by 1937, while Kays still offered one style of heeled and shaped-leg rain boot, most of the women's boots featured in the catalog were regular "Wellies." And by 1960, all the boots shown were ankle-length and, critically, were advertised as a practical option for bad weather. As far as the young and the stylish were concerned, they also had a significant image problem. For the teenage Lesley Hornby and her friends, growing up in the London suburb of Neasden,

With the disappearance of the Russian boot at the beginning of the 1930s, the only tall boots for women were rubber rain boots. (Everett Collection/Shutterstock.)

In the 1940s and '50s, shoe manufacturers regarded boots as utilitarian items, separate from fashionable shoes. Even stylish pairs, like these ankle boots, were seen as something to be worn only when the weather was bad. (Everett Collection/Shutterstock.)

it was better to go through an entire winter with your legs frozen to the bone than wear boots. "Nobody wore boots," Hornby, who was to become famous worldwide as sixties supermodel Twiggy, recalled. "Boots meant ankle boots, brown with a zip, the sort of things old ladies wore."[113]

To a large extent, this view was shared by the people who made boots. Shoe manufacturers and retailers saw boots as a separate category of footwear from shoes,[114] to be worn for protection from bad weather or for work. Unlike shoes, boots did not have to be fashionable, only practical. This was the world that Beth Levine set out to change.

THE FIRST LADY OF SHOE DESIGN

Beth Katz Levine was born in December 1915, one of five children of a Lithuanian dairy farmer from Patchogue, New York.[115] Maybe her passion for boots came from the days she spent in riding boots, in the saddle on the farm's horses.[116] Certainly in later years she would say that her mother thought a fine pair of shoes was a necessity, while her father's work with horses and cows meant she knew about leather. In 1939, looking for work in New York City, she answered a job advertisement for a shoe model. She had a dainty pair of size 4½B feet that, she claimed, not only made the shoes look better but also reduced the weight of the sample bag that the salesmen had to drag around.

In those hardscrabble days at the end of the Depression, Levine had to fulfill multiple roles: model, secretary, and receptionist. This may have run her off her perfectly formed feet, but it also provided priceless exposure to the actual business of making and selling shoes. Combined with

The fashion industry was slow to grasp the significance of the Levines' early fashionable boot styles, such as this pair from 1959. From their first appearance in 1952, it took nearly ten years for the fashion boot to take even the first steps toward widespread acceptance. (Image copyright © The Metropolitan Museum of Art. Image source: Art Resource, NY.)

her natural eye for design, and more than a touch of inborn moxie, it gave her a great start for what would become her life's work.

In 1944, Beth Katz, as she was known at the time, interviewed for a design job with the Andrew Geller shoe company. The man interviewing her turned out to be her future husband, a sales and advertising manager named Herbert Levine. Herbert was a graduate of Dartmouth College who had worked as a journalist for various fashion papers before moving into marketing.[117] He didn't design shoes himself, but he had a nose for business and could promote Beth's groundbreaking work.

In 1948 they founded their own label, which they called Herbert Levine Inc. because, in Beth's words, "the name sounded like a shoemaker." Beth freely admitted that the risks she took as a designer resulted from a desire to keep Herbert amused; along the way, she produced sandals with an Astroturf instep, shoes that looked like racing cars or Aladdin's lamp, and an "upper-less" shoe that was little more than a sole that attached to the bottom of the wearer's foot with a strip of adhesive.

During the 1950s, shoe design was dominated by European fashion houses. America was admired and imitated for its casual footwear, such as loafers and saddle oxfords, but there were very few American designers inspiring international fashion.[118] Beth Levine changed this, and it was her work on boots for women that made the Levine name internationally known.

The Levines first experimented with a fashionable boot in 1952. It was made from white kid leather, around 8" from heel to toe, with a stiletto heel. It had an elasticated band around the top of the shaft that gripped the calf tightly.[119] Afterward, Beth couldn't remember exactly why she felt a "boot mood" coming on,[120] but it's unlikely that she and Herbert could have predicted the response of shoe retailers when she modeled them, which was general hilarity.[121] Boots were not fashion. Boots were for rain and snow. Everyone knew that. Beth's little white boots did not sell.

Rain Boot, EARLY 1960s

For most women at the beginning of the 1960s, a pair of boots was something that you wore to keep your feet dry in rain or snow. But that didn't mean that they couldn't be fashionable as well. This boot, from the first years of the decade, is a good example of that. It's made from rubber but has an applied finish that makes it look, at least from a distance, like leather. It is also cut to emphasize the wearer's ankle and the lower curve of her calf. The interior is lined with faux sheepskin for insulation.

Boots like this were relatively common in the 1950s and the early '60s, and although, as the decade wore on, they were replaced as fashionable wear by a newer generation of fashion boots, waterproof and/or lined boots remained a popular item through the 1970s and beyond; they made up around a third of the boot styles available in U.K. mail-order catalogs.

This ankle-length rain boot from the early 1960s mimics the fashion boots of the period, down to the textured pattern of the rubber, which gives the appearance of leather.

THE TIDE TURNS

Rejection seems to have awakened a stubborn streak in the Levines. Their first pair of boots might have been produced on a whim, but for the rest of the fifties their collections invariably included boots, some of which are preserved in the collections of New York's Metropolitan Museum of Art; these include risqué stocking boots, which combined a high-heeled shoe with a fishnet silk stocking upper that climbed to midthigh;[122] kitten-heeled knee-length boots in Dalmatian spotted leather;[123] black leather ankle boots with spike heels;[124] and black silk evening boots with large bows at the ankle.[125] None of these designs was successful. One wonders what the buyers from Neiman Marcus, Saks, and Bloomingdale's thought about this determined woman coming back year after year with the same unsellable designs. Beth Levine's genius was clear. But what was this seemingly endless obsession she had with boots?

Not that the shoe market of the fifties was completely hostile to the boot. If you look through magazines like *Vogue* from this period, there are a surprising number of ankle-length boots around and they are not all utilitarian rain boot/galoshes affairs. Some are very stylish. The model for these seems to be the Perugia-type ankle boots from the very end of the 1930s. These persisted through the forties and fifties as a very distinctive style of boot: low-heeled, barely skimming the ankle, and often with a small V-shaped cutout at the vamp. During the late '50s they were frequently paired with slim-fitting ski pants.[126] And their appearances became more frequent as the decade drew to a close.

But there was still the problem that boots were seen as protective winter gear, not fashion items. The early Levine boots even came with a warning insert in their box for those who might be confused. "Treat me kindly. I am a fashion shoe . . . called a boot," the label explains. "I was created to be soft, light, elegant, and divinely comfortable. I was not intended to be a snow boot or a rubber boot. I have kid leather insides. I am not water repellent . . . not waterproof, or scuff proof. I am the finest boot ever made, and a delightful experience to wear. But, I cannot be guaranteed beyond normal shoe wear."[127]

As it turned out, the Levines were not the only ones experimenting with new styles of fashionable boots. In 1957, Capezio produced what the *New York Times* described as a "narrow, near knee, flat-footed ballet boot."[128] Today, the term "ballet boots" is usually applied to a form of fetish wear that holds the foot permanently *en pointe*, but in 1957 it was quite literal; as a company, Capezio was particularly noted for its dance shoes. The 1957 boot seems to have had little impact, but it was the precursor of a more successful range of footwear that came into vogue in the very early 1960s. An example designed by Bonnie Cashin ("a long-time advocate of boots," as the *Times* described her[129]) in 1961, currently in the collections of the Metropolitan Museum, is a low-heeled boot of soft, pink leather; it was pulled on and came almost to the knee.[130] This same style of boot was featured by a number of designers, including Evan-Picone (taupe and camel suede with skirts and sweaters) and Rudi Gernreich (patent leather boots over tights with jacket and dress ensembles).[131]

By 1958, the press was finally beginning to pay some attention. "The news in shoes is the city boot," Joan Rattner reported in the *Herald Tribune*. "Some go all the way up to the knee, others reach the calf, and some just touch the ankle bone. All are made of leather." Rattner's article highlighted two offerings from the Levines: purple crushed-suede boots with rhinestone heels and a brushed-leather "Cossack boot" in beige.[132] By now, other designers had started to experiment with boots. David Evins was a renowned shoemaker who had won a Coty Award in 1948 for his creation of the shell pump, a shoe with a low-cut top that had the effect of showing more of a woman's foot.[133]

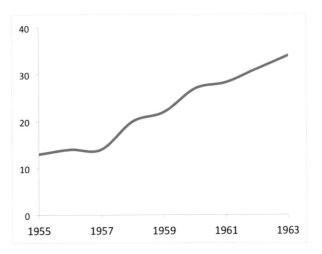

Starting in the 1950s, the frequency with which the word "boot" appears in publications like *Vogue* and the *New York Times* steadily rises. As boots begin to be regarded as a fashion item rather than a utilitarian one, the attention devoted to them by the press begins to increase.

His design ethos was aimed at making shoes for women that were lighter and more comfortable, and he had a host of high-profile clients, including Marilyn Monroe, Judy Garland, and Ava Gardner.[134] But in 1958 he was also producing boots; Joan Rattner's piece included more designs from Evins than it did from Beth Levine, including 24-karat-gold kid knee boots and shoe boots in silver kid with a high-riding tongue.

But if the late fifties showed evidence of growing acceptance of the fashion boot, their first emergence was not so much as boots *per se*, but through the adoption of what the *Atlanta Constitution*'s Raymonde Alexander termed "the boot shape" in both high-heeled evening shoes and more casual daywear. "Demi-boots have below-ankle toplines," he wrote in July 1960, "that are cuffed, stitched, elasticized, or fringed. True boots may be ankle high or higher, sometimes on stacked heels."[135] The first rumblings of real change can be seen in the number of times the word "boot" appears in the *New York Times* compared to the fashion journals *Vogue* and *L'Officiel* during 1961. It's clear from the spike in mentions that the *Times* was on to something, and that becomes even more evident when you examine the references in detail. In August, for example, the paper reported that, for casual wear on campus, "Shoes will become boots." It rhapsodized over that season's knee-length patent leather boots lined in bright red fuzzy pile and tapering sharply to an elegant toe. There were also black leather boots that rose just to the anklebone and glove-tight multicolor suede boots.[136]

Later that same year, the *Times* devoted a whole piece to "the boot in fashion." "The boot," the paper announced "promises to be one of fall's smartest fashions. Cropped at the ankle or knee high, boots this season boast all the characteristics of the newest shoes, such as squared or oval toes, heels of many shapes and heights, and handsome leathers."[137] The article went on to highlight some of the practical features of the new-style boots, such as being lined for warmth and treated to repel rain and snow. But it

ANKLE BOOT
Early 1960s

This stiletto-heeled ankle boot from 1961–62 is typical of the first generation of sixties fashion boots. With its pointed toe and sharply tapering heel, it has much in common with the popular shoes of the period. The upper is made from cowhide, which has been dyed to resemble zebra skin. It's a decorative finish, and it also marks this boot as a fashion item rather than the more utilitarian boots of the period; it would have been completely unsuitable for wet weather.

These styles were very popular during the first wave of fashion boots, but the fall collections of 1963, with their emphasis on taller, low-heeled boots, made this daintier design obsolete.

A pair of fashion boots from the early 1960s, made from cowhide dyed to resemble zebra skin.

was also made quite clear that, while they might be practical, these boots were also about style. Some designs combined fur or fabric with leather, while others were made for evenings out, curving low around the ankle, bejeweled and embroidered, and set on slim, midheight heels.

This was far more detailed coverage than anything yet published in *Vogue*. True, both the magazine and the newspaper devoted significant attention to Roger Vivier's square-toed ankle boots for Dior,[138] but at this point it was only the *Times* that recognized the wider trend. *Vogue* was still treating boots as an extension of the fashions of the previous decades, when ankle-height styles were moderately commonplace and practical. The most noteworthy things about the Dior boots, in Vogue's opinion, were their square toes and oval heels. By contrast, the *Times* had recognized the emergence and potential importance of knee-length styles, something that would become even more marked the following year.

THE BOOTS CRAZE

In December 1962, Virginia Rusk, the wife of the U.S. secretary of state, threw a lunchtime fashion show for the spouses of a visiting delegation of Japanese politicians. While their husbands were closeted in economic talks with the secretary, the kimono-clad women watched "wide-eyed" at a selection of elaborate outfits that American women were supposed to go through during a typical day. Among the various ones modeled for the appreciative audience was an outfit for the American wife doing "station wagon chores," described as "a pleated skirt, long sweater, corduroy coat, with hood, and knee-high boots . . . to make the chores fun."[139]

Mrs. Rusk, who had not intended the show to be quite as elaborate as it eventually turned out, felt moved to explain that the procession of outfits was more a case of what a typical American woman might *wish* to wear, as opposed to what she could actually afford. Nonetheless, even just a few years earlier, it would have been almost unthinkable for boots to feature in an exhibition of the best of American fashion, let alone something that the average woman might desire. But American women, or at least, those women on the cutting edge of style, had caught on to boots in a big way. And while we tend to think of the French as fashion trendsetters, where the fashion boot was concerned it was American designers and manufacturers—Capezio, Beth and Herbert Levine, Bonnie Cashin—that made the early running. Even when French designers like Roger Vivier entered the picture, the French press was slow to catch on. This was never more true than in 1962.[140]

That was the year when the sixties boot craze started to take off, at least in the press. Looking back eight years later, *Daily Mail* fashion writer Iris Ashley remembered that in May 1962 "there was only one pair of boots (not counting Wellingtons and riding boots) in the whole of London. . . . Hand-made they were by Anello and Davide, and I nearly got shot for photographing them in the rain and getting them dirty."[141] She went on to recall thinking that the emerging popularity of boots would mark the end of the stiletto heel in the early sixties. "This time next year [i.e., summer 1963] stiletto heels will look tarty and when the time came, they did. And for that matter, do" she added, as a little zinger.[142]

Ashley took credit for spotting boots as an embryonic fashion trend, but she was not the only one. "Boots will put the kick in fashion this fall and winter," Raymonde Alexander wrote in the *Atlanta Constitution* in July. "Not just foul weather boots, but boots for fair days and nights. There will be low boots, stopping short at the ankle; boots that climb to the knee; and any number of other boots stopping at various points along the way." Even though not everyone would want boots, Alexander noted that price levels, heel heights, and materials would vary enough to suit any wearer.[143] At the New York collections in June, the *Times* reported that there were "high, narrow boots" by Vera Maxwell and black patent riding boots by John Weitz. Patty Peterson's fall forecast for the paper, in August of that year, predicted "boots for all occasions" as a major accessory trend,[144] while the paper's fall shoe review describes new styles of boots "as low as the ankle and as high as the knee," in patent plastic or black alligator, with low or high heels.[145]

In the Toronto *Globe and Mail*, Olive Dickason reported that the fashion world was "eyeing boots,"[146] which were providing most of the fashion conversation for that season. Sophisticated women in cities like New York, London, and Paris were choosing boots for casual suburban wear, for trips to the city, and even for cocktail parties. While gilded leathers were popular, especially for those evenings on the town, "those in the know" preferred to coordinate their outfits by having boots and dresses made from the same material. Ankle boots were the most common, but some of the leather styles rose almost to the knee. Sadly for Dickason's Toronto readership, however, she had to report that "they will rarely be seen in Canada . . . most Canadian women will content themselves with low cut shoes."[147]

It's fair to say that boots for women emerged relatively early in the wave of artistic and cultural change that became known as the sixties "youthquake." The year 1962 was not yet the era of miniskirts and Mary Quant. The Beatles were still in Hamburg, the preternaturally ancient Harold Macmillan was in 10 Downing Street, and America had taken only the first, tentative steps into the mire of Vietnam. Even if the frothy New Look frocks of the forties and fifties were disappearing, a lady still wore gloves and a hat to go out. The somewhat masculine cut of the first generation of tall sixties boots—low-heeled, straight, and relatively loose-fitting—complemented the heavy tweed skirts and sober suits of the time.

This can be very clearly seen in the 1962 Paris fall collection of Balenciaga. The French may have seemed a little boot-phobic, but at his show Balenciaga revealed something quite startling: the first over-the-knee fashion boots for women, side-zipped in leather and suede, worn with checked and pleated skirts, white blouses, and wool and leather coats and gloves.[148] The *Daily Mail* hailed the emergence of "a new sporting type of woman, one who can walk the countryside with elegance in very high leather boots and leather jerkin,"[149] while the *Atlanta Constitution* described it as "an unexpected group of country clothes."[150] The chic and the daring duly took note. "Keep an eye on the young . . . ," the *Daily Mail*'s Iris Ashley urged in October. "The under twenty-fives. . . . These are the girls who made long hair piled high into fashion, the girls who've been living in tunic dresses and Chanel-type suits—these are the girls who are going mad for capes. For daytime, they wear them with high boots."[151] By November, Ashley herself had caught the boot bug. "The boots craze has gone all the way now," she declared, enthusiastically. "From the high Russian style—black patent, to some of the prettiest little gold jobs imaginable." The latter were the first item she had decided on for a party thrown by designer Hardy Amies that night. "These boots I must wear. The are irresistible. They are ankle high in gold leather with gold mesh fronts . . . 8 gns at Harrods."[152] That same month, a *New York Times* interviewer reports that French fashion buyer Jacqueline Barry entered the room in "a charcoal-checked suit and knee-high boots."[153] And here, once again, is Beth Levine, whom another *Times* interviewer describes as stalking round her office in "size 4, high-heeled suede boots."[154]

(A) WHITE LEATHER BOOTEE. Elegantly modelled in the height of fashion. Leg is 7½ inches high in popular Russian style with warm contrast lining throughout. Features include 2¼-inch stiletto heel with metal heel-tip, pointed toe with decorative white button. Hard-wearing sole.

Sizes: 3, 3½, 4, 4½, 5, 5½, 6, 6½, 7.

Weekly 4/6

P.6401 White . . . . Price 89/6

Fine Quality Ladies' Bootees

ELEGANCE AND COMFORT IN WINTER WEATHER

(B) BLACK SUEDE BOOTEE beautifully modelled in a design that is increasing in popularity and demand. Plain vamp and quarters with attractive pointed toe. Complete ankle warmth and comfort with the elasticated mock Astrakhan collar. Bootee is finished with a sensible, dainty 2¼-inch heel with metal tip. Hard-wearing sole.

Sizes: 3, 3½, 4, 4½, 5, 5½, 6, 6½, 7, 8.

Weekly 3/6

P.6815 Black . . . . Price 69/6

(C) LOW-LEG SUEDE BOOTEES. Designed in the latest low leg style with self-adjusting toggle fastening. Sheepskin-lined leg and sock with leather inside counter to avoid excessive stocking wear. Quarters are contrast stitched with mock apron to match. Leather bound with decorative pull-on loop. Microcellular sole and wedge heel.

Sizes: 3, 3½, 4, 4½, 5, 5½, 6, 6½, 7, 8.

Weekly 3/–

P.6779 Black . . . . Price 59/6
P.6573 Coffee . . . . Price 59/6

Please see Pages 179, 180 and 181 for a further selection of Kays Ladies' Bootees.

A page from the 1960 autumn/winter catalog from the British mail-order company Kays shows some of the fashionable boots typical of this period. Ten years on, the selection of boots available through such catalogs would run to many pages and encompass all lengths, from ankle to over the knee. (University of Worcester.)

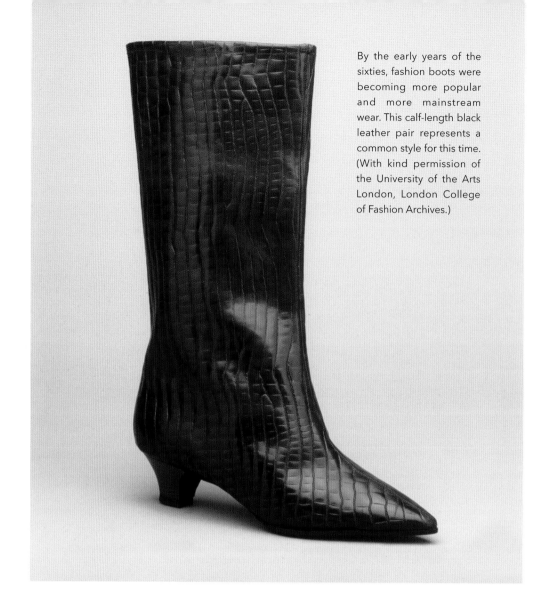

By the early years of the sixties, fashion boots were becoming more popular and more mainstream wear. This calf-length black leather pair represents a common style for this time. (With kind permission of the University of the Arts London, London College of Fashion Archives.)

Boots for the Liberated Leg

In time, Levine's persistence in the potential of a fashionable boot for women was amply rewarded. She went on to design boots for a host of celebrity clients, including Barbra Streisand, Marlene Dietrich, Mamie Eisenhower (black velvet knee-high boots), Pat Nixon (who took some persuading, because she thought boots were unfeminine; Beth eventually coaxed her into a pair of black knee-length ones), Jacqueline Kennedy (Levine made her a custom pair of thigh-high boots in burlap, with a stacked heel), and Jane Fonda—although not, as is often reported, for Nancy Sinatra, a story we'll look at later.[155] "Women adored Levine boots," Vivian Infantino wrote in 1975, at the time when the Levines were winding up their fashion house. "They knew they were in exquisite materials, made to last, fashion-right, and sinfully comfortable."[156]

Levine continued to innovate in boot design throughout the 1960s and beyond. The stretch vinyl boot was another of her brain waves, developed from an upholstery fabric made in Italy that utilized a urethane/nylon mix to smooth the material over the furniture. Levine persuaded the manufacturer to adapt the material for boots, the result being the zipperless, knee-length "Female" boot—in Levine's words, a boot for the "liberated leg."[157] "Before stretch boots, a skinny-legged woman in boots looked like a rooster wearing socks," was how she described it.[158] According to Levine, in a 2004 interview by Helene Verin,[159] the popularity of the Female boot was down to a sample pair that was shipped by mistake to Saks Fifth Avenue; a customer who tried them on refused to take them off and wore them out of the store, creating "a fashion frenzy."

ANKLE BOOTS

Ankle boots were by far the commonest style of fashion boot in the 1800s and the first decade of the twentieth century. They're also the only real example of a unisex style of fashionable boot, and they are still around and massively popular today. So when we're looking at the evolution of fashion boots, you'd think that ankle boots would be one of the earliest branches of our family tree, coming right off the very base.

As it happens, however, there are some problems with this idea. First, there really isn't much to speak of in the way of ankle boots from the 1920s to the 1930s. Then there's a brief attempt to revive the fashion boot at the end of the 1930s by designers such as André Perugia, which doesn't go anywhere.

After that comes Beth Levine's early attempts at designing a fashion boot during the 1950s, many of which are essentially ankle or calf-length styles, before we get into the 1960s and the various ankle and calf-length boots of the middle part of the decade,

These Chelsea boots by the British company Hobbs are from the middle years of the 1990s, but they could just as easily be from three decades earlier. Ankle boots are one of the most enduring styles of boot for both men and women.

among which those of André Courrèges are probably the best-known type. Then there is another gap, from the late 1960s to the late 1970s, during which high-legged boots predominate, before shorter styles come back into fashion during the late 1970s. From these initially high-heeled designs came a whole range of high- and low-heeled ankle boots that flourished during the eighties and are still with us today.

And just to complicate things, the whole process of the evolution of the fashion boot from the 1930s through the early 1960s took place against a backdrop of ankle and calf-length rain boots, which we don't call fashion boots because of their utilitarian nature, but from which the various designers of boots

Prior to that, retailers had not known what to make of these form-fitting boots, which had a distinctly sexy edge.

By the end of the sixties, boots were so popular that the Levines were able to create a specialized retail outlet, called Beth's Bootery, on the fourth floor of Saks Fifth Avenue in New York. The Bootery opened for business on February 16, 1970, and because Beth was given considerable leeway to sell new colors and avant-garde styles, and turnover was high, it became something of a design laboratory. It was also a roaring commercial success, and Saks opened new branches in Washington, D.C., Detroit, Chicago, and Beverly Hills.[160]

In 1967, Levine was presented with the Coty American Fashion Critics Award. It was the first time in more than a decade that it had been given to a shoe designer. The award recognized Beth Levine for "design innovations that overcame traditional boundaries of footwear." Perhaps none of those boundaries was quite as high as the one between practical and fashionable footwear that was represented by the boot. But once it was broken, the fashion boot surged to levels of popularity that may have surprised even its creator.

CHAPEAU
MELON ET
Bottes De Cuir

A girl strides through an English country graveyard. She's dressed in a leather jerkin and breeches and tall black leather boots, blonde hair flowing behind her. Confronted by a mountainous villain, she seizes hold of him and hurls him into an open grave.[161] Meet Dr. Cathy Gale, widow, archaeologist, judo black belt, British intelligence agent, and TV sensation—a smart, resourceful woman who can handle herself in a fight. In 1963, British television had never seen anything quite like her before.

The 1960s saw significant changes in the role of women that were not confined to the TV screen. With the approval of the oral contraceptive pill, women gained an unprecedented level of control over their fertility. While social conservatives tut-tutted about promiscuity and extramarital sex, the major impact of this new contraceptive technology was in transforming women's economic role. By uncoupling the onset of sexual activity from the age that women first married, it allowed them to invest in education and other forms of human capital as well as generally becoming more career-oriented. Soon after the birth control pill was legalized, there was a sharp increase in college attendance and graduation rates for women.[162]

Reviewing a September 1963 episode of *Naked City*, Iris Ashley described how fashion could be used on-screen to quickly paint a picture of this new breed of woman. The "blonde and beautiful" heroine lived alone in an apartment, where she played records and lounged around in black leotards and a turtleneck sweater. When a man called to take her out, she was able to swiftly pull on a slim skirt over the tights, a heavy V-neck sweater over the turtleneck, and add tall boots and a fur-trimmed raincoat.[163]

chapter
4

Like no heroine seen on television before, *The Avengers*' Cathy Gale had the academic background, resourceful nature, and physical combat skills that ushered in a new breed of liberated woman for the 1960s. Her leather "fighting suits" and tall boots, seen in this 1964 publicity shot of Honor Blackman and Patrick Macnee, were an integral part of her image. (PA.)

Modern readers may struggle to see anything radical in this, but for a generation of women reared on the elaborate femininity of 1950s fashion, the idea of this relatively mannish take on evening wear—let alone the fact that she was able to make the change in the time it took her date to climb the stairs to her apartment—must have seemed little short of revolutionary.

The changing position of women in society is also reflected in many films and novels of the time; a prime example of this is *The Country Girls Trilogy*, written by the Irish author Edna O'Brien and published between 1960 and 1964.[164] By the last volume, *Girls in Their Married Bliss*, its two protagonists, the young Irishwomen Caithleen "Kate" Brady and Bridget "Baba" Brennan have moved to London to live a life that might, for earlier generations, have been the tale of a rakish young man—or at least it would in Baba's case. Her married lover, a wealthy builder, requests that she buy a pair of boots. As Baba remarks, "'Twas around the time that women were wearing high leather boots to dinner parties and everything." In order to please him, she ends up purchasing a pair of boots so tall that she "looked like a general in them."[165]

For most of the 1960s, there were three main styles of fashion boot: ankle-length, knee-length, and the over-the-knee boots known as *cuissardes*. These differing styles all share two characteristics—they are low-heeled and relatively loose-fitting. The low heel sets them apart from the earlier generation of stiletto-heeled ankle boots, while the loose fit contrasts with the more shaped leg of the late sixties and early seventies.

THE *Sixties* BOOT

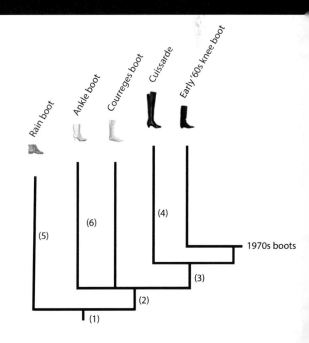

The development of the boot during the first half of the 1960s, as mapped by shared characteristics: (1) shaft length less than 6"; (2) low heel; (3) shaft length greater than 12"; (4) shaft height at or above the knee; (5) rubber or other waterproof material; (6) high- or low-heeled

Boots, Boots, Boots

It wasn't only Baba that was out buying boots. Reading the fashion press for 1963 leaves you in no doubt that, for that year, boots were the big fashion story. "Boots, a seemingly unlikely prospect for fashion honors in the women's shoe industry, are making a big splash in the marketplace," wrote Leonard Sloane in the *New York Times* of May 12. "The transformation of boots from bulky, strictly functional foul-weather gear to an item in milady's wardrobe for both indoors and outdoors is one of the more important shoe fashion stories since modern shoe-making was born in 1862."[166] "Boots will be putting a kick into fashion like no foot fashion in years," Raymonde Alexander wrote in the *Atlanta Constitution* in July. "They are expected to go anywhere a shoe is worn." There would be boots for walking and boots for town, he went on to report. "They may barely reach the ankle or climb to the knee. . . . The favored shape is expected to be the slender leg-hugging knee-high boot of leather so soft it won't stand alone." This soft style of boot was worn crushed like a glove. Regardless of height, the tops of the boots tended to be angled, notched, or softly curved. "They may be plain or collared, banded, furred, or folded."[167]

The year 1963 saw the continuation and more general cementing of a style that Balenciaga had introduced the previous year, a countrified look that Alexander called the "Sportif"; this blended tall boots with tweed vests, shirts, and brown, figure-conscious skirt suits, in which lightweight stretch materials like Lycra were used to maintain a neat body line.[168] Alexander described the Sportif as a country look that had come to the city and was expected to learn city ways, without losing its relaxed, outdoorish manner.[169] The *Times*'s reports of the Paris fashion collections that year include knee-high kid boots by Cardin and tall boots by Jacques Griffe. At YSL, "snug as leggings, the boots by Roger Vivier wrapped the leg to midthigh." Balenciaga showed plaid capes and matching suits "worn with boots that reached to the knee or just above the ankle."[170] "Boots set the pace of fashion this season," agrees Jeanne Molli on August 29, "whether in couture or ready-to-wear collections."[171] But by September the paper is reminding readers that "months before Paris made so much of tall boots, Capezio had designed over-the-knee back laced boots for women."[172] "Boots are everywhere," wrote Patricia Peterson.[173]

This was a sentiment echoed in the pages of *Vogue*. "Boots take over," the magazine announced in the fall of 1963, "for every weather, total chic."[174] In August of that year, a piece titled "For Kicks—Legs" noted the popularity of "boots, boots, boots—marching up and down again in reaches from ankle to over-the-knee" and "stockings that end up boots—long sheaths of satin attached to little rounded shoe-shapes," the latter a reference to Beth Levine's stocking boots. The same article featured black stretch satin evening boots, reaching over the knee with rabbit-fur garters, imported from England by Saks Fifth Avenue.[175]

Vogue's reporting of the New York and Paris collections featured knee-length styles in port-wine suede by Mancini and thigh-high boots in white elkskin by Nina, but there was no doubt about the iconic look of the year.[176] Spread across two pages, we have "the most feminine foot, the most luxurious boot—black crocodile . . . musketeer boots—

shiny, thigh-high, shapely as legs. With this look they brought down the house at St. Laurent." Roger Vivier's iconic boot was paired with a black suede jerkin, a visored leather cap/hood, a strap-sleeved short coat, leather gloves, and tights. In contrast to the other collections, which, if they featured boots at all, tended to pair them with respectable twinsets and suits, this was radical stuff.

Vivier had originally designed the boots for Rudolph Nureyev's performance as the prince in *Swan Lake*. It took the genius of Yves Saint Laurent to recognize the subversive effect of putting a princess in the prince's shoes, much as he adapted the men's suit as women's wear three years later, when he created *Le Smoking*. Saint Laurent was, in effect, reimagining the pantomime principal boy for the haute couture set, recognizing that maybe there were some women out there who would like to play Prince Charming.

It certainly created a splash. "Yves

Yves Saint Laurent's fall collection from 1963 was a radical departure from the "New Look" of the previous decade. In place of nipped waists and full skirts came visored caps, black leather jerkins, and Roger Vivier's towering cuissardes in black crocodile. (© John French/Victoria and Albert Museum, London.)

brings on the beat look in tweed," the *Daily Mail*'s Iris Ashley announced in her July 30 report on the Paris shows. Saint Laurent had covered the legs, but not with the expected dropped hemlines. Instead he had employed boots and heavy stockings—tweed jerkins that ended just above the backside, narrow slacks, and boots that came halfway up the thigh. Black clothes with high boots in crocodile gave what Ashley called "a real space girl effect . . . the boots are tight to the leg and as far as I could see zipped up the side or the back. This is the Beat Look with a dash of cayenne and no mistake."[177]

If anything, *L'Officiel* has even more boots than *Vogue* in 1963—as well as the YSL alligator-skin boots, there are also knee-length styles by Cardin and Durer, cuissardes by Celine, and even a first sighting of Courréges's white kidskin ankle boots, a style that would become a much bigger deal over the next two years. For the most part, all these boots were flat-heeled and—*Vogue*'s enthusiastic verbiage aside—fairly loose-fitting. The shock value here was all about masculinity, and in 1963 it made for a big splash.

"Will you wear the Robin Hood boots?" Iris Ashley asked her readers in the *Mail*, referencing Saint Laurent's mock-croc thigh boots.[178] The paper devoted an entire page to London's reactions to the new fashions. Predictably, romance novelist Barbara Cartland hated them. "I think the collections are perfectly hideous. They are severe, masculine. Designers these days are making women more masculine and men more feminine. It's a *dreadful* mistake." But others, and particularly younger women, were much more enthusiastic. Diana McLeod, the daughter of British Conservative politician Iain McLeod, was very taken with the boots in particular. "I love the boots, they are so different . . . way out, kinky. You've got to be an extrovert to wear them, you can't be a mousy type and just trail along in those boots." The *Mail* sent an actress, Lucille Soong, out on a shopping trip in Hampstead wearing a pair of cuissardes ("twenty five guineas") with a green suede jacket and pink patterned trousers. All too predictably, a stir was caused. "Traffic and trade was brought nearly to a standstill," the paper reported; an accompanying photo shows Ms. Soong examining a greengrocer's wares, while a group of skeptical Hampstead housewives examine her.[179]

Meanwhile, shoe manufacturers prepared to make a killing. In a warehouse on London's Wardour Street, a Mr. Sidney Silbey presided over a newly received inventory of nine thousand pairs of women's boots. "They're going mad," he declared, cheerfully. "You know what they are when something goes to their heads," he continued. "No smart woman is going to be without boots this winter. Look at these, leather-finished plastic, only 52s. 11d. High boots with a Cuban heel and a bit of braid to finish

This selection of outfits, designed by Pierre Cardin and exhibited at the 1963 *Sunday Times* Fashion Awards, clearly demonstrates what Raymonde Alexander of the *Atlanta Constitution* dubbed the "Sportif" look: countrified hats, scarves, tweed suits, and tall boots. The flat-heeled boot styles worn by most of the models contrasts with the one pair of kitten-heeled pumps, representing the more typical conservative footwear of the time. (Daily Herald Archives/Getty Images.)

'em off with. Or these, 14 gns., real leather. Or these—we [are] smothered with orders . . ."[180]

The rapidly growing popularity of fashion boots demanded a new set of rules for wearing them, outlined by Judy Innes in the *Daily Mail*. Don't pair immaculate hair and an elegant coat with boots more suited for Maid Marian. Don't wear boots so wide they look like waders, especially if you're short. Avoid boots with decorations that shout for attention or draw attention to the horizontal line at the top. Watch how you walk—"there's a millimeter . . . which makes all the difference between looking gay and casual and looking like a guardsman on his day off." Wear stockings that are the same color as your boots to make the gap between skirt and boots less obvious. "Any girl that wears high heeled red boots with a shiny black mac is asking for trouble." And above all, if you're going to wear thigh-length boots, remember that you'll need "the personality to make the result look like a girl in boots rather than boots on a girl."[181]

DR. GALE, I PRESUME?

There was one girl who *did* have that sort of personality, and she was generating an enormous amount of public attention for one of the leading television shows of the period. *The Avengers* started life in 1961 as a rather dour procedural series that paired medical doctor David Keel (Ian Hendry) with criminal investigator John Steed

CUISSARDES

Whether worn with jeans and a leather jacket or lighter, floral skirts and dresses of the sort seen here, cuissardes give any outfit a defiantly masculine swagger. (William Moss/Shutterstock.)

The very name has a swashbuckling ring to it. Cuissardes are what the French call women's thigh-length boots, although the term can also be applied to fishermen's waders. The name comes from the French noun *cuisse*, which means "thigh."

Riding boots of this style were widespread in the seventeenth and eighteenth centuries, and conjure up images of cavaliers, pirates, or muske-teers. So a woman wearing boots like this was immediately playing fast and loose with gender roles, something both scandalous and a little exciting. Hence, the enduring appeal of the pantomime principal boy.

Playing with gender identity was part of the attraction of boots in the 1960s. In his excellent history of the boot, Bradley Quinn makes the argument that putting women into boots was one way of rejecting the froufrou femininity of Dior and the New

■ CONTINUED ON PAGE 60

Look.[182] So over-the-knee boots, that most dashingly male of styles, made their appearance relatively early.

There had been a tiny but thriving underground market in handmade women's thigh boots for fetishists as far back as the late nineteenth century. Their earliest appearance in mainstream fashion was in 1962, when Balenciaga's fall collection featured a tall boot by Mancini that just covered the knee, but the one that fashion history tends to focus on is the 1963 alligator-skin thigh boot in Yves Saint Laurent's autumn couture collection.

Cuissardes hung around for much of the sixties. They really took off at the end of the decade and tend to be associated with the more adventurous women of the sixties—none more so than Brigitte Bardot. Anyone who's watched Bardot in black leather thigh boots straddling a gleaming chrome motorbike while crooning Serge Gainsbourg's "Harley-Davidson" will know exactly what I mean (see Chapter 5).

Over-the-knee boots have ebbed and flowed in popularity, and there have been several different incarnations since the emergence of the cuissardes: in the late 1960s to early 1970s; the late 1970s; the late 1980s to early 1990s; the turn of the Millennium; and their current round of popularity, which began in 2009. But none of these boots is really related to the other over-the-knee styles. Each has its origins in the prevailing styles of the time, and their emergence is based on similar, but independent, cultural influences.

(Patrick Macnee). The two initially teamed up to solve the murder of Keel's fiancée by drug dealers, continuing to work together on other crimes. But when Hendry left at the end of the first series, a replacement was needed. Enter Dr. Cathy Gale (Honor Blackman).

Gale was a radical departure from any female character previously seen on TV. Her backstory was that she was an anthropologist married to a farmer in Africa. During her time in Kenya, she had learned to hunt, shoot, and fight. When Mau Mau insurgents killed her husband, she came to London to study for a PhD, and became the curator of a museum. It was there that she met Steed. Originally she was supposed to be one of a rotating cast of partners for Steed, but by the beginning of the third series, in September 1963, it was clear that Cathy Gale was more than enough to carry the show on her own.

From the outset, Gale's character was seen as not just self-assured but also possessed of a high degree of physical prowess. Though she occasionally carried and used a gun, she was far more likely to tackle adversaries physically, using a mixture of judo and other martial arts to incapacitate her opponents with kicks, throws, and karate chops. It was because of this physicality that the original costume designer, Michael Whittaker, made the decision to dress her in leather "fighting suits" that were both tough and allowed freedom of movement.[183] As well as jerkins, jackets, trousers, and breeches, the fighting suits also featured a variety of styles of boot, from calf-high to over-the-knee in length.

The *Daily Mail*'s Iris Ashley hailed the changes in TV represented by shows like *The Avengers*, which recognized the existence of fashion intelligently. In the first series, Gale's costumes veered too close to fancy dress, Ashley believed, but the hiring of a new designer, Frederick Starke, to create the clothing for the third series had the potential to create in Dr. Gale, "black leather, high boots and all," a new prototype for women "who want to look as she does—even if they can't throw their man over their shoulders."[184]

The boots had a significant cultural impact. They quickly became one of the signature features of the show, along with Patrick Macnee's bowler hat and tightly rolled umbrella. In France the show was called *Chapeau Melon et Bottes du Cuir* (Bowler Hat and Leather Boots), which has an admirable sense of Francophone panache. It even spawned a pop record, a lamentably awful affair called "Kinky Boots," "sung" by Blackman and Macnee. Written by the humorist Ned Sherrin for the groundbreaking British satirical show *That Was The Week That Was* (aka TW3), "Kinky Boots" was originally an instrumental piece that was played as backing to a segment on the growing popularity of fashion boots. But then someone had the bright idea of capitalizing on the popularity of *The Avengers* by adding lyrics and having the show's stars sing it.

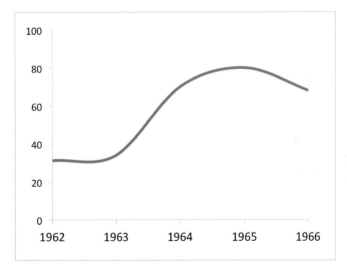

The middle years of the 1960s showed the boot consolidating its role as a key element of the fashions of the time, as shown by the number of times it is mentioned in publications like *Vogue* and *L'Officiel*.

The song might have been atrocious, but there was no doubt that the boots had attracted widespread public attention. Which makes it all the more surprising that the next year, 1964, shows a marked drop in coverage by both *Vogue* and *L'Officiel*. In the case of the French magazine, the drop is precipitous—down from more than forty references to *bottes* and *cuissardes* to barely a tenth of that.[185] Could it be that there was a boot backlash going on?

There are a few things in favor of this interpretation. First, it's clear that some fashion editors were suffering from boot overload. "After a winter of boyish boots . . . fashion is pointing itself in the opposite direction," the *New York Times* notes on February 20, 1964.[186] "Spring shoes are feminine and frankly pretty." It's also apparent that the "youthquake" met with some early resistance. "Pant suits, giddy boots, and above-the-knee hemlines have separated the girls from the women in loud warfare," Angela Taylor wrote on December 5, 1964,[187] "with cries of 'squares' and 'reactionaries' on one side and 'unbecoming' and 'unfeminine' on the other." Saint Laurent himself, the father of the thigh-scraping "Robin Hood" boot, expressed dismay at how widely they had been adopted. "I meant them for country or spectator sports," he protested, in January 1964. "I think boots are ghastly when worn with suits or dresses. So anti-feminine."[188] And in the same year, we also have Genevieve Dariaux's splendidly dismissive statement that "boots are usually a superfluous accessory, more at home in a college girl's closet than in the wardrobe of an elegant woman"[189]

WHITE HEAT

Not that the college girls would necessarily have disagreed. In 1965, Angela Taylor interviewed a gaggle of Vassar, Wellesley, and Bryn Mawr coeds for the *Times*.[190] All the students in question were working in campus branches of various department stores and were unanimous that boots were for cold weather only—"you get kidded a lot otherwise." The only dissenting voice was Pat Brennan, a University of Pennsylvania student, who opined that her Courréges boots were "so comfortable, I love them. And boys might like them better than high boots."

It seems part of the problem was that the boot hadn't completely shaken off its utilitarian roots. The *Times* bucked the trend with an increasing number of boot references,[191] but looking at them in detail reveals a schizoid pattern. Coverage of the fashion shows in 1964 highlights thigh-length boots by Rudi Gernreich, tall black suede boots by Feraud, high-heeled boots by Simonetta et Fabiani, and, of course, those ubiquitous little white Courréges boots. But the advertisements for boots in the paper tout qualities of warmth and water-resistance as much as stylishness. Even for pure fashion boots, the plethora of styles that had emerged from the previous year's shows was causing confusion. "By next winter, fashion boots will have worked out their wild vicissitudes," the *Guardian*'s Alison Adburgham predicted hopefully. "Thigh-length Robin Hoods, moc-crocs, pseudo-riding boots, patent spat boots will have had their moments: but some fashion boots will survive to see other seasons because they have proved themselves both practical and smart."[192]

But there were other cultural forces in play, and not just those that referenced warrior women. These were the years of the space race. In 1961, Alan Shepard became the first American in space; in 1962, John Glenn orbited the planet and President Kennedy pledged that the United States would go to the moon; and from

THE *Courréges* BOOT

The early sixties saw a split in the evolutionary path of the fashion boot. One direction rapidly led upward, over the knee; this was the cuissarde. The other hovered in the region between ankle and midcalf. This style, which had more than a little in common with its progenitor, the rain boot, was probably the most common fashion boot of the years 1963 to 1965.

The best-known examples of these are the boots that were produced by the French designer André Courréges. Courréges was one of the major promoters of modernity in fashion. Along with Mary Quant, he led the drive toward radically shorter skirt lengths in the sixties. His space-age collection of 1964 featured clean, uncluttered geometric designs in white or bright primary colors and the use of novel materials such as metal and PVC. Courréges accessorized his clothes with quirky details such as visors, goggles, and—of course—boots.

The Courréges boot was a low-heeled, calf-length white leather style. It was rapidly copied by other designers and became very widespread. The problem with it, as with all calf-length boots, is that it drew unblinking attention to one of the widest sections of the wearer's legs. Fine if you're a skinny 1960s model with a boyish physique; not so good if you are a real woman, and especially the sort of wealthy matron who could afford couture clothes like the ones made by Courréges. This effectively guaranteed that boot

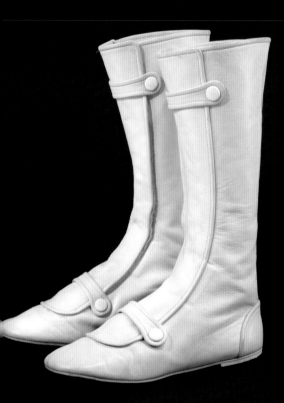

Andre Courrèges's iconic little white boots of the mid-1960s were often imitated but never equaled. This pair is one of the later versions, from 1967. (Image copyright © The Metropolitan Museum of Art. Image source: Art Resource, NY.)

heights would rise again, and before long they did, leaving the Courréges boot an icon, but a dated one. "Ignore anything the fashion wizards insist is a 'must,'" June Wilson advised in the *Atlanta Constitution* of January 25, 1966. "Don't you feel a little embarrassment for the girls who bit on the Courrèges boots?"[198]

1963 onward, the pages of *Life* and other periodicals were filled with images of the astronauts of the Mercury and Gemini projects in their bright white and silver space suits. In Britain, Labour leader and future prime minister Harold Wilson warned his audience at the 1963 party conference that a "new Britain" would need to be forged in the "white heat" of this "scientific revolution."[193] In the middle years of the sixties, eyes were fixed firmly on the future.

So instead of the swashbuckling pirates, princes, and principal boys of the past, designers searching for an assertive image of womanhood increasingly looked forward, to a bright and shiny future that would be delivered by that technological revolution. It would be another twenty years before an American woman went into space,[194] but in 1963 the Soviet Union had already launched its first female cosmonaut, twenty-six-year-old Valentina Tereskova, into orbit around the earth. Fashion designers duly took note.

Among the host of space-age costumes—silver miniskirts, plastic visors, and matching bootees—there is one designer in particular who stands out. André Courréges was born in 1923.[195] His father, a butler, didn't think much of young André's desire to go to art school and wanted him to be an engineer. André obliged, attending the École Nationale des Ponts-et-Chaussées. He went on to become a pilot in the French Air Force during World War II, and it wasn't until the ripe old age of twenty-eight, when he joined Balenciaga in an entry-level role, that he became part of the fashion world. He formed his own fashion house in 1961.

It was Courréges's 1964 "Space Age" collection that thrust him into public view. Rejecting the old norms of elaborate draping and decoration, Courrèges tapped his background in engineering and his love of modernism—he was a great fan of Le Corbusier—to produce clothes that were a celebration of freedom in the form of "truncated A-line dresses, a palette of astronaut-friendly white and silver with an occasional shot of lime and tangerine, and, above all, a miniskirt."[196] But he's probably best remembered for the boots that accompanied these designs: the flat-heeled, white leather, calf-length boots that bear his name.

Courréges's mid-decade collections, with white-gloved and stiff-helmeted models, presented, for some, an unnerving vision of the females of the future. It was an aseptic technology-driven dream, especially when Courréges used clear plastic made from vegetable fibers, not petroleum. In a world that was fantasizing about a designed future, Courréges contributed to the mood, with moon girls whose short skirts exposed their thighs and whose feet were free to hop, skip, and jump in bootees of white kid or clear plastic.[197]

Boots for a New Generation

Courréges may have been accused by Coco Chanel of preferring toddlers to real women,[199] but it was clear that youth was "in." Across the English Channel, another of the sixties' pivotal designers, Mary Quant, was pursuing her own youth-driven vision of fashion. Like Courréges, Quant's clothes were designed for activity—as she described it, "I was making

British designer Mary Quant set out to make fashion both affordable and fun for a new generation of young working women. Key to this was the use of new materials, like the plastic mackintosh and boots seen in this image from 1965. (Central Press/Getty Images.)

The "GO-GO BOOT"

The term "go-go boot" turns up with monotonous regularity in almost every piece of writing on sixties fashion. It's a shorthand term for "a fashion boot of 1960s vintage." But does it have any real meaning? Is there actually such a thing as a go-go boot? Part of the difficulty is that the term is contextual. It implies youth on the part of the wearer; an upbeat, party mood; association with other clothing types, such as miniskirts or hot pants. Go-go boots are less an item of footwear and more a cultural term, defying easy definition. And when you look back at the sixties and see what can be observed based on the magazines, movies, and TV shows of the time, a pattern becomes clear.

In the early years of the decade, prior to around 1965, boots were mostly low heeled and straight-legged. They came in three basic varieties: ankle- or calf-length boots, which were a continuation of those seen in the fifties; knee-length boots; and thigh-high boots, or cuissardes. But from the mid-sixties onward, there is a change in the knee-length boot. The heel became a little higher and blockier, though it didn't reach the heights seen in the following decade. Also, crucially, there was a move from a straight leg to a more fitted style that hugs the calf while remaining relatively loose at the ankle.

So rather than a monolithic "go-go boot," we actually have two distinctive styles of sixties boot, one more masculine, the other leaning toward femininity with its shaped leg and high heel. It's another manifestation of the style pendulum that we noted at the beginning of this book.

The middle years of the sixties saw the remorseless rise of the knee-length fashion boot, such as this example from 1965. (With kind permission of the University of the Arts London, London College of Fashion Archives.)

easy, youthful, simple clothes, in which you could move, in which you could run and jump."[200] As with Courréges, boots were a key element of Quant's designs, culminating in the launch of her own line of footwear, Quant Afoot, in 1967. The difference between Quant and Courréges, however, was one of price. Courréges was designing for the couture market; by contrast, Quant made clothes that could be afforded by shopgirls and typists. For boots, this was the key market. "Much of the credit for the current craze for boots and the boot look can be given to the teens," Raymonde Alexander reported in 1965. "They were the first to latch onto the look as a group. It wasn't long before all ages wanted to look unmistakably young—the boot being the foundation."[201]

By 1965, even *The Avengers* had changed. Cathy Gale had gone, replaced by the more famous Emma Peel (Diana Rigg). In the first season after this transition, the opening credits of the American edition of the show have Peel in a leather catsuit, accompanying Steed as they examine a body on a human-scale chessboard. Steed pours a glass of champagne as Peel tucks a gun into the top of her knee-length boot.[202] But this sequence is deceptive, because in the show itself Mrs. Peel's outfits were quite different; gone were the heavy leather and high boots of the Gale era, replaced with figure-hugging jumpsuits and white ankle boots more suitable for the female astronaut or jet pilot of the future.[203]

Despite this, by the fall of 1965, the trend for boots was upward again, and not just in terms of number of mentions. Although the ankle and calf-length Courréges-influenced styles still dominated the fashion press, taller boots, with taller heels, were gaining ground. The *Atlanta Constitution* reported that in London shoe shine boys had changed their prices from a flat rate to 1 pence per inch to cope with the ever-increasing height of women's boots.[204] The roots of this trend lay back in 1963; "boots on the way up," *Vogue* noted, referencing a new, almost knee-length style by Roger Vivier.[205] This boot showed an important advance on the earlier styles; it was "set on new, incurved, stacked heels." This is a key step in the history of boots in the sixties; it is the development of the stack-heeled boot that marks the final, irreversible shift from footwear that still had strong utilitarian roots toward a pure fashion boot.

By 1966, this was very obvious. The number of references to boots in the *New York Times* may have dipped slightly, but the paper absolutely nailed it on December 23, 1966, when Angela Taylor wrote that the "boot ideal is tall and skinny enough to show the curve of the ankle."[206] This is the look that can be seen across the *Times*, *L'Officiel*, and *Vogue*: high-legged boots, in leather, suede, patent, and—increasingly—new materials like plastic or vinyl, with a stacked heel and the shaft slightly curved to emphasize the shape of the ankle. Manufacturers duly took note. Alison Adburgham reported in the *Guardian* that the British shoe firm Ravel had "decided, not without trepidation, to back boots again this autumn and put into production 30 different kinds of high boots for their Pinet, Mondaine, and Ravel shops." Other British shoe firms were also awaiting the first reports from Paris with anxiety, Adburgham continued. If the Paris shows did not feature high boots, manufacturers and retailers would be left with undersold stock—"Boots on their hands," as Adburgham put it, a possibly unintentional pun. "But Paris *has* shown boots—so everyone is talking, writing, and photographing boots. Paris is a confirming place."[207]

Previous generations of women had regarded a pair of shoes as a serious investment. By contrast, the young women of the sixties "youthquake" put more emphasis on affordability. Plastic boots, like the example shown here, may have been short-lived, but they were also massively popular.

These tall boots were the solution to cold knees exposed by short skirts, Raymonde Alexander wrote in July 1966. Reporting on a collection by designer Pauline Trigère, he noted that Trigère chose glove-soft leather boots that reached above the knees because she disliked the effect of shorter boots, which cut a woman's silhouette into three parts.[208] Others had no problem with a gap. Describing the Italian fashions of 1966, John Hart declared that "[Italian designer Rocco] Barocco is the leader of the cool, swinging in postilion boots that look like Italy. Odd they never thought of that before. The super-Italian boots zip up the back and cover the kneecaps in front, fitting almost as closely as a stocking. A stretch of real stocking is still exposed between boot top and mini-length hem, which suddenly seems not so short after all. Barocco proved it neatly with a lavender suit of nattier wool."[209]

The year 1966 brought the winter of the long, swashbuckling coat, made from cloth or fur and worn with a buckled belt and high boots. Sometimes a cape was worn instead, which reached to midcalf or even the ankle, "but neither the long coat or the cape look well unless there are boots below them." Gloria Emerson cautioned in the *Atlanta Constitution*.[210] In the Paris collections that year, *Vogue* reported coats that fall to midcalf with their "hems striking six inches below the tops of tall boots." These are "Boots for a heroine," the magazine exclaimed. "What she knows is this: boots have never been more exciting . . . vital to the new hemlines in fashion now . . . snugged against the leg, tipping the base of the knee, to wear with coats to mid-calf and dresses above the knee."[211]

There's a poignant moment in "The Forget-Me-Knot," an episode from the sixth series of *The Avengers*. Emma Peel's husband, thought to be long dead, has been found and rescued; Peel is leaving Steed to be reunited with him. As she descends the stairs from Steed's apartment, she meets her replacement, Tara King (Linda Thorson). Peel, that habitual wearer of midsixties ankle boots, is being supplanted by King, who is sporting culottes and a pair of leg-hugging, thigh-high latex boots. Peel gives her a critical piece of advice—"He likes his tea stirred anti-clockwise." The guard has changed. By the end of 1966 boots had, in the words of the *New York Times*, "become a fashion way of life."[212]

The greatest kiss-off in the history of pop was recorded in 1965 and released in February of the following year. To appreciate its impact, you need to understand that in the early sixties, women's reactions to deadbeat boyfriends, at least in popular culture, were those of Lesley Gore, crying in a corner at her party because Johnny hasn't shown up. Nancy Sinatra wasn't crying. Her response to her lying, cheating man was to walk out the door. Right over the top of him.

"These Boots Are Made for Walkin'" was written by Lee Hazlewood, a longtime collaborator with Sinatra. He infamously instructed her to sing like "a fourteen-year-old girl who fucks truck drivers," but with its shameless swagger she actually sounds more like an woman who drives a truck. It's not at all a flirtatious song. And in this context, it is most definitely a song that plays on the masculine side of boot wearing.

When we gaze back at the sixties, we tend to think of the whole miniskirt-and-boots look of the mid-decade as distinctly feminine, an *Austin Powers* vision of disposable, swinging dolly birds. But the emergence of boots as a fashion item in the early sixties was more of a reaction to the frills-and-petticoats delicacy of the New Look era, an anti-feminine movement.

The first generation of sixties fashion boots—low-heeled, loose-fitting, and worn with rugged, tweedy suits—tended to emphasize masculinity when compared with the delicate shoemaker's confections of the previous

Nancy Sinatra about to start walking, April 1966. (Keystone Pictures USA/Alamy Stock Photo)

decade. It wasn't until the mid-sixties, when Sinatra's record was released, that fashion boots first began to acquire the kitten-heeled, form-fitted characteristics that made them distinct from their distant progenitor, the riding boot.

So while Nancy Sinatra may have danced her way across America's TV screens in cute little go-go boots, the lyrics and intent of the song were more about giving her man a hard kick from a pair of work boots. Those boots are a sign of assertiveness and liberation.

The claim is often made that Nancy's first pair of iconic white knee-length boots were purchased from Beth's Bootery, the newly opened boot store at Saks Fifth Avenue that featured designs by Beth Levine.[213] It makes for a nice story, linking the two women who arguably did the most to popularize and mainstream the idea of the boot as a fashion item for women.

Unfortunately, it's not true. The Bootery did not open its doors until five years after Sinatra's record was released and, according to the lady herself, quoted by Rachel Bergstein in *Women from the Ankle Down,* she actually picked up the pair in question in London's Carnaby Street. "Some of the boots [came from Levine], but I was getting boots mostly in London and that's not Beth Levine." Nancy was more inspired by the looks being pioneered by Mary Quant, and though she did later acquire some pairs from the Levines, when she started having boots custom-made, "my official boot maker was [Pasquale] De Fabrizio here in Los Angeles, and he made a lot of wonderful boots that I used on stage."[214]

THE AGE OF
The Boot

Paris, the autumn of 1967. In a television studio, on a set made up to look like an auto repair shop, a massive, chrome-plated Harley-Davidson is surrounded by hanging chains and red-and-white oil drums . . . astride it stands arguably the most famous woman in France, "black leather miniskirt; shiny, high-heeled boots that climb up to her thighs; the dark eyes; that blonde mane of hair,"[215] singing an outrageous song that freely blurred the lines between riding a bike and riding a man.

The term "icon" is heavily overused, but there's a good case to be made that Brigitte Anne-Marie Bardot is just such a thing. She was, in 1969, the first woman chosen to be the official personification of Marianne, the national symbol of the French Republic, representing liberty, reason, and the triumph of republicanism over monarchy. You don't get much more iconic than that. As Beth Levine once said, the boot, like the Pill, was a symbol of women's new freedom and emancipation.[216] So the idea of Bardot as a booted Marianne has a lot going for it.

The reality is a little different. Bardot *was* an early adopter of boots—a series of photos from 1963 shows her mingling with adoring fans in London while filming the movie *Une ravissante idiote*; she wears narrow pants tucked into calf-length leather boots. Then from the middle years of the decade, we have a few images of miniskirts and knee-length boots. But most of the photos we think of as "typifying" the star come from a relatively brief period of her life, spanning 1967 and 1968, a period that marks the start of an age when the fashion boot reigned supreme.

Brigitte Bardot straddles her Harley during the filming of her 1967 French TV special. (INA/Getty Images.)

A Year-round Phenomenon

There's a very famous scene in *The Wizard of Oz* (1939) where Dorothy's house, swept up by a tornado, has crash-landed back to earth. She opens the door and steps from the sepia-toned world of her Kansas childhood into the bright Technicolor of Oz. It's one of the great moments of cinema. You get much the same sensation when you open the September collections edition of *Vogue* from 1967. Previous years had been full of monotone imagery, stark black-and-white contrasts. But now we have an extraordinary riot of color. It provides a strange counterpoint to the history of the sixties. By the end of the decade, the optimism of the early to middle years—faith in technology, progress in social change and equal rights, the sweeping away of Old Guard politics—had been replaced by something darker and more pessimistic. These are the years of Altamont and the Manson family, the Tet Offensive and the murders of Bobby Kennedy and Martin Luther King Jr.[217]

In the light of these events, some violent, many tragic, it seems almost trivial to report that fashion, too, was being roiled by change. "Fashion is in a state of flux," Phyllis Heathcote wrote in the *Guardian*, describing the Paris collections. "Kid fashions for everybody have had their day . . . what we want is adult clothes with a young look. We have had enough of the mini and all its works." Heathcote believed that the new look would concentrate on three points, "the only ones that matter. Where, if anywhere, you place your belt; how close your clothes lie to your body, how much leg you show." This meant a more natural waistline, longer skirts, and a more fitted line. The new breed of fashions would have more femininity and more romance. Boots were a key component of this, because they would counteract the

During the mid-sixties a fashion footwear war was raging between those two great rivals, the boot and the shoe. Thanks to the efforts of Beth Levine, Mary Quant, and others, the boot had escaped from the galoshes-and-gaiters ghetto of rainwear. But now the shoe had a new ally–the kneesock. One effect of the sixties fashion "youthquake" was a desire on the part of designers to make grown women look like little girls. The fashion papers were filled with a new generation of big-eyed, small-breasted, narrow-hipped models. Making the fashionable woman look like she was an escapee from the local parochial school, with a plaid minikilt and kneesocks, was the logical next step.[219]

Of course, there were good, practical reasons why you might opt for socks rather than boots. A rise in the price of leather during the mid-sixties made a decent pair of boots an expensive proposition. Socks were more forgiving of variations in calf shape–they didn't hang off skinny legs or strain uncomfortably against fuller ones. And the shoe/sock combination was more flexible–you could always ditch the socks in favor of tights or bare legs. Of course, socks were less suited to cold, wet weather and you couldn't get the shiny, space-age effect that boots could add. In 1964 there was a brief and not very successful flirtation with gaiters–leather sleeves that would clip over the shoe to give the effect of a boot but with the flexibility of a sock. It didn't catch on. What was needed was a cheap boot that would give the leg-hugging silhouette of a sock but the shiny, waterproof appearance of more expensive styles.

Enter the vinyl boot. A product of the explosive growth in popularity of man-made materials, it had a two-part construction—a semirigid plastic shoe to which was attached a one-piece sleeve of stretchable vinyl that formed the vamp and shaft of the boot. An elasticated strip or, alternatively, a strap and buckle around the top of the shaft, helped to prevent the boot from sagging. By the end of the 1960s, vinyl knee boots were hugely popular. They came in a variety of colors—white or black were the most common, but red, green, blue, or more exotic shades were not unknown. They were cheap to make, cheap to buy, and cheap to replace when they fell apart, which they all too frequently did. They remained popular well into the early 1970s, when real leather became more affordable and artificial leather substitutes more widely available.

And as hemlines continued to climb, the vinyl boot rose with them, over the knee and higher. So high that at times it was hard to tell them apart from stockings. Some of them even came with a garter belt to hold them up. Unlike their contemporary, the cuissarde, these ultrahigh boots were something entirely new. The cuissarde looked backward, to the swaggering boots of cavalrymen and pirates, appropriating their masculine panache for the liberated women of the 1960s. The late-sixties thigh boot looked forward, utilizing new materials to give legs a sleek, futuristic look. It's not coincidental that glossy black thigh boots were one of the main accessories of Pierre Cardin's space-age collections of 1967 and '68.

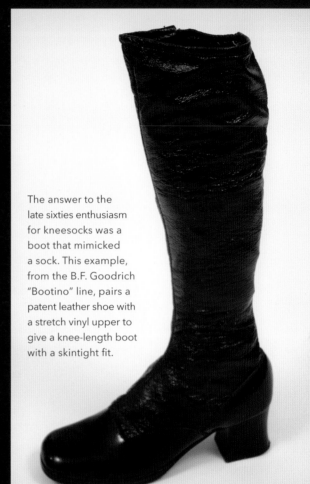

THE *Vinyl* BOOT

The answer to the late sixties enthusiasm for kneesocks was a boot that mimicked a sock. This example, from the B.F. Goodrich "Bootino" line, pairs a patent leather shoe with a stretch vinyl upper to give a knee-length boot with a skintight fit.

Vinyl was only one of the materials utilized. Designers also experimented with latex, leather, nylon, and various other types of fabric. The key feature, and the one that set them apart from the cuissarde, is that the boot clung tightly to the leg. If the knee-length vinyl boot was an alternative to knee-length socks, these much taller boots were intended to replace stockings, pantyhose, or leggings.

Ultraboots dominated the fashion papers for a couple of years but never really gained widespread acceptance. They looked amazing on the models in *Vogue*, but in real life they were challenging to wear. If your legs were too thin, they would sag inelegantly. Too stout, and they would look overstuffed. And the garter belt was unnecessarily fiddly for a generation that had already abandoned stockings and garters. By the end of the decade, the tall vinyl boot still survived but now as a more conventional design, a longer version of the knee-length boot that just covered the knee. It lasted into the early years of the 1970s before finally disappearing for good.

more unflattering effects of a midcalf skirt and help to maintain the fitted silhouette. But Heathcote cautioned against regarding boots as a catchall solution. "Boots help. But who in their senses wants to trail around in boots all day—especially the new peel-on, above-the-knee, clinging, claustrophobic 'stocking boot'?"[218]

Phyllis Heathcote may have been a boot skeptic, but she was in a minority. That exuberant explosion of color seen in *Vogue* most definitely included boots, a regular cornucopia of boots with a color pallete that matched and complemented the rest of the outfit—not just traditional black leather, but red, white, blue, silver, yellow, and orange, and in materials like patent leather, suede, PVC, and any manner of exotic products of the laboratory. This was the beginning of the first great peak in boot popularity, at least as measured by citations in the fashion press, which started in 1967, dipped just a little in 1968, and then soared to new heights in 1970. It's pretty much consistent across all the publications surveyed. And what makes this period so unique is the pattern of boot references.

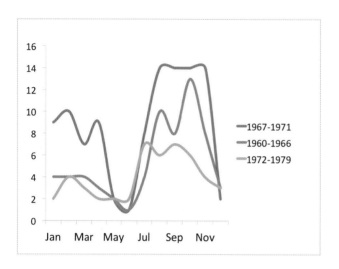

By and large, and unsurprisingly, interest in boots is strongly seasonal. It starts as fall fashions begin to arrive in the stores during September, rises through the autumn and early winter, then drops off sharply in January and February, when thoughts turn hopefully (and optimistically) to spring outfits and swimwear. Enter the term "boot" into Google Trends, which shows interest measured in Web searches, and you can see this pattern clearly: a series of regularly spaced seasonal peaks, year after year, starting when Google began to record search metrics in 2010. We don't have Google Trends for the 1960s, but tracking the average number of mentions of "boots" in *Vogue* per month reveals pretty much the same pattern for the years 1960 to 1966. The peak comes a little earlier than Google shows it, because of the traditional pattern of fashion publishing (fall previews in July/August, party clothes in December, spring/summer previews in January). But it's still recognizable. It's also there for most of the 1970s, albeit the peak period lasts longer—a reflection, perhaps of just how common a footwear item the fashion boot was in the middle and late seventies. But the real surprise is the pattern for 1967–71.

During that big, decade-straddling peak, boots had almost year-round popularity. The only real decline is at the height of the summer fashion coverage, in May and June. For the years 1967–1971, boots were a part of fall, winter, spring, and even summer

Compared to the periods before and after, between 1967 and 1971—the peak of its popularity—the fashion boot was a year-round object of interest in the press. The number of mentions dips only at the height of summer fashion coverage in June and July.

outfits, at least in the high-fashion world represented by *Vogue*. And while today's boho fashions may flirt with the idea of a summer boot, it seems that in the history of footwear those four years beginning in 1967 were the only time when this was the case.

Before the summer of 1967 had even ended it was clear that boots were a big deal in the fashion world. In an August 16 *Washington Post* article on boot pioneers Beth and Herbert Levine, Eugenia Sheppard wrote, "Boots have been so big that it was hard to believe the fashion would last another year." But it did, and the Levines knew why: "What else can women wear when winter's cold and skirts are still short?" Sheppard went on to report that almost one-third of the Levines' production in the fall of 1967 would be boots.[220] Sheppard herself had already called the trend back at the beginning of the year. "If there still exists that kind of hackneyed old thing called a status symbol in fashion," she declared "that status symbol, right at this minute, is absolutely and certainly the right pair of boots. Boots, if they have class are, besides hair, the things most women are willing to invest in rather heavily."[221]

At the same time, across the Atlantic, Alison Adburgham was seeing the emerging trends in the stores. "September is the start of a new fashion year as far as fashion is

THE *Boots* OF LATE '60s

The mid-sixties saw a move from the low-heeled designs of earlier years to a higher, stacked heel. A worldwide rise in the cost of leather, combined with the emergence of a range of artificial fabrics, led to the development of new styles of close-fitting boots of knee length and higher. Even leather boots of this period favored a shaped calf. It was this second generation of "go-go boot" that was to give rise to the next generation of fashion boots in the 1970s.

The development of the boot during the late 1960s. Rather than a monolithic "go-go boot," there are actually four distinct styles: an early and a later variant of the knee-length boot and two styles that use artificial materials to achieve a skintight fit that mimics a sock or stocking. (1) Shaft length greater than 12″; (2) shaft fitted to the curve of the calf; (3) heel height greater than 1″; (4) stretch upper of vinyl or other artificial material; (5) shaft height at or above the knee.

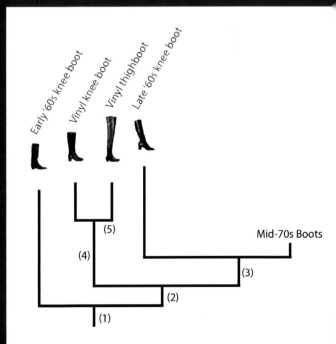

KAYS 44

A typical look from the golden age of the fashion boot—thigh-skimming winter coats with black knee-length boots. This example is from the British mail-order company Kays. (University of Worcester.)

concerned," she reported in the *Guardian* on August 30. "It is amusing to spot the post-Paris accessories . . . the chain belts, and the wide leather belts with important brass buckles; dark brown and black stockings, dressy blouses with frothy fronts . . . And the boots. Those glove-fitting, thigh-high boots that were in so many of the Paris shows already have their counterparts at 89s 11d in the West End branches of Dolcis."[222] In the *Daily Record*, Felicity Green was inspired to channel Sir Walter Scott. "Breathes there a girl with soul so dead she doesn't own at least one pair of high boots."[223]

New Styles, New Materials

In truth, this was all about new materials and new colors—the fashion equivalent of Dorothy's multicolored landing in Oz. Covering most of the leg in tight, shiny, brightly colored vinyl or glovelike leather, the glove-tight fashion boot of 1967 gave women a sleek but exuberantly colorful look that had never been seen before. In January of that year, Sheppard reported that Mancini's "Danou" boot (retailing for the princely sum of $59.95) was the choice of well-heeled society matrons, including Doris Duke, Jackie Onassis, and Amanda Burden: "easier to get into than some, because it zips up the side, comes to just below the knee . . . it crushes like a glove and is snug enough to stay up without support."[224] By March, the *Washington Post* was reporting that stewardesses in "miniskirts and mod boots" had been making "test" flights on American's nonstop Los Angeles to New York flights.[225] And when the Levines won the 1967 Coty American Fashion Critics Award, celebrity clients such as Marlene Dietrich and Barbra Streisand modeled their boots.

Reporting on Pierre Cardin's 1967 collection, Phyllis Heathcote and Alison Adburgham were unenthused about the opening moments, "in which men and girls wandered around traumatically in astronauts' gear" to the sound of "cosmic music," but once this curtain-raiser was done and the main show began, they were pleased to see no radical changes to the basic influence that Cardin had exerted over fashion styles for the last few seasons. "The Cardin girl is the same little sophisticate, just six months older. She still loves swinging shifts. But her skirts are a little longer. Her

Thigh-Length BOOTS LATE '60s

This pair of thigh-length boots dates from 1967–1969, the period when boot length reached its apogee; the heel is relatively low, but the leg is unbelievably high—29" from heel to thigh, compared with around 14" for a regular knee-length boot. At that height, they were more hip boots than thigh boots. Another striking feature is just how narrow the calves and tiny the ankles are. Even taking into account that women's legs were less aerobically sculpted fifty years ago, you'd need the physique of Twiggy or Jean Shrimpton to get into them. Not only are the calves and ankles tiny, but the top of the boot is equipped with a couple of circulation-challenging elastic gussets that would have kept it clamped brutally tightly to the thigh. There was no need for garters with these boots.

The foot is lined with sheepskin—a nice touch that would have kept the wearer's feet warm in the depths of winter. Lined boots are not uncommon, but it's rare that the lining is confined to the foot. The most likely reason is that the sleek lines of the boot would have been spoiled if the lining had extended into the shaft. Certainly there would be no room for both sheepskin and leg in those tiny ankles.

This was a time when boots reached skyscraping heights. This one, from the late 1960s, reaches almost to the hips.

dresses brush the top of the knee, and sometimes her coats just cover it." Footwear was "sturdy" with squared heels about an inch high. Aluminum was used to outline welts and heels, and to circle the tops of the boots. In 1967 there were "no thigh-high boots, mercifully . . . they are all well below the knee."[226]

Born in Venice to French parents in 1922, Cardin trained as a tailor, working for a number of different fashion houses, including "New Look"-era Dior, before starting his own company in 1950. He is probably best known for his avant-garde designs of the 1960s, when he was one of a number of designers to tap into the technocentric space-age ethos of the sixties. His geometric designs were the antithesis of the ultrafeminine New Look. In keeping with the futuristic theme, he emphasized the use of nontraditional materials—plastic, vinyl, and metal. Given this, it's not surprising that boots were a significant part of the Cardin designs of the late sixties. He used close-fitting, high-legged styles to provide a sleek silhouette and shiny materials like patent leather to emphasize the high-tech look.

Worldwide, the popularity of boots was plain to see. A good sense of this can be gleaned from the pages of *Australian Women's Weekly*, whose readers plainly hungered for pictures of the latest fashions from the Northern Hemisphere. So here we find Madame Guy de Rothschild walking with Maria Callas, Elizabeth Taylor, and Richard Burton at the races at Longchamps and wearing black patent leather thigh boots with a matching bag and mini Persian lamb coat.[227] Taylor herself was pictured in hip-high leather boots and an ermine coat, departing from Heathrow on a flight to New York,[228] while Down Under, at the Randwick races, a red Russian fox minicoat and thigh-length brown leather boots were the choice of Susan Palmer, worn with a matching fur hat and high-necked bone wool dress. And in June 1968, on the streets of Sydney, junior home economist Christine Nossiter was "eye catching in black leather thigh-high boots, worn with a hand-knitted Italian wool dress in an unusual sludge color."[229]

BEBÉ AND SERGE

And then there was Bardot. By 1967 she was not quite the "sex kitten" of collective memory. She was thirty-three years old, eighty percent of her film output was now behind her, and she was only six years away from retiring from acting altogether. As John Lennon tartly commented after meeting her in 1968, "I was on acid, and she was on her way out." He wasn't referring to the door.[230] And yet, Lennon apart, she could still exert a powerful spell on men. Unhappily married to German millionaire Gunter Sachs, she engaged in a string of affairs. One of her lovers from this period described how "she dealt with her conquests like a praying mantis . . . [they were] zombified by Bardot. That woman had a supreme talent for grinding men into rubble."[231]

Then in October 1967, she met with Serge Gainsbourg to discuss music for a TV special. He had a song that he thought might be just right for her, a song about motorcycles. Bardot had no particular interest in bikes, but she was more than a little interested in Gainsbourg, a chaotic artistic genius who was the antithesis of every man she had been with before. They broke the ice with a little champagne. Things progressed. By the time they got around to recording "Harley-Davidson," the two were embarked on a torrid affair.

In the words of his biographer, Gilles Verlant, Gainsbourg took the fading star and made her hip again. He took total control of the visuals for the TV show, picking Bardot's wardrobe according to what he thought would suit her. So it's tempting to think that he was the one who chose those thigh-high boots—which also turn up in another number, "Comic Strip." The boots were made by Roger Vivier. His list of accomplishments as a designer of footwear is a long one, and he's already earned his place in the history of fashion boots because of the groundbreaking women's cuissardes he designed for Yves Saint Laurent in 1963; his second major contribution was giving Bardot her boots for "Harley-Davidson."

And Bardot's boots kept on walking, through airport terminals and on the streets of Paris, Rome, and Saint-Tropez, through 1968 and beyond. My particular favorite from this period is a photo taken in Grenada, Spain. Bardot, hair back and resplendent in leather miniskirt and thigh boots, saunters along, oblivious to the frankly lustful stares of two men, one young and one old, both sets of eyes glued to the expanse of thigh revealed between skirt and boot top.

She wasn't the only one wearing boots in 1968. Their popularity showed no sign of abating as winter turned to spring and summer that year. "Boots will be off on a big new kick this autumn," *Australian Women's Weekly* reported in February. "The long vinyl boot could be the single biggest item to dominate the fashion scene, striding round town under a mini, more often than not topped by a swinging cape."[232] In July, the *New York Post* reported, silver boots for evening wear "sported a golf ball size cluster of rhinestones at the place where one would expect spurs. Another clump of fancy stones was attached at the top of the boot, just below the knee."[233] For those of a more organic or hippie-ish bent, Desco was selling squaw boots "made exactly the way American Indians once made them." "It's the big new look" a Desco spokesman declared. Quoted in the *New York Times*, Herbert Levine was delighted. "When boots are selling in August in Lubbock, Texas, then I know boots are going to be big this year."[234]

Once again, it was mostly the very tallest of boots that made the headlines. The Levines were marketing a stocking boot, which was a jersey or nylon upper, chemically treated so that it looked like leather, attached to a leather shoe. The boots hooked up to a belt ("sold separately" of course—Herbert Levine was a canny businessman). Meanwhile Delman produced black Corfam boots with white scrollwork detailing that climbed past the knee; a plainly baffled shoe salesman was quoted by the *Times* as saying they "would be nice to go wading in, or fishing out West."[235] Rudi Gernreich teamed long suede boots with dresses and coats that were "the length of pages' tunics." But it wasn't all about principal boy outfits—Roger Vivier produced jodhpur boots specifically designed for women who wanted to wear pants—still seen as a challenge even in those radical times.

But if the late sixties were golden years for the fashion boot, it was in the first two years of the next decade that it truly hit its apogee. "Boots go with almost anything now," Frances Cawthon wrote in the *Atlanta Constitution* in September 1970. "What do you wear with boots? It's easier this season to ask what you DON'T wear with boots."[236] A week later, Enid Nemy described boots as being snapped up like peanuts at a cocktail party. "The boot phenomenon, now in its second year, is all but inexplicable," she wrote. "Some women are buying them for the first time; others are adding to already extensive boot wardrobes. A surprising number have worn them through the recent heat wave, and certainly they are seen with every skirt length." Harold Kaplan, a buyer for I. Miller Shoes, summed it up succinctly: "If they can walk, they're buying boots."[237]

In trying to break down the complex underlying causes for the soaring popularity of boots, Nemy proposed that it was the interplay of six different factors, which are worth looking at in detail here. The first of these was the massive expansion in the range of available styles, colors, and textures. Courréges's little white boots aside, the predominant look of the early sixties had been black leather. Striking, for sure, but also hard and a little masculine. Now women could pick from boots that were smooth, shiny, dull, stretch, suede, snakeskin, alligator/crocodile, satin, or velvet. They could, in Nemy's words, mix chic with femininity.

Youthful fashions from the 1970 autumn/winter catalog of U.K. mail-order company Freemans. The boots are ubiquitous, in a variety of colors and materials. (Freemans Grattan Holdings.)

There was also a much greater emphasis on the total "look" of an outfit. Whereas the first generation of fashion boots had sat a little uneasily with tweeds and twinsets, now boots were matched to the color pallete of the outfit. The contemporary elaborate costumes of the period were receptive to including decorative boots, and the growing reaction to the modernity of the mid-sixties, in the form of the Edwardian revival that began in 1966–67, provided a huge boost in popularity to lace-up boots that drew for inspiration on the footwear of the turn of the century (see Chapter 6).

While boots in the sixties are most strongly associated, at least in the contemporary imagination, with miniskirts, they were also very suitable to the new midi-length skirts that became popular at the end of the decade. The length of the skirt, which just skimmed the top of the boot, was ideal for that style

Over-the-Knee
BOOTS EARLY '70s

This bright red leather boot dates from 1969–1971. The style is typical for the period, but the material is not. These knee-skimming boots were more often fabricated from man-made materials, which guaranteed a skintight fit and shiny finish at the expense of longevity. That may be one reason why this pair survived the last five decades while so many of its contemporaries did not.

The strap-and-buckle details at the instep and the top of the shaft are very typical of this period and are entirely decorative; it's not possible to adjust the fit with the top strap, as was the case with some contemporary boots. Instead, the close fit of this boot is achieved by the cut of the shaft, which is narrow at the ankle and tightly curved to follow the line of the calf. In contrast to the vinyl designs of the period, there is little flexibility, which would have made these boots a challenge to wear.

Tight-fitting, buckled over-the-knee boots were very popular at the beginning of the 1970s. This one is unusual in being made from leather—the most common styles had uppers made from artificial stretch materials.

of footwear. Women who liked the look of boots with their short skirts in 1969 were able to transfer the same boots to the new skirts in 1970. The end of the sixties was also the time when designers finally got around to tackling the problem of fit; the sagging and bunching that plagued earlier generations of fashion boots—going all the way back to the Russian boots of the 1920s—was finally eliminated, not just by using new, stretchable materials that clung to the leg but also by employing leg-hugging tops, buckles, and laces. Better fit meant more feminine boots.

As befits footwear that began as a utilitarian item, boots were (and are) inherently practical. "In cold weather and slush, good-looking boots are better than soggy shoes," Nemy declared. But, most important, by the end of the sixties boots for women were no longer seen as strange or *avant garde*. "Boots aren't a fad anymore," Nemy quotes one designer as saying. "They've been around for almost seven years and they have become a way of living and moving. They're comfortable, useful, easy to wear, and even sexy."[238] Describing the fashions of winter 1970, the *Guardian* reported that Parisians "mostly wear their overcoats covering the knee, except those—and there are many—who wear long, above-the-knee boots. These are worn with skirts just short enough to leave a gap above the boots of a few centimetres—a very seductive gap."[239]

Changes in skirt style went beyond the mini and the midi. The microskirts of the late sixties may have driven the rise of the boot to new heights, but it was lengthening skirts at the end of the sixties that pulled the attention of designers back to the ankle. Boots became a medium for decoration—contrasting colors of leather, snakeskin, fur; canvas boots with embroidered flowers; and "front interest" features such as buckles, lacing, or zippers. These boots were, for the most part, shorter than the towering ones of the previous few years—stopping just short of the knee—but they had higher heels—2 to 2.5″ on average.

GAUCHOS, SHORTS, AND HOT PANTS

It wasn't just midi- and maxiskirts that helped to sustain the popularity of the boot. There was a new craze—gaucho pants. In April 1971, Dale Cavanaugh wrote in the *Washington Post* that women were grabbing cropped pants "because of that pair of great-looking boots you bought. You hate to cover up all that style with long pants. Besides, you discovered that long pants don't tuck into boots all that conveniently. That's when you decided that knickers and boots were made for each other."[240] The ideal pair of knickerbockers, she decreed, should fall 4″ below the kneecap or 2″ below the top of knee-length boots. "The Boot is unequivocally the shoe to wear with gauchos," the *Atlanta Constitution*'s Frances Cawthon decreed. "And the gaucho is unequivocally one of the leading silhouettes for 1970. It's not just a sportswear look for leisure: it's a serious contender for the daytime city costume and often replaces the skirt for a new suits look."[241]

Angela Taylor wrote that gauchos were an antidote to the perception of the midiskirt as "matronly"; the cropped pants were so popular that women "finding them scarce in stores at first, began cutting off pants legs or tucking pants into boots for a knicker effect." But something even more radical was on the way; short shorts, or "hot pants" as they came to be known. Writing in the fall of 1970, Taylor reported that "short pants are getting the fashion whirl for spring and summer. In Paris, young girls are reportedly wearing them right now, over tights, with boots and long coats," while in New York, according to the *Times*, Mrs. Harilaos Theodoracopoulis, "wife of a shipping executive and mother of two," was teaming tweed shorts by Halston with capes and tall boots.[242]

"The boot is the accessory for the 1970 daytime dress—BUT," warned Francis Cawthorn, "you have to be careful with your choice. One which crinkles too much, or is of heavy leather, often looks untidy with the more supple fabrics of which one-piece dresses are made today. If your boot isn't smooth, then it's best to substitute a stocking-boot with a more sleek fit." In a marked change from the earlier generation of boots, Cawthorn advised that the new rule to follow was that the hemline should reach to the boot tops or a little below. For evenings, boots could be used to accessorize ethnic eveningwear, "since many folkloric costumes around the world DO feature a boot of some sort for women. . . . Good choices this fall will be the laced, fitted versions or those with special trim such as embroidery." For evenings, Cawthorn recommended a stocking boot, "perhaps of sparkling lame or stretch fabric. It can be worn under ankle-length dresses also."[243]

As we've already seen, the numbers do not lie: this truly was the period when boots became not only a daytime and evening staple but also a year-round fashion for women. "Boots will march right on into spring," Eugenia Sheppard declared in November 1970, and although "almost anything that can be done has

The photographer John Hendy took many street shots recording fashions in London's Kings Road during the early 1970s. Here, a young woman photographed in 1971 wears shiny, leg-hugging stretch boots with an above-the-knee dress. (John Hendy.)

been done to boots," designers continued to push the limits of the possible. "They don't have to look like boots," Mary Ann Crenshaw wrote in the *Times* in February 1971. "With no-one quite certain whether hemlines are up, down, or gone, show designers have made the wrapped leg their answer to any fashion question. To them, a wrapped leg can mean anything from a sandal strapped thigh-high to a boot that has an open toe, open heel, open front—in fact, almost no boot at all."[244]

The summer of 1971 saw a profusion of summery boots. The Chelsea Cobbler had in previous years sold a popular canvas boot; their 1971 version was open at the front, with scallops, and tied loosely with "big, floppy bows." Then there were "caning boots," in which the wearer's bare leg was wrapped with thin, woven leather straps, which had an unfortunate habit of trapping toes. And what of the thigh-high sandal? True, the straps tended to slip down around the ankles, meaning the wearer had to either tie them so tight it cut off her circulation or tie them around thigh and knee and hope for the best. But those suede or leather straps snaking up the leg . . . in the words of shoe designer Laura Tosato, they were part of the "new femininity, sensuality, and sexuality in fashion."[245] Even if no one could agree whether they were boots or not.

PEAK POPULARITY

What was not in doubt was the popularity of boots. Enid Nemy's report on the "Great Boot Boom of '70" makes it clear that this was something special, with a rush on boots (variously described as "unbelievable," "incredible," and "fantastic") that began in the midsummer of 1970. "We sold as many boots in the last week of July this year as we did in all of August last year," Nemy quotes Irwin Mervish, the merchandise manager of shoes at A&S, as saying. For the customers interviewed by Nemy, the word "addiction" is not an unfair description. "I like the look. I bought three pairs last year, two pairs today, and I'm going to get two more pairs. I have suede, wet look, and leather boots and I'll probably get a pair of evening boots later," said Victoria Abbate, a young shopper at Saks. "I like them with both short and long clothes. I have six pairs now and I'll probably get another two," says Mrs. William Skinner, a housewife, at Macy's. But an unnamed woman writing a check for $400 for five pairs of boots has probably the best answer. "Why am I buying boots? I'm buying them for a very simple reason. I want them."[255]

Raymonde Alexander, writing for the *Atlanta Constitution*, would have agreed. "[I]t is definitely a fact that boots will continue to be important in the shoe wardrobe again this season. You must have them—several pairs if you're going to keep pace in fashion's fast company." Alexander described the toe shapes for the new season's boots as a gently rounded square. Heels "take on more balance and sometimes flare at the back or both back and front. This type treatment is said to better balance the new look in fashion—that silhouette with the smaller look at the top and longer midi-hemline in the skirt." It was that drop in hem height, in Alexander's opinion, that was driving the popularity of boots, with designers promoting boots as a cure for any hostility that might be directed toward the new midi-length skirts. "According to recent predictions in New York, boots will actually help put across the new and more extreme looks in fall and winter fashions . . . there was some mention of compatibility between the boot-covered leg being an extension of the shoe to meet the hemline." Also, "you won't feel that flapping of material around your leg as much through a layer of boot."[256]

For younger women, affordability was also an important factor. There were shortages of leather in the mid-sixties, which led to a rise in prices, but at the same time designers like Mary Quant were experimenting with other materials, such as PVC and Corfam, the latter being a shiny artificial leather produced by DuPont. These materials were significantly cheaper than real leather, but also much less durable (you'll notice if you visit vintage clothing stores that there are very few shoes and boots from this period still around today). However, Rachelle Bergstein, in her 2012 history of women's shoes in the twentieth century,[257] proposes that this may actually have driven the growing popularity of boots. Unlike their mothers, who had lived through rationing and postwar austerity and regarded a good pair of shoes as an investment requiring many years of wear, the young women of the sixties were more open to the idea of disposable fashion—inexpensive, trendy items that could be quickly replaced as and when they went out of fashion.

In a plaid minidress and shiny black knee boots, Bernadette Devlin looked a little out of place in the pillared splendor of Derry's Bishop Street Courthouse.[246] Even more incongruous was her reason for being there. On that damp day in December 1969, the diminutive twenty-two-year-old was appearing in court charged with inciting a riot. The fact that she was also an elected Member of the British Parliament only made the whole scene more bizarre. In the witness box, Sergeant Francis Flynn of the Royal Ulster Constabulary testified that he had heard Devlin railing against residents of Derry's predominantly Catholic Bogside neighborhood as they faced off against the riot police of Ulster's Protestant government. "What sort of fucking buggers of Irishmen have we got," she had yelled, by way of encouragement. "Can you not see you have the black bastards [i.e., the police] beaten? They're out of [tear] gas. We have the stuff if you're men enough to use it. I can supply all the petrol bombs you need and more."[247]

Devlin, then and now a passionate believer in a thirty-two-county socialist republic of Ireland, was one of the more colorful figures to emerge in the early days of what became known, with characteristic Irish understatement, as "The Troubles"; she was memorably described by one Ulster Unionist politician as "Fidel Castro in a miniskirt."[248] But she was also part of a global phenomenon in the late 1960s, as radical left-wing activists, often students, took to the streets to confront the war in Vietnam and the injustices of poverty, racism, and colonialism. In its early days these movements, for all their outward idealism, were quite sexist in nature. It was not unusual for male activists to see the role of "their" women as supporting the revolution by cooking and providing sex.

But by the end of decade, women like the German activists Ulrike Meinhof and Gudrun Ensslin, and the Black

Described by one of her Ulster Unionist oppon as "Castro in a Miniskirt," Bernadette Devlin wa youngest female MP elected to the U.K. Parliar and an example of a new breed of revolutio women politicians. (PA/Alamy Stock Photo.)

Panther Party's Kathleen Cleaver began to take a much more active role. They were talented lead and activists, but image was also a major factor. Cleaver, "instantly recognizable by her iconic Afro a knee-high leather boots," [249] was memorably photographed toting a shotgun in leather jacket, m boots, and shades, a look adopted by many of the Panther women. Black leather boots were descrik as the "trademark" of Marilyn Buck,[250] another sixties activist who spent more than two decades in because of her activities as an "anti-imperialist freedom fighter"[251] after she became an urban guerill the seventies. Bernardine Dohrn, one of the leaders of the Weather Underground, was noted for wea expensive Italian leather boots, often thigh-length, with miniskirts and oversized, chic sunglasses.[252] Fel Weatherman Bill Ayers describes Dohrn speaking to the crowd during the October 1968 Days of R in Chicago in a "short skirt and high stylish black boots. . . . Her blazing eyes . . . allied with her elegance . . . a stunning and seductive symbol of the Revolutionary Woman."[253] And then there was Bernadette Devlin, frequently attired in boots and a miniskirt, who "defiantly exposes her body to the elements."[254]

For these warrior women, leather provided the edge necessary for an urban guerilla, while boots were both stylish and symbolized power. Devlin was a particularly effective symbol of change because of the contrast between her and the overwhelmingly male, conservative, Unionist political establishment of Ulster. At the time when she was elected as an MP, wearing a mini and boots still seemed like a radical option. Later, as the struggle for women's rights gained equal status with the campaigns against imperialism and racism, the mood swung against styles that might be seen as feminine rather than feminist. The radical women of the mid- to late seventies tended to go for a more unisex look.

The American company B.F. Goodrich was better known as a manufacturer of tires, but during the twentieth century they also applied their durable, waterproof products to a range of athletic and fashionable shoes and boots. These are examples of fashion boots from the sixties.

As Bergstein notes, a knee-length boot crafted out of leather would be significantly more expensive than one made from an artificial material like PVC. That would place it beyond the reach of teenagers and young women, and make it available only to the sort of older, wealthy clientele less likely to take on radical new trends. But instead, the go-go boot became widely adopted by a new breed of young, fashion-conscious, independent, and sexually and politically liberal women. So you could say that the cheap plastic boot opened the way for the widespread acceptance and adoption of boots in the following decade. It is certainly true that the early seventies featured boots in a plethora of trademarked artificial materials, most of which have long disappeared from view. A 1970 article on boots by the *Atlanta Constitution* featured a 10" pant boot, made from a new material called Futuran; knee-high boots in camel-tone stretch Vynarich complementing a leopard-patterned coat; a 17" boot with side zipper, draped vamp treatment and a decorative buckle; and a slim-fitting knee boot with a flared heel and a new style of zipper curved to follow the line of the boot around the ankle. "Your choice of boot height will most surely be determined by several factors," the article advised. "The longer slit in the skirt at the front or side will call for the highest. Pants or poncho looks will require another." But whatever the outfit, "somewhere within the height range from below-the-knee to mid-calf to just-above-the-ankle level, there is just the boot to stand up to the looks of vest, scarfs [sic], fringes, and beads."[258]

"Boots have been so big that it was hard to believe the fashion would last another year,"[259] the *Washington Post*'s Eugenia Sheppard had written back in the fall of 1967. "One might almost say . . .that everything has to be worn with boots," Alison Adburgham wrote in the *Guardian* in July 1970. "In our centrally heated lives, can we really wear boots day and night? If we do, we are the fools of fashion."[260] And yet women seemed to be quite happy to play the fool where boots were concerned, and for five years it appeared less and less likely each year that their popularity would decline. Strangely, just when it seemed the march of the boot was unstoppable, that's exactly what happened.

For Bardot, the decline in popularity had already begun. By the time her TV special aired, on New Year's Day 1968, she was back with her husband and her affair with Gainsbourg was all but over. In its dying days, the two mismatched lovers recorded a song that stands as a memorial to the *folie* that existed between them at the height of their passion. Bardot's cuckolded husband, Sachs, hated "Je t'aime . . . moi non plus" so much that Brigitte was forced to plead with Gainsbourg not to release it. He acceded, and Bardot's marriage lasted another two years before the couple finally divorced. In 1970, Bardot donned another, pink, pair of thigh boots for a comedy called *L'Ors et la Poupée* (the bear and the doll), in which she pursues a man because she's infuriated that he doesn't find her attractive. Reviewing the film in the *New York Times*, Vincent Canby noted that "charm is the ingredient that is in singularly short supply . . . largely, I suspect, because Miss Bardot, once a sex kitten, now approaches middle age with all of the grace of a seasoned predator."[261] By the time she finally retired from acting, in 1973, the fashion boot was also, apparently, in a state of decline.

Boots ON THE SCREEN

Bree Daniel's life is falling apart. Convinced that she is being stalked, she has seen one of her friends turn up dead in suspicious circumstances, she has had tapes of her own voice played back to her on the phone, her apartment has been ransacked, and she has just tried to stab with a pair of scissors one of the few men she can trust. She flees into the crowded streets of New York in a vain attempt to see her therapist, weaving through the crowd in a short brown trench coat, belted blue wool minidress, and towering black leather thigh boots.

This is a scene from Alan J. Pakula's movie *Klute* (1971); Bree is a struggling actress in New York City who supports herself through moonlighting as a call girl. She was played by Jane Fonda, who won the Academy Award for Best Actress that year for her performance in the role. Ann Roth, who designed this costume and the others worn by Fonda in the movie, chose the boots not for any association with prostitution, but because that was what smart young women in New York were wearing at the time; many of the clothes—including those thigh-length boots—came from Fonda's own closet.[262] The boots are supposed to be a badge of style.

Klute was made toward the end of the greatest period of sustained popularity in the history of the fashion boot, and its costumes reflected that. Roth designed a succession of outfits for Fonda, most of which featured boots of one sort or another. It provides a window into a time of extraordinary diversity for the boot, which saw the emergence of new styles, new materials, and new ways of wearing them.

Jane Fonda in her Oscar-winning role as call girl Bree Daniels from the movie *Klute* (1971). The frequency with which boots appeared in her wardrobe for the film was not because of their historical association with prostitution but because this is what fashionable young women in New York were wearing at the time. (Rex.)

Klute is not the only movie that captures this era. From France there is *Manon '70* (1968), starring Catherine Deneuve, the opening credits of which show the chaotic backstage area of a fashion show, with models having a succession of vinyl thigh boots peeled on and off; another French production, *Eugenie de Sade* (1970), with an eponymous antiheroine, played by Soledad Miranda, who goes through a series of fashionable booted outfits during her descent into incestuous murder and madness; and two more films starring Jane Fonda—*Barbarella* and the "Metzengerstein" segment of the omnibus film *Spirits of the Dead* (both 1968). But it is *Klute*, more than the others, that best captures the flavor of the time, as bright sixties optimism transitions into something darker and

Everything
OLD IS
NEW AGAIN

In the late 1960s, Kasia Charko was a student at the Leicester College of Art. It was a time when design and fashion were becoming heavily influenced by Art Nouveau, Art Deco, and 1940s themes. The students, including Charko, began to scour market stalls in Leicester looking for original 1930s and 1940s clothing, which they worked into their own outfits or took apart in order to understand how to mimic the designs. Then, one day, "a girl in the fashion department came to college in the most beautiful maroon suede knee length boots. Somebody told me they were from a shop in London called Biba and that the clothes there looked old and they had the most wonderful makeup."[263]

Eventually Charko was to work as a graphic designer for Biba, a classic London fashion store of the sixties and seventies that was the creation of designer Barbara Hulanicki and her husband Stephen Fitz-Simon. With its fusion of Art Deco style and rock-and-roll excess, Biba was probably the best-known example of a newfound enthusiasm for retro fashions that began in the late 1960s and reached its apogee during the early years of the seventies. The "Biba boot," which was one of the store's best-selling items (see sidebar), is one example of how this passion for vintage-themed fashions affected all items of clothing, including boots, but it is by no means the only one. Other styles, including lace-up "granny" boots and platform-soled boots also benefited.

FOR MEMBERS ONLY

Haya Kazubes, Miss Israel 1973, poses on the terrace of the House of Commons prior to that year's Miss World contest. The towering platform soles and knee-skimming tops were typical of boots from this period, at least on that side of the Atlantic. (PA.)

One of the most striking examples of the late-sixties passion for nostalgia was the emergence of vintage-flavored lace-up boots of the kind shown here. For most of the 1960s, boots were a popular symbol of modernity, but they were also by far the most common style of women's footwear in the late nineteenth and early twentieth centuries. So designers in the late 1960s were able to take the ubiquitous sixties boot in all of its leather, suede, and vinyl variants and, by adding design accents such as lacing or buttons, create an instantly "Edwardian" boot, like the one shown here, to complement the retro fashions of the time.

Starting in the latter part of the 1960s, there was a surge in nostalgia for Victorian and Edwardian fashions. These lace-up knee boots date from the early 1970s; they could easily be from seventy years earlier.

Curiously, this comes at a time when the mainstream fashion press shows a precipitous decline in the popularity of boots. "Mostly you're in shoes," said *Vogue*, discussing the fall fashions of 1972.[264] But this is not mirrored in the mail-order catalogs of the time, which still reflect a robust market for fashion boots of all kinds. Neither does it seem to have affected the clientele of Biba and similar stores. The demographic for Biba was teenagers or twenty-year-olds, "postwar babies who had been deprived of nourishing protein in childhood and grew up into beautiful skinny people: a designer's dream," as Hulanicki described them.[265] Women over thirty years old were considered old in the Biba store, and if the Biba girls were even reading *Vogue*, they weren't greatly influenced by it.

BACK TO THE FUTURE

By and large, the history of the fashion boot in the sixties was part of the move toward modernity that typifies the decade—the beginning of the liberation of women (as signified by the co-option of a formerly masculine mode of footwear), the emergence of new

1 **HIGH LEG BOOT** shows off a perfectly plain
suede upper styled with a flattering knee
high 18 inch leg and full length side zip
fastening. Chunky 2½ inch heel and resin rubber
sole. Average girth of leg top 13½ ins.
Sizes: 3; 3½; 4; 4½; 5; 5½; 6; 6½; 7.
Q.6826 Beige   Q.6851 Dusty Pink
Q.6854 Grape   Q.6855 Grey
All One Price £10·95 20 wks 55p 40 wks 28p

The tall, brightly colored boots produced by the London
store Biba spawned a host of imitations. These boots are
from the 1973 autumn/winter catalog of the British mail-
order company Kays. (University of Worcester.)

materials like plastics and vinyl, and the obsession with the space race and the "white heat of technology." But by the end of the decade, a backlash to this technocentric view of the world had taken hold. It came in a number of different forms. The one that is most commonly associated with the late sixties is the hippie movement, and, as it happens, hippies had their own styles of boots (when they bothered with footwear at all), which tended to be softer, loose-fitting suede designs, often worn by both sexes. But there was another movement, perhaps more Anglocentric, that was a contemporary of the hippies.

This particular style could best be described as "neo-Edwardian" and represented nostalgia for the past days of the British Empire. Male fashions were often based on the military uniforms of that time, while women adopted longer skirts and dresses, with lace and petticoats, and hair pinned-up rather than flowing free. Stores like I Was Lord Kitchener's Valet and Granny Takes a Trip specifically catered to this market. It was ironic that a clothing movement that celebrated one of the most reactionary periods of British history should have occurred at a time when the United Kingdom was rapidly divesting itself of the last vestiges of empire and society was going through the most profound period of liberalization since the Renaissance. The young people who adopted these fashions were living alongside the aging relics of the Edwardian era and, for the most part, rejected utterly the attitudes and politics of that time.

As Deirdre Clancy points out in her history of post-1945 costume, by the beginning of the 1970s any women over the age of thirty had lived through more changes in fashion than at any other time in history.[266] From a feminist perspective, a small coterie of relatively distant and unconcerned male designers had been dictating "looks" that, while they had started out as liberating, now seemed more like exploitation—and exploitation that frequently carried a perverse air of underage sexuality, driven primarily by dubious male tastes.[267]

So perhaps it's no surprise that, as Clancy argues, women in the late sixties and early seventies were addressing their independence by choosing to turn away from the looks of the previous decade in favor of a more graceful and covered-up style of dress. It was also clothing that gave the wearer greater control over her personal style. Women like Kasia Charko began a hunt through the flea markets and thrift stores in a search of romantic clothes, drawn not just from the past but also from the four corners of the earth, mixing, matching, and layering them. The look created was, in Clancy's words "intensely romantic and expressed a great yearning for a purer, more handcrafted past."[268] This spread beyond fashion into interior design, with a rediscovered enthusiasm for Victoriana, prints by William Morris and Liberty, and the combination retro-organic looks promoted by Terence Conran's Habitat chain of stores.

BOYISH CHARM

This was a nexus of opportunity for the fashion boot—boots were already popular in the 1960s, as we've seen, and they were also by far the most common style of women's footwear in the Edwardian era. By adding design accents like lacing or buttons, designers

THE *Biba* BOOT

Biba boots were much in evidence on London's Kings Road during the early 1970s; this pair is from 1971. (John Hendy.)

"I finally made it to Biba's for the first time. . . . We all went on an excursion to London and decided to go to Biba's on Kensington High Street. . . . I gasped at the rows of beautiful suede boots in plums, rusts, purples and greens."[269]

The boots that so entranced Kasia Charko were designed by Barbara Hulanicki in 1969, against the wishes of her business partner (and husband) Stephen Fitz-Simon, who thought Biba should get out of the business of selling shoes. The Biba boot proved him wrong. It was impossible for the store to keep up with the demand for them; women would queue out of the door and down the street, and buy boots in different colors— and sometimes even different sizes— than they had intended, just to get a pair. Problems with shoplifting were so chronic that customers were allowed to try on only one boot; they got the other one at the counter when they were ready to pay.[270]

The boots continued to be sold until Biba folded in 1975, changing somewhat in style; the earliest designs were over-the-knee and had a Louis heel, whereas the later ones were knee-length and the heel was higher and slimmer. They came in a kaleidoscope of colors and were notoriously tight-fitting; the tops of the boots were darted to give a close fit—so close that the Biba boot was reportedly tight enough to cut off circulation.[271]

Biba's boots originally retailed for £8 19s 6d, and were immediately assailed by cheaper knockoffs—Sacha produced a similar style for £7 7s, for example—and other retailers were reduced to rummaging through the discarded boot boxes in Biba's trash cans to see what colors were selling best. The cash-strapped sometimes went to more elaborate lengths. Kasia Charko "found a cobbler who made a pair of black canvas Biba style boots for me for a couple of quid. Well, it was a start."[272] Unfortunately, because the boots were designed to match Biba's other clothes, only the genuine boots looked right.

were able to create an instantly "Edwardian" boot—the "granny boot," as it was known. The longer maxiskirts of the period—whose popularity was also sparked by the late-sixties trend for nostalgia—frequently had a split at the front to allow for ease of movement, which revealed flashes of the boot as the wearer walked. Decorative features like front laces and colored patterns capitalized on this, acting as eye-catchers.

In the winter of 1969–70 a new trend emerged in fashionable areas of London such as the Fulham Road. As reported by Sally Fawkes in the *Daily Mail*,[273] women bored with another winter of trousers started tucking their pants into their elegant knee-length boots, creating the "Cossack" look. Unfortunately, tucking 12" of trouser into an expensive pair of boots did neither the boots nor the pants any favors. And so another fashion flashback to the early twentieth century occurred: the rediscovery of knickerbocker pants. "It's a fashion strictly for the young," Fawkes cautioned, "but it's a great way to break the eye in on the boot-top level. And it's this winter's international look." Worn with short jackets or vests and a newsboy cap, they gave the wearer a distinctly boyish swagger, but in the *Guardian*, Alison Adburgham, like Sally Fawkes, had words of warning. "This fashion should be considered with caution. Good fun and most fetching on lithe figures with slim legs; but one only has to think what mature actresses look like when playing the principal boy to realize that breeches are not for everyone."[274]

Boots worn over trousers were a feature of another fashion throwback, which mimicked the costume adopted by women drivers and aviators in the first three decades of the twentieth century; in the *Washington Post*, Nancy Ross described these as bearing "a suspicious resemblance to a lumberjack or WW1 doughboy's gear."[275] All those laces could be problematic, but many of the boots were "mercifully . . . provided with skate-type hooks." In the *New York Times*, Angela Taylor reported that the shoe store Orbach had come up with something special for the impatient: "a boot with fake lacings—a hidden zipper at the side does the trick."[276] "In spite of the lashings of proper shoes, the preference is for Zane Grey high-heeled boots, laboriously lacing up the front and leveling off to accommodate any skirt length below the knee, even with chiffon party dresses," the *Guardian*'s John Hart wrote in April 1970. At knee-length they could accommodate plus fours, or half-leg pants with wide cuffs. "Long pants," Hart concluded, "have just about had it."[277]

Fashion's early-seventies nostalgia trip was not limited to footwear. The period also saw the return of knickerbocker pants, which proved to be the ideal accompaniment to knee-length boots. (John Hendy.)

Mostly in Shoes

As we saw in the previous chapter, boots were at the height of their popularity in women's fashion during the fall and winter of 1970–71. So it's quite a surprise to leaf through back issues of *Vogue* from 1972 and 1973, where there are virtually no boots to be seen. When we look at the number of references to boots in *Vogue*, *L'Officiel*, and the *New York Times*, we observe the same thing: a steep plunge from the peak of 1970–71 to a deep trough in the years 1972–73.[278] If your perception of the early seventies is a riot of platform-booted glam-rock dollies, this comes as quite a shock. What was going on?

There were a number of factors in play during this period, and if you dig into those contemporary magazines and papers, you start to get some clues about what might have been happening. First, there was a great enthusiasm for pants. More than half the outfits in the editorial content involved trousers of some sort or other, usually wide-legged. Skirts tended to just skim the tops of the knees. Hats were common, as was shorter hair. And the shoes—and almost inevitably they were shoes—had high, chunky heels and platform soles. The overall look was very reminiscent of the fashions of the 1930s, the golden era of Hollywood glamor. And, indeed, that was a look that many designers and retailers sought to capitalize on. Biba based its entire design ethos around trying to replicate this era, perhaps as an escape from the unremitting grittiness of early-seventies Britain.

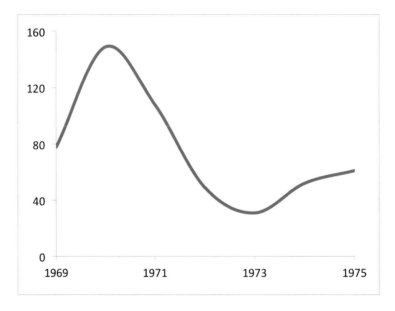

After the rise, a great fall—coverage of boots in the fashion press plunges to an all-time low in 1972 and 1973, despite the continuing popularity of fashion boots on the street. The emergence of a new, loose-fitting style of "baggy boot" in 1974 marks a renewal of interest.

So where does that leave the fashion boot, only a year on from its pinnacle of popularity? At first sight, the simple answer is: out in the cold. "The explosion of shorts, complete rout of midi skirts, retreat of boots . . . these are the most dramatic results of the Paris spring campaign," Alison Adburgham reported in the *Guardian* on February 9, 1971. She identified two major beneficiaries as being the manufacturers of tights, because women would no longer be able to hide ladders under their boots, and the shoe industry. "For while a girl could get by on one pair of fashion boots that she wore with everything, there is no such getting by with one pair of shoes or sandals. These need to be more deliberately appropriate to the clothes they accompany."[279]

"Boots continue with pants," *Vogue* declared, in 1972,[280] "and against the weather. *Mostly you're in shoes* [their emphasis]—lifted by platform and higher heel." Pants demanded ankle boots, the only style of boot to be greeted with enthusiasm. This shorter boot had an important role in ensuring an unbroken line from the vamp of the shoe to the cuff of the pants. In an editorial piece on winter weather fashions, *Vogue* hailed "a beautiful new boot with the fit and suppleness of a shoe, simply extended on the leg and rubber-soled against icy streets." But even so, the best footwear for winter was "a good leather shoe with the sturdy lift of a thick rubber sole that's proof against cold winter streets."[281] Leg protection—once the preserve of the tall boot—is now provided by long coats, ribbed stockings, or those ubiquitous pants.

Something like this had happened before, at the end of the 1920s; the link between the popularity of thirties-style fashions and the fall of the fashion boot was not accidental. Russian boots declined sharply in popularity as women sought out more feminine fashions—footwear that was daintier and less restrictive than a tall, enclosing boot. "A lighter, prettier, more feminine shoe," as *Vogue* declared in a 1973 review of fall accessories; that same review featured eight pairs of shoes, but only one boot: a slim, black leather ankle boot that provided the "smoothest line for pants."[282] In the actual 1930s, this had been enough to kill off the fashion boot—in all but its shortest form—for the better part of three decades.

But its seventies incarnation proved to be more resilient, in part because the role of women had changed dramatically. Far more of them were going out to work, and if the idea of braving the elements in a knee-length skirt, wooly tights, and a pair of chunky shoes sounds all well and good in theory, any woman who has commuted in winter will tell you that tights get wet, shoes fill with water, and an extra layer between your legs and the bitter chill of a cross-street wind can be very welcome. Ultimately, boots were not just stylish but practical, and it was that practicality that made the difference. Describing her experience as a student living in freezing-cold accommodation during the winter of 1971, Kasia Charko wrote, "At least now we could wrap ourselves in fashionable long coats[,] midi and maxi skirts and long leather boots; they were most welcome."[283]

The early 1970s were the heyday of the very short shorts known as hot pants. Like the contemporary knickerbockers, hot pants went well with boots, whether the late-sixties incarnation of the knee-length boot or its taller early–seventies cousin, the Biba boot. (John Hendy.)

Platform Boot, EARLY 1970s

These boots are from the United Kingdom and were made in the first half of the 1970s. The most obvious feature is the platform sole—a solid block of plastic 2" deep that has the effect of raising the heel of the boot to 5". The platform is angled inward at the toe to make it easier to walk, but it still must have been quite a challenge.

Another challenging feature shared with boots of this period is the tightness of the shaft and ankle. This created a very sleek, leg-hugging silhouette, but would have made the boots an uncomfortable proposition for any woman with less-than-skinny legs. As Kasia Charko wrote, "I had difficulty zipping up mine too and went around with numb legs for a while."[287]

One of the most distinctive aspects of the boot, and the one that most clearly places it in the first half of the seventies, is the line of the top of the shaft. This swoops upward in a low curve from the back of the leg, so that the front of the boot more or less covers the knee. It's neither a knee-length boot nor an over-the-knee style but something in between—a "knee-scraping" boot, perhaps.

This particular pair is relatively conservative, being made from black leather, but platforms were definitely seen as "fun fashion" and came in an appropriately wide variety of colors and materials. Commenting on her time working at the London shoe store Sacha, Kasia Charko reported that by far the best-selling boots were the white leather platforms. "Girls loved to wear them with hot pants or miniskirts."[288]

A pair of women's black leather platform boots from the first half of the 1970s.

STACKED HIGH AND SOLD CHEAP

By 1973, many of those long leather boots had towering platform soles. Platforms were another reflection of the new enthusiasm for retro fashion. The style has deep roots, stretching back to Classical Greece, where actors wore cork-soled platform sandals, called *kothorni*, of differing heights to indicate the social status of their characters.[284] In more recent times, during the eighteenth century, they were used to lift the wearer above the filth of polluted city streets. But by the twentieth century, it was all about style. Platforms were a way of dramatically increasing height with less pain and discomfort than was caused by regular stilettos. Prior to their 1970s renaissance, the last time platform shoes had been popular was in the 1930s and '40s, so it's not surprising that when stores like Biba began to mine those decades for inspiration, the platform was one of the first things to be resurrected.

The platform boot was a fortunate coincidence of the enthusiasm for platforms and the practical reliability of the knee-length boot. These boots are often considered the most flexible—and flattering—style of boot, and this was reflected in the fact that sales of this style far outstripped those of its more outré contemporaries. Which is not to say that the "go-go" boot didn't evolve during the sixties. While the earlier versions tended to be loose-fitting, later boots were cut to hug the curve of the calf, mimicking the tight-fitting vinyl styles of the period. Heels also began to increase in height as the decade wore on. Platform soles

The platform sole was another example of nostalgia in fashion, in this instance the golden years of Hollywood glamor in the 1930s and '40s. This knee-scraping suede pair from the British mail-order company Grattan are tall enough to cover the leg completely below the hem of the coat. (Freemans Grattan Holdings.)

allowed heels to rise even higher, because platform boots had one important advantage over shoes. With a shoe, it was quite possible to fall "off" a towering platform, twisting or even breaking one's ankle.[285] With boots, the additional support at the ankle and calf helped reduce this risk and make it easier to walk.

Platform boots came in a variety of shapes and sizes, but the most common style was a chunky-heeled boot that just skimmed the knee, making it arguable whether it was knee-length or over-the-knee (see sidebar). This boot is almost completely absent from the major fashion magazines of the time; you can search the pages of *Vogue* and *Harper's* in vain, but its popularity becomes very clear when you look at mail-order catalogs from this period. First appearing in 1972–73, by the following year platforms are easily the most popular style of boot, making up more than 60 percent of the pairs on sale.[286]

There was, unarguably, something quite cartoonish about the platform boot, especially when paired with the light, flow-away dresses of the period, which fitted the ethos of the wide-eyed waif-woman that was promoted by stores like Biba. Platforms were most definitely marketed toward a younger audience; skimming through mail-order catalogs from the period, you find pairs of boots in metallic blue or brown,[289] silver,[290] or shiny black vinyl with a red and yellow striped instep.[291]

Kasia Charko, by that time working in a branch of the shoe store Sacha on London's Oxford Street, was wearing boots year-round, even during the summer. "The Sacha boots as well as being the highest heeled were also the tightest. We had a terrible time zipping them up on all but the skinniest of legs. Once we got them zipped up we told customers to keep them on as long as they could so they would stretch. Sometimes we had to resort to the 'stretching' machine out the back in the stockroom i.e. two girls pulling either side of the unzipped boot leg with all their might." Another problem was the tendency of the shanks of the boots to break because they couldn't take the strain of the high heel. "This was quite comical and could be seen everywhere and not only on Sacha boots. The sure sign was people walking along with the heels of their footwear flopping around because they had lost all stability."[292]

Tight boots were certainly a problem, and not one that many manufacturers were taking time to address. "The fashion for boots has been a long time with us, yet to the best of my knowledge only one firm has given a thought to the girls with fat calves," Alison Adburgham complained in 1972. The brand in question, the "Maxi-Top Boot" by Portland, came in a variety of suede and leather styles, together with a shiny white boot with a rubber sole and foam lining. Retailing for £12, the Maxi Top's 14.5"-leg length was complemented by a gusset that allowed the calf dimension to expand from 17" to 19". "That's quite some thighs," Ms. Adburgham commented, approvingly.[293]

It wasn't just a matter of comfort. In the winter of 1970, Paul Steel, a physician from Atlantic City, New Jersey, had noticed a spate of unusual cases at his surgery. The patients, who were all women between the ages of fifteen and sixty, were suffering from pain in one or both of their legs. The symptoms, which included redness and swelling, were typical of a condition known as thrombophlebitis, in which blood clots form in a vein. Investigating, Steel concluded that the common factors of age, sex, season, and "style consciousness" pointed to an unusual cause: in his words, "abrasive

Tall suede boots from the British mail-order company Kays, 1973. (University of Worcester.)

irritation and constriction from the upper end of malfitting dress boots, which had been so enthusiastically accepted by the chic, well-attired ladies." Describing the new condition, which he termed "boot-leg phlebitis," in the *Journal of the American Medical Association*, Steel reported that the condition was common, usually of intense patient concern, but relatively simple to treat by means of local soaks, rest, leg elevation, and abstinence from boot wearing. "Fears of embolization are real," he concluded, "but the removal of the exciting source make resolution of this problem a rewarding experience for the attending physician."[294] The noted podiatrist William A. Rossi was less inclined to find humor in the situation. "Doctors warned that thrombophlebitis caused by continued wearing of these leg-tight boots could even prove fatal," he wrote in 1976.

This pair of boots was manufactured in Brazil, in all likelihood between 1974 and 1976. The first thing that strikes you when you look at them is how small they are.[296] The ankle is unforgivingly tight, and the shaft has been folded and stitched at the top to give them a wicked curve that is only partly relieved by having a very long, elasticized gusset on the inner surface of the shaft. These are absolutely a young woman's boots, and they reflect the comments made by contemporary writers about having to stretch boots in the back of the store to make them fit.[297]

The next thing you notice is that these are very definitely platform boots, but that the sole is much thinner than the classic platform boot of the period. Another feature of the sole and heel is that they are made from laminated layers of wood, built up to provide both the platform sole and a high, stacked heel. These contrasting wooden accents were another distinctive feature of boots from this period; most boots before and afterward had soles and heels that were made from the same material as the uppers. Today, wooden heels are more of a novelty, used to give the boots a retro feel.

The toe of the boot is rounded—again, this is indicative of the first half of the seventies. Before and after, boots tended to have more of a pointed toe, as they do today. The round toe was seen in both shoes and boots from early to mid-1970s, and reflects the more "organic" or "rustic" design ethos of the seventies, compared to the space-age vibe of the sixties and the overt modernism of the eighties. Round-toed boots are quite rare today, even in styles that are consciously retro.

THE MID-'70s
Knee boot

These fashion boots from the mid-1970s are a more practical variation of the contemporary platform boots, although they were still tight enough to put the wearer's circulation in peril.

"But not one woman was known to discard her sexy fashionable boots despite the warnings. Women were ready to die with their boots on."[295]

With the onset of winter in January 1974, the real reason for the enduring popularity of boots came into play. "From a fashion point of view, boots haven't had much of a look-in this winter," the *Daily Mail* wrote. "But there comes a point where fashion goes by the board and plain old practicality takes over." A combination of icy weather and the unheated offices that resulted from an apparently never-ending series of strikes paralyzing British industry brought the boot firmly back into fashion. Perhaps as a result of fashion's earlier dismissal of the style, "there are lots of very good boots drastically reduced in the shoe sales at the moment," the *Mail* continued, softening the blow of a major purchase for those who thought last year's boots were looking old and tatty. Of the five examples pictured by the *Mail*, four were platforms: one ankle-length and the remainder knee-length. Crepe soles and stacked heels predominated, and the boots came in a riot of colors; in addition to the usual black and brown, there are also red, green, olive, camel, navy, beige, gray, maroon, caramel, and orange pairs.[298]

Teenage Rampage

In 1964, while Andre Courréges was wowing Paris with his space-age clothes and little white boots, fifteen-year-old Susan Kay Quatro was playing bass and singing in an all-girl garage band called the Pleasure Seekers. Initially working the cabaret circuit in their hometown, Detroit—where attention focused on their looks rather than their music—the Pleasure Seekers opted for matching outfits of miniskirts and knee-high boots. Ten years later, and on the other side of the Atlantic, Susan—her name now shortened to Suzi—had swapped these for platforms and a leather catsuit and was pounding out a succession of chugging hard-rock/pop songs penned by Nicky Chinn and Mike Chapman. As Philip Norman wrote in 1975, "[O]f all female rock singers, she appears the most emancipated: a small girl leading an all-man group . . . a rocker, a brooder, a loner, a knife-carrier; a hell-cat, a wild cat, a storm child, refugee from the frightened city of Detroit."[299]

This was the era of glam rock, and towering platforms definitely fitted its trashy design aesthetic. But Suzi Quatro was something of an oddity. Most of the contemporary glam rockers, such as Slade, The Sweet, Mott the Hoople, Wizzard, and the somewhat edgier American equivalents like Iggy Pop and the New York Dolls, were male. Platform boots were a unisex phenomenon, but mostly because, to a greater or lesser extent, these bands embraced a cross-dressing aesthetic that went along with glam's emphasis on androgyny and sexual and gender ambiguity.

Which is not to say that there weren't women who could carry off the look. Probably the best known of these were the Runaways, an all-female rock band from Los Angeles that had a series of hits between 1976 and 1978. Members of the Runaways, who included Cherie Currie, Joan Jett, and Lita Ford, frequently wore towering platform boots onstage, along with leather jumpsuits, lingerie, and other provocative clothing, while pounding out hits like "Cherry Bomb" and "Queens of Noise."

But for more mainstream audiences, the memories of platforms are more likely to come from the Swedish pop leviathan ABBA. From the mid-seventies to the early eighties, the quartet of Agnetha Fältskog, Björn Ulvaeus, Benny Andersson, and Anni-Frid Lyngstad dominated pop charts worldwide. Their record sales ran into the hundreds of millions and they continue to sell heavily today, more than thirty-five years after the group disbanded. The female members of ABBA, Fältskog and Lyngstad, wore a wide variety of boots on- and offstage—the stage versions tended toward the extreme, because of a quirk of Swedish tax law; stage outfits could be tax deductible, but only if they could not be worn other than for performances.[300] So it was that on April 6, 1974, when ABBA seared themselves onto the public consciousness by winning the Eurovision Song Contest with "Waterloo," Agnetha Fältskog faced her adoring public in an electric-blue satin knickerbocker suit with knee-scraping metallic silver platform boots. Even from the perspective of today's nostalgia for seventies fashion, it was an eye-watering combination.[301]

THE BOOTS of the EARLY TO MID-SEVENTIES

Three styles of boots are united by a high stacked heel and close-fitting leg and ankle. In the earliest versions of these boots, the shaft was tall enough to skim the kneecap. As heel heights rose, so did the thickness of the soles. The later versions of these boots had a reduced shaft height and slightly lower platforms—a more pragmatic version of the earlier styles. By the late seventies, these tight-fitting boots had all gone, replaced by looser, more comfortable designs.

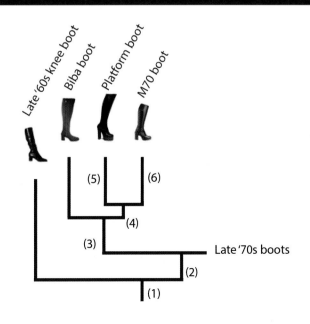

The early 1970s saw the appearance of a cluster of related boot styles in Britain and Europe, not all of which achieved popularity across the Atlantic. (1) Knee-length, fitted leg; (2) stacked heel; (3) fitted ankle, shaft partly covers the knee; (4) platform sole; (5) sole height greater than 1"; (6) shaft height below the knee.

The Collapse of the Platform

Platforms were popular, but they were also relatively short-lived. At the height of their popularity in the winter of 1973, they made up more than half of the pairs of boots appearing in British mail-order catalogs; two years later, this proportion had dropped to 25 percent, and for the remainder of the decade, there were no more than one or two pairs offered. The last year they appeared was 1978, by which time the style looked truly archaic.[302]

Part of the problem was that, with their cartoonish look, platform boots were definitely not for anyone over the age of twenty-five. When they first appeared, the main alternative was the late-sixties incarnation of the knee-length boot. But by 1975 this had been superseded by a new boot that was effectively a watered-down version of the platform boot, retaining the tightly fitted leg and stack heel, but with a much-reduced sole—less than an inch deep in most cases. This mid-70s style makes up the bulk of the knee-length boots seen in the 1975–76 and 1976–77 editions of the catalogs (see sidebar).

The platform phenomenon was largely confined to one side of the Atlantic. After the sharp dip in references in the fashion press during 1972 and 1973, 1974 saw a big resurgence of interest in fashion boots. The department stores were filled with an incredible variety in height, detailing, and colors. But there was one style that was conspicuous by its absence, as Enid Nemy pointed out in a *New York Times* article from September of that year. "Few [boots] are carrying the exaggerated platforms so popular in shoes this summer."[303]

That's not to say that the platform boot was completely missing from the United States. Nemy goes on to describe how "the higher than high heels and platforms that seem to stretch into infinity have been translated into boots at a number of specialized shoe stores throughout the city. They particularly line West 34th St between 5th and 6th Avenues, and the color range is impressive."[304]

So the platform boots were there, but were strictly the preserve of specialist stores. In the United States, the evolution of the fashion boot had followed a different path, but one that was about to merge with that of Europe.

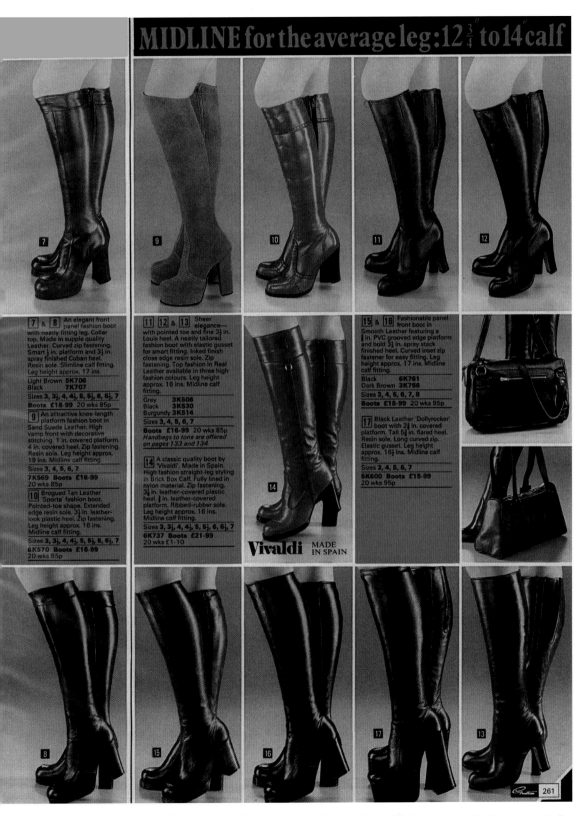

7 & 8 An elegant front panel fashion boot with neatly fitting leg. Collar top. Made in supple quality Leather. Curved zip fastening. Smart ¾ in. platform and 3½ in. spray finished Cuban heel. Resin sole. Slimline calf fitting. Leg height approx. 17 ins.

Light Brown **5K706**
Black **7K707**
Sizes **3, 3½, 4, 4½, 5, 5½, 6, 6½, 7**
Boots **£18·99** 20 wks 95p

9 An attractive knee-length platform fashion boot in Sand Suede Leather. High vamp front with decorative stitching. 1 in. covered platform. 4 in. covered heel. Zip fastening. Resin sole. Leg height approx. 19 ins. Midline calf fitting.
Sizes **3, 4, 5, 6, 7**
7K569 Boots **£16·99** 20 wks 85p

10 Brogued Tan Leather 'Sports' fashion boot. Pointed-toe shape. Extended edge resin sole. 3½ in. leather-look plastic heel. Zip fastening. Leg height approx. 16 ins. Midline calf fitting.
Sizes **3, 3½, 4, 4½, 5, 5½, 6, 6½, 7**
6K570 Boots **£16·99** 20 wks 85p

11 12 & 13 Sheer elegance—with pointed toe and fine 3½ in. Louis heel. A neatly tailored fashion boot with elastic gusset for smart fitting. Inked finish close edge resin sole. Zip fastening. Top fashion in Real Leather available in three high fashion colours. Leg height approx. 16 ins. Midline calf fitting.
Grey **3K506**
Black **3K530**
Burgundy **3K514**
Sizes **3, 4, 5, 6, 7**
Boots **£16·99** 20 wks 85p
Handbags to tone are offered on pages 133 and 134.

14 A classic quality boot by 'Vivaldi'. Made in Spain. High fashion straight-leg styling in Brick Box Calf. Fully lined in nylon material. Zip fastening. 3½ in. leather-covered plastic heel. ¾ in. leather-covered platform. Ribbed-rubber sole. Leg height approx. 16 ins. Midline calf fitting.
Sizes **3, 3½, 4, 4½, 5, 5½, 6, 6½, 7**
6K737 Boots **£21·99** 20 wks £1·10

Vivaldi MADE IN SPAIN

15 & 16 Fashionable panel front boot in Smooth Leather featuring a ¾ in. PVC grooved edge platform and bold 5½ in. spray stack finished heel. Curved inset zip fastener for easy fitting. Leg height approx. 17 ins. Midline calf fitting.
Black **6K761**
Dark Brown **3K766**
Sizes **3, 4, 5, 6, 7, 8**
Boots **£18·99** 20 wks 95p

17 Black Leather 'Dollyrocker' boot with 2½ in. covered platform. Tall 5½ in. flared heel. Resin sole. Long curved zip. Elastic gusset. Leg height approx. 16½ ins. Midline calf fitting.
Sizes **3, 4, 5, 6, 7**
5K600 Boots **£18·99** 20 wks 95p

261

Ten years earlier, mail-order catalogs featured only a limited selection of boots. But by 1976, companies like Grattan could offer a boot to fit every woman's taste. (Freemans Grattan Holdings.)

THE NEW
EASE IN
Fashion

In January 1975, *New York Times* reporter Georgia Dullea attended a mysterious boot sale at 34th and 8th Avenue in Manhattan. In a room were twenty-five clerks, six cashiers, a dozen other staff, and "stacks and stacks of boot boxes. Above them, dangling from clotheslines, were 10 styles of boots." The identity of the seller was a mystery, but the story was that he had been caught with a large stock of boots that needed to be sold quickly. "Nobody likes to say 'hey, we got clobbered,'" one of his staff said. "We've got one million boots to sell. We've got warehouses all over the country, bulging with boots for ladies."[304]

They were priced to sell quickly, at $2.99 or $3.99 a pair. But they were also, in the words of Ms. Dullea "calf-clingers. . . . They are made of vinyl for the 'leather look' and the 'crinkle look.' Many have fake laces." They were not "the Boot-of-the-Year. Such a boot sells for $65 and up and comes in bunchy, buttery leather. It barely touches, never clings to the calf. It gives you the Cossack look."[305] Six years earlier, women couldn't get enough of those skintight, wet-look vinyl boots, or the high, laced "granny boots." Now manufacturers were left with warehouses full of unsold stock that they could barely give away.

In the late 1960s, boots were all about youth culture. Ten years later, the generation of women who wore those boots had grown up, and the boots had grown up with them. The brightly colored, leg-hugging, thigh-grazing boots in brightly colored vinyl had been replaced by loose-fitting pairs in leather and suede. The key difference was price. Back in the sixties, cheap and cheerful vinyl had supplanted leather, as designers like Mary Quant made boots that were affordable for shopgirls and typists. But now boots were, in the words of *Times* reporter Enid Nemy, "a sybaritic adventure in consumerism."[306]

Prices ranged from $35 to $150, around 35 percent higher than a typical pair from the end of the sixties. As Herbert Levine pointed out in the same article, "[O]ur boots sell for $100 and $150 because they use the same amount of leather as six pairs of shoes."[307] And yet women bought them. At Bloomingdale's, in the late summer of 1974, "taller, wider, creamier, crushier" boots by Yves Saint Laurent sold like crazy, despite a price tag of $105 and temperatures in the eighties. And despite the fact that some women might be "questioning the droopy look," in the words of designer David Evins, there were some significant advantages. Those baggy ankles and loose legs were a lot more forgiving on shorter legs than the calf-hugging styles of 1970.

By the second half of the 1970s, the young women who had embraced the fashion boot in the '60s had grown up. The boots had grown with them, evolving from youthquake exuberance to something more practical for day-to-day wear. (Freemans Grattan Holdings.)

GOING UP THE COUNTRY

The 1960s had started out as an age of great optimism. It was the time when society swept away the fossilized political and social norms that had been in place for much of the first half of the century. There were great liberal advances in the law, equality, and civil rights; an explosion of creativity in the arts, music, and fashion; and dramatic reforms of education. But as time went by, this sense of optimism was clouded by the human and social costs of the war in Southeast Asia, violent demonstrations on the streets, and political assassinations. By the end of the decade, the mood was much darker. If the early years were about the bright promise of technology and the space race, by the beginning of the 1970s the story was one of Altamont, the Manson murders, Mỹ Lai,[308] and Tet. And this mood continued into the following decade, which turned out to be one of economic fallout from the OPEC crisis, industrial action, and terrorism.[309, 310]

Under the circumstances, it's perhaps not surprising that people took refuge in nostalgia, a longing for simpler times. We've already seen, in the previous chapter, how this affected fashions in Britain, with stores like Biba selling clothes that were heavily influenced by the styles of the interwar years. This spilled over in the design of boots from the period, with the growth in popularity of lace-up and platform-soled styles. On the other

Frye
CAMPUS BOOT

The Frye boot company had been around since 1863, but the Campus boot was truly a 1970s icon.

By the 1970s, the tan leather, knee-length Frye boot was widely seen on university campuses, being the boot of choice for coeds across the country. The company even called the style "The Campus Boot." There were other rivals, such as Dingo boots, but Frye was the original and has given its name to the general style, regardless of manufacturer. It was so distinctive that when the Smithsonian was searching for items to best represent America during the sixties, it chose a pair of Campus boots.

The Campus is not a delicate item. The leather is thick and doesn't have much in the way of flexibility, which is fine because the boot is loose-fitting anyway. There's no zip-fastener; the straight shaft is pulled on, with a couple of canvas boot straps on the inside to give extra purchase. The heel is a massive stack, built up from alternating layers of dark and light wood, and the seams and stitching can best be described as rugged. All of this makes for a supremely durable piece of footwear. Ann Roiphe wasn't kidding when she wrote in the *New York Times* about looking like you expected a horse to step on your toes.[314]

Frye boots waned in popularity at the end of the seventies, but the company continued to prosper, selling boots for riding, motorcycling, and a variety of utility purposes, and in 2002 the brand started a triumphant return as a fashion object with cult status. With an enormous archive of classic boot styles to draw on, and adoption by fashion-conscious celebrities like Jennifer Aniston and Sarah Jessica Parker, Frye was discovered by a new generation.[315]

Frye boots like the Campus are important to understanding the history of the fashion boot, not just because of their past popularity or the company's current renaissance. Their emergence as a women's boot in the seventies also marks a significant divergence between dress boots and more casual styles. That divergence persists to the present day; the high-heeled dress boot represents the former, while the current crop of low-heeled boots, usually worn over pants, is the end point of a path that can be traced all the way back to the Campus boot.

side of the Atlantic, however, things followed a different path. There was a strong "back-to-the-land" movement;[311] this is most closely associated with the hippie counterculture and communes, but certain aspects of it also came to pervade mainstream fashion. Throughout the 1970s there was a great enthusiasm for clothing associated with rural work wear: cotton, gingham, and denim. And for the fashion boot, one particular style prospered above all.

The Frye Company, founded in 1863, claims to be the oldest continuously operating shoe manufacturer in America.[312] Frye made its reputation producing harness and engineer boots, but during the late 1960s its rugged, knee-length, pull-on boots became popular among both men and women of the Woodstock generation. The company may have refined its skills and designs making utilitarian riding and farm boots, but its 1970s boots were inarguably fashionable. While the design and manufacture were 100 percent traditional Frye, the ethos was very much that of the seventies fashion boot and influenced by other contemporary boot styles (see sidebar).

"This winter," Ann Roiphe wrote in the *New York Times* in January 1976, "in the cold climates, every boy and girl from 13 to 22 will be wearing a down jacket and Frye boots."[313] The Frye boot first became popular in the winter of 1974-75, but it had taken time for the word to filter through to the buyers in the big stores. Now they were everywhere. The boots had to be bought a size small, so they could stretch out. As Roiphe described it, "[Y]oung people of both sexes have blistered and bled, limped and suffered until at last the stiff thick leather has given in and stretched—and then it doesn't stretch, it sags. Frye boots—and they are everywhere around you—bag at the ankles so the wearer looks like a basset hound with old legs, wrinkled from the hard life it's known."

By now, you'll have gathered that Roiphe was not a fan of the Frye, which she contrasted unfavorably with the ultrafeminine fashions of her youth. "Why are they being worn to and from classes in some of our elitist institutions? Why are our young people living as if they expect a horse to step on their toes?" Despite this, Fryes remained enormously popular for much of the decade. They also had a profound influence on other boot styles. Even the U.S. versions of the leg-clinging boots of the early seventies showed strongly "countrified" tendencies, often mimicking the tan color and heavy stitching of the Frye boot.

FASHION RELAXES

The boom in popularity of the Frye boot was part of a wider shift in design, what *Vogue* referred to as "the new ease in fashion,"[316] slightly oversized, but still well proportioned and with an emphasis on comfort. "Fashion for girls is going BIG again this autumn," Barbara Griggs announced in the *Daily Mail* in August 1974. In pursuit of comfort, women would increasingly be adopting and adapting pieces of menswear to produce loose-fitting, casual outfits. Griggs heralded the return of the "Sloppy Joe," a large sweater that represented a complete turnaround from the lean, tailored look of previous seasons. "You wear your

THE NATURAL CHOICE
Fashion boots from KAYS

The new styles of straight-legged boots were easy to wear over pants, adding to the casual "country" look of the time. (University of Worcester.)

Sloppy Joe striped and bulky, with a narrow skirt and tall-heeled, beautifully polished boots," Griggs decreed.[317]

Critically for the history of the fashion boot, this period also saw a shift away from pants toward skirts. This was a full skirt, pleated or folded to allow for ease of movement, and to accompany it, "go with a boot," *Vogue* decreed, "it's a leg lengthener."[318] Dresses were made of jersey, midi-length, or slightly longer, and could be belted tightly or worn loose and floating according to choice. Paired with the new style of loose-fitting, "baggy" boots and a headscarf, it gave the wearer a "peasant-style" look, as the *Daily Mail*'s Barbara Griggs termed it, which was in keeping with the new, relaxed, countrified feel of fashion. The length of the dress was such that it just skimmed the tops of the tall boots.[319]

So it is that, in the July 1, 1974, edition of *Vogue*, we see the emergence of a new style of fashion boot, and the emphasis is clearly on easy living: "For country dressing/weather dressing—the boot. The new softness of a boot—glove soft, supple on the leg, with a higher, straighter, prettier heel. To wear in the country with heavier, textured tights, a longer suede skirt . . . to wear for cold weather anywhere."[320] Early on, these skirts tended to end on or just above the knees, leaving a small exposure of leg between the top of the boot and the hem of the skirt. In the second half of the decade, skirts lengthened, to cover the top of the boot, while shoes—all the rage just a year earlier—were definitely out. "It's boots with almost everything," Kathryn Samuel wrote in the *Daily Mail*, looking at the fall fashions for 1974. "They're knee-length, wide round the ankles, and high heeled."[321] "One may as well go barefoot," Enid Nemy declared in the *Times*, "as wear a simple pair of shoes with the longer skirt."[322]

"We'll most probably be wearing baggy boots at Easter," Barbara Griggs predicted, looking at the likely fashion developments of 1975. "They're such an integral part of the current fashion look," which was midlength skirts, big-sleeved shirts, baggy sweaters, and no jeans. The new year's crop of boots would feature a range of colors that would keep them appropriate for spring: blue, peach, cream, and olive green.[323] Meanwhile in Paris, Bernadine Morris reported, "[P]opular booteries, such as Renast on the Rue Tronchet, hand out tickets to women standing in line on the sidewalk, as if they were selling meat or pastry."[324] Renast's boots, which were especially popular with working women, sold for around $100 a pair. But the chicest boots in Paris were those at François Villon, and they were selling for two or three times that price. "It's not absolutely obligatory to wear high-heeled boots with the long skirts," Morris noted, but most women did, and visiting Americans were buying boots in Paris and wearing them home on the plane. The number of citations in the fashion press reflect that popularity, and they're remarkably consistent. From the deep dip in boot citations that we saw in 1972–73, numbers rise steadily through 1974 to 1976, reach a peak in 1977, and then drop off toward the end of the decade.[325]

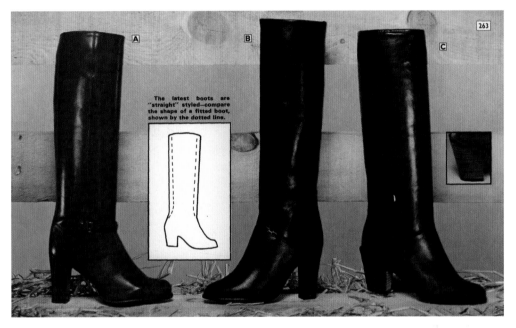

Mail-order companies like Grattan felt obliged to explain the new boot styles to customers who were accustomed to a closer fit. (Freemans Grattan Holdings.)

The Cossacks Are Coming

Every now and again there's a pivotal moment in fashion history, and for the fashion boot one of these occurred in 1974, when Yves Saint Laurent created a Russian-themed collection. As we already saw in the 1920s, designers have frequently drawn on Russia—with its exotic mixture of Asian and European influences and potentially exciting mix of materials like furs, silk, and gold—for inspiration. Saint Laurent's collection featured full skirts that fell below the knee, thick sweaters, capes, quilted gold jackets, velvet and satin knickerbockers, long fur coats and matching fur hats, and a new, and very distinctive, style of knee-length fashion boot.[326]

In contrast to the zippered, calf-hugging styles of the day, the new boot was loose-fitting, touching the leg rather than clinging to it, and falling in extravagant folds as the

KNEE
LENGTH BOOT
Etienne Aigner

Etienne Aigner was born in what is now Slovakia in 1904. He made his name in the years after World War II making high-end leather accessories for haute couture fashion houses in Paris. He moved to New York in 1950 and set up in business for himself, producing belts, handbags, shoes, wallets, and other luxury items.

This knee-length boot by Aigner dates from the late 1970s and has a number of features that are typical of this period. First, in contrast to the mid-seventies boot we looked at in the previous chapter, the leg is relatively straight and the ankle quite wide; it's a much easier fit than the earlier generation of boots. It still has a stacked heel, but instead of the polished wood of the mid-seventies boot, this one is covered in leather that is the same color as the rest of the boot. And unlike the round toe of a few years earlier, this boot has a toe that is not entirely round but not strongly pointed either—from below, the sole looks almost egg-shaped.

The color itself is a common one for the period, oxblood, which is a dark red with purple and brown undertones. Colors like oxblood, maroon, and burgundy were popular shades for seventies boots and have come back into fashion in recent years. There are a couple of interesting design accents: the broad, double seam that runs the length of the shaft is similar to that seen in western-style boots like those made by Frye, while at the back of the heel is a metallic inset that is based on Aigner's monogram, a horseshoe-shaped letter *A*.

Etienne Aigner had begun his career producing high-end accessories for the Paris couture houses. By the 1970s, the company that bore his name was producing highly desirable bags, shoes, and boots. The oxblood color of this boot was a popular shade in the later years of the decade.

soft leather crushed around the ankle. Rather than having heels that were covered in the same material as the boot itself, the new boot featured stacked heels in material like wood. And with thin, rubber soles, they were eminently practical for walking on slippery winter sidewalks.[327] Inevitably, given the Russian theme, the new boots quickly became known as "Cossack boots," although they had little in common with the felt *Valenki* of the Russian winter. Instead, with their loose-fitting ankles, decorative stitching, and an occasional trimming of fur, they harked back to the original "Russian boot" of the 1920s—that abortive attempt at developing a fashion boot for women that we looked at in a previous chapter.

By 1975, the *New York Times* was referring to this style as the "Boot of the Year."[328] "Boot of the Decade" might have been more appropriate, as this was by far the most common style of fashion boot from the mid-1970s to the early years of the 1980s, at a stroke consigning the leg-hugging styles of the late sixties and early seventies to obsolescence. This is not to say, however, that the transition from clinging boots to loose-fitting ones was entirely a smooth one. Just as had been the case with the Russian boots of the 1920s,[329] many women weren't quite ready to embrace a boot that sagged so spectacularly around the ankles. "Baggy boots" is how the U.K. fashion press and mail-order catalogs were referring to them in 1974 and 1975,[330] a marketing strategy that seems less than appealing. Nonetheless, enough women wanted them that a shortage of boots was a big deal.

"Mystery of the Missing Baggy Boots," the *Daily Mail* reported in November 1974. "Just why aren't the shoe shops of this country simply bursting with Baggy Boots?" Barbara Griggs asked. "That's what I—and most of my readers—want to know." The boots were so integral to the season's new looks that their absence was causing alarm. Partly it was a case of demand far outstripping supply, but for stores like Elliotts, who were manufacturing their own style of the boot, there were also technical challenges. "Modern lightweight heels have to be put on by machine," Adrian Elliott explained. "And with the ordinary boot that zips up from the ankle that's no problem. But to put the heel on an unzipped baggy boot, we've had to invent a new machine with an arm long enough to reach down inside the boot and put that heel in." Getting the requisite amount of folding was also a challenge. "If it's wrinkled all the way up it's a nightmare," Elliott went on to explain. "Smooth at the top it's a classic and looks like being with us for quite a while."[331]

As we saw in the previous chapter, for most of the mid- to late seventies close-fitting boots still prevailed, but in a different form from those of the late sixties and early seventies. These mid-70s boots were made from suede or leather and shared a stacked heel with the Cossack boot, but clung tightly to the ankle and calf. Initially platforms, over time the depth of the sole decreased until in the end it was basically regular thickness. You can see this pattern of replacement if you look at mail-order catalogs from this period.

First appearing in 1972–73, by the following year the platform-soled boot was easily the most popular style as measured by the number of pairs offered in the catalogs. But this popularity dropped sharply through 1975–76, and the style disappeared completely after 1978. The tight-legged, mid-seventies design makes up the bulk of the knee-length boots seen in the 1975–76 and 1976–77 editions of the catalogs, but drops off markedly thereafter. It is replaced by the Cossack boot, which first appears in 1975–76. This takes

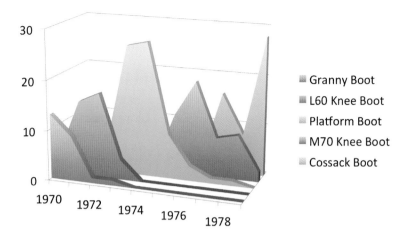

30
20
10
0

1970   1972   1974   1976   1978

- Granny Boot
- L60 Knee Boot
- Platform Boot
- M70 Knee Boot
- Cossack Boot

Changes in the popularity of different styles of fashion boot during the 1970s, as measured by the average number of pairs that appear in British mail-order catalogs during this time.

a couple of years to catch on (perhaps because of the "baggy boots" label), but by 1977 there are twice as many of them as there are the older styles, and by the end of the decade they account for more than 50 percent of all women's boots on offer, and twice as much as the next largest category.[332]

SHORT BOOT, *Late 1970s*

The late 1970s saw a split in fashion boots, with knee-length styles increasingly supplemented by boots that were either taller or shorter. This casual boot, from the last years of the decade, is an example of one of the shorter styles. In keeping with the comfort-driven ethos of the fashions of this period, the shaft is made from warm sheepskin, but the shoe is water-resistant, camel-colored leather. The heavy wooden heel and pointed toe reference the western-themed styles of this period, while the sturdy, ridged sole ensures traction on icy city sidewalks and muddy country paths alike.

As the seventies drew to a close, there was a growing enthusiasm for shorter styles of boot. With its soft suede upper and shearling lining, this example blends high fashion with casual comfort.

This period also saw the emergence of some new styles of fashion boot. In 1975, Mary Ann Crenshaw noted in the *Times* that while "boots have unquestionably become a fashionable winter wardrobe essential . . . this year there's a different boot afoot."[333] She was referring to a shorter style of boot, ending at midcalf, that was often worn with thick, ribbed woolen stockings, sometimes layered with kneesocks to bridge the resulting gap between boot top and skirt. They were not cowboy boots, but like the contemporary Frye boots they frequently employed western-style themes like scalloped tops, pull tabs, buckles, or decorative stitching.

"It's lucky that shoemakers are almost all bootmakers too," Barbara Griggs reported from the 1977 Paris fall collections. "Otherwise they'd be grimly facing bankruptcy." Griggs estimated that around 90 percent of the models on the Paris catwalks that season were wearing boots of some sort. "Ankle-high boots, calf-high boots, knee-high boots, and thigh-high boots. Boots that laced-up and boots you simply slid into. Boots made of soft sheepskin, shiny calf or dressy satin. Boots that invariably had low heels for daytime." The variety of boots seen in Paris was, in Griggs's words, "staggering."[334]

Ankle-length fashion boots as seen in the 1978 autumn/winter Freemans catalog. (Freemans Grattan Holdings.)

The year 1977 saw the reemergence of the over-the-knee boot after a six-year gap. Reporters covering that year's fall ready-to-wear shows in Paris were full of praise for Karl Lagerfeld's collection for Chloe.[335, 336] Lagerfeld had been much taken with Federico Fellini's *Casanova*, released in December of the previous year, and decided to produce a collection based on the eighteenth-century costumes seen in the movie. But rather than women's clothing from that period (which he declared to be "uninteresting") Lagerfeld chose to design a collection for women that was influenced by the flamboyant male clothing of the period. So we have broad-brimmed Cavalier hats, capes, velvet and satin breeches, lace-trimmed blouses, and lots of swaggering over-the-knee boots.[337]

Or, specifically, three styles of boots, which were described in a review by Nina Hyde in the *Washington Post*.[338] "Black satin high heeled boots that are thigh high, a boot for sports wear that looks as if you are wearing pants, and "puss n' boots" boots that are very soft and draped, that give a new proportion with the very full skirt." Lagerfeld had the boots made in Italy because, in his opinion, the French *bottiers* weren't up to the task. His major innovation for Chloe was a full, flowing dress in very thin, delicately patterned, and softly colored material that wafted around the body when walking. The dresses were long, but they were split high on the front, and they were also adaptable; they could be worn hiked up on one side or with the hem buttoned in such a way that it

Karl Lagerfeld's 1977 fall collection for Chloe featured thigh-length boots inspired by those of the eighteenth century. He paired these heavy boots with full, flowing dresses in very thin, delicately patterned, and softly colored material. The type of boot shown here, one of three styles in the collection, was designed to give the look of wearing leather pants. (Arthur Elgort/Getty Images.)

seemed to ripple over the wearer's boot tops. Alternatively, one part of the hem could be hiked up and tucked into the boot tops or into the waistband of the tights underneath. The combination of very high boots and thick, ribbed tights ensured that even through the dresses were split almost to the waist, there was no excessive exposure of flesh. The whole ensemble was *outré*, but it was also quite modest.

The look caught on. By May 1977, Bernadine Morris was reporting in the *New York Times* that a growing number of retailers on 7th Avenue were featuring knee-baring dresses for fall, also noting that high boots and thick tights should be used to offset increased leg exposure. At Gino-Snow, Richard Assatly was experimenting with short styles, such as a bloused jacket worn with over-the-knee boots. "That's for the young contingent," Morris commented, rather tartly.[339] By the time the glossies started covering the fall fashions, in their July editions, over-the-knee boots were high on the list of accessories. In its review of shoes for the 1977 fall season, *Vogue* hailed "a great-looking new over-the-knee boot to wear with a tunic top and textured legs . . . or a thick Shaker sweater and matching leggings. Or to pull on over the narrowest narrowed pants and cuff down (boots are that soft this year!) sometimes to show its cozy shearling lining."[340]

The year 1977 also saw the return of the mini, albeit in a new form suited to the easygoing fashions of the time. The late-seventies mini, as interpreted in the Paris collections of that year, was a big sweater or baggy tunic top, worn with wool stockings and low-heeled boots of all heights from ankle length to thigh high. In the *Daily Mail*, Barbara Griggs commented that, in tunic and thigh boots, half the models looked like pantomime principal boys.[341] Describing the buccaneer styles of Lagerfeld et al., Griggs had some reservations. "If I had fantastic legs, I'd love to show them off in a brief tunic or huge sweater," she wrote, a little wistfully. "Leggy girls will love the Paris Principal Boy style. The rest of us will go for something rather more girly."[342]

The August edition of *Vogue* offered a Helmut Newton–shot feature on the Paris and Milan collections that focused heavily on Lagerfeld's work.[343] Reclining on the grass below the Arc de Triomphe, a model demonstrated the "new way to be in a dress . . . Karl Lagerfeld's soft slide-y ecru challis dress, held by a waist-wrap of knitted burgundy sleeves. With a matching burgundy knit cardigan, lace flower, with over-the-knee leather boots . . . All by Chloe." Another Newton image showed "Karl Lagerfeld's oversized turtleneck in white ribbed knit. The big news—the way you wear it: pulled down over matching leggings, with over-the-knee boots and a soft slit-front grey flannel skirt—you haven't seen anything like it before!" the magazine concluded excitedly.[344]

This new iteration of the over-the-knee boot had more in common with the first generation of cuissardes from the early 1960s; it was a relatively bulky, loose-fitting boot, and although it had a heel that was quite high, it was also heavy and blocky. If Karl Lagerfeld and his imitators were intending to produce footwear that would bring to mind a cavalryman or buccaneer of the eighteenth century, then they certainly succeeded. In fact, the next time over-the-knee boots were back in fashion—at the end of the 1980s—they would once again look to the same period and aesthetic for inspiration. And once more, it would be Lagerfeld—now designing for Chanel—who would lead the charge.

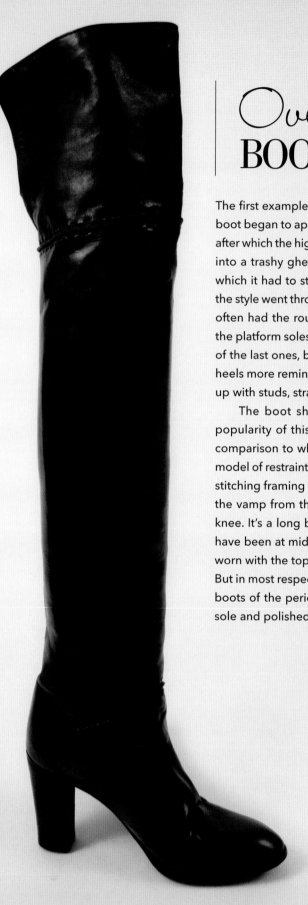

Over-The-Knee
BOOT, LATE 1970s

The first examples of the seventies' take on the over-the-knee boot began to appear around 1976; the last ones during 1982, after which the high-heeled, thigh-high fashion boot descended into a trashy ghetto of bikers, rockers, and sex workers from which it had to struggle mightily to escape. During that time, the style went through a fair amount of evolution—early versions often had the round toes, shaped legs, and sometimes even the platform soles of early- to mid-seventies boots, while some of the last ones, by companies such as Wild Pair, had toes and heels more reminiscent of cowboy boots and were toughened up with studs, straps, buckles, and the like.

The boot shown here, however, dates from the peak popularity of this style of boot, between 1977 and 1979. In comparison to what went before, and what came after, it is a model of restraint. The only decorations are two double rows of stitching framing the major seams of the boot—one separating the vamp from the shaft, the other encircling the shaft at the knee. It's a long boot—on most women, that flared top would have been at midthigh level, although this style could also be worn with the top turned down to form a cuff below the knee. But in most respects, it is just an elongated version of the dress boots of the period, and it shares with them the egg-shaped sole and polished, glossy leather finish.

Fashion boots reached new heights in the last years of the 1970s, with a rediscovered enthusiasm for over-the-knee styles.

By 1978, the new-style over-the-knee boot was cementing its popularity. In the *Toronto Star*, Shirley Morris reported that the longest boots that fall "are over the knee and made from fine glove leather that can be rolled back. They're intended for straight-legged pants or, more spectacularly, worn only over leotards with a big sweater."[345] The reference to the turndown cuff highlighted one of the key features of this boot: adaptability. With the flap down, it gave the wearer a piratical swagger; with the flap up, it could be used to cover the unsightly bunching of fabric around the knee that was inevitable when jeans were tucked into boots. The ability to turn down the top of the OTK boot to make a cuffed knee boot was an important selling point because, as much as anything, 1978 was the year of the convertible boot. Faced with a plethora of choices of shaft length, some women plumped for a boot that could be any length you wanted, cuffed above or below the knee, or scrunched down to the ankle, depending on the outfit.[346] Why buy three pairs of boots when you could wear the same pair in three different ways?

Over-the-knee boots could also be worn with the top turned down, as seen here in the 1978 autumn/winter Freemans catalog. This provided not only flexibility of wear but also a certain piratical swagger. (Freemans Grattan Holdings.)

Looking Good, Feeling Good

By 1977–78, the fashion boot had hit a new peak of popularity. A single article from the *Guardian* of September 9, 1977, gives a snapshot of the remarkable diversity of styles that were available that winter.[347] These included a calf boot in natural leather with sheepskin lining; a shiny boot with attached multistoried leg warmer; a flat, rust leather riding boot with a sheepskin lining; leather and canvas gaiters paired with a lace-up ankle boot; a red stacked-heel ankle boot; calf-length leather and fur boots; a black soft ankle boot; a leather stirrup boot in black or brown; a beige suede-and-leather boot; a brown suede knee-length lace-up boot; and a thigh-length white sheepskin patchwork boot. The western boot was also popular in various styles that bridged the gap between traditional cowboy boots and the various short-legged fashion boots of the time. If popularity was measured solely by diversity, then boots were in a pretty good place.

This was the time when a pair of boots began to be looked at as an "investment"—not surprisingly, given the hike in prices, but a definite shift from the more disposable boots of the sixties. Newspapers like the *Toronto Star* featured articles full of tips on prolonging the life of a leather or suede boot (admittedly a particular challenge in the Canadian winter).[348] Above all, the practicality of the boot was emphasized. "It's a revolution I heartily applaud," Barbara Griggs wrote in the *Daily Mail*. "I love not having to worry

A selection of shorter boot styles from the 1978 autumn/winter Freemans catalog. (Freemans Grattan Holdings.)

about laddered tights as I climb back into a pair of comfortable, low-heeled boots."[349] "Boots not only look good, they feel good," said *Cheap Chic*, a 1975 style guide. "How far and how fast can you walk in a pair of high-heeled pumps?"[350]

Well-made, expensive, practical, a good investment . . . it's clear from the articles of the time that boots were a solid proposition for the fashionable women, but these are not exactly terms that set the pulse racing. And while there were plenty of articles reporting the popularity of boots, the number of references to them was steadily declining. The tide of fashion was turning against high boots. "Paris styles kick long boots out of fashion," the *Atlanta Constitution* announced in August 1978, reporting that for most collections midcalf boots with very high heels had replaced the taller boots seen the previous year.[351] The emergence of new, shorter styles of boot was linked to wider changes in fashion, away from the relaxed, comfort-driven clothing of the mid-70s toward something sharper and more obviously tailored. New youth culture demanded new styles of boot, and by 1977 changes were starting to appear.

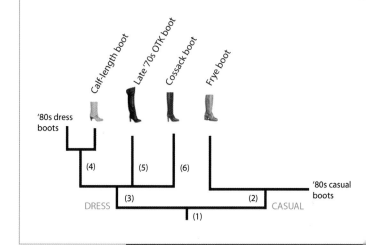

The middle years of the 1970s saw a fundamental split between casual and dressy styles of fashion boot—one that persists to the present day. (1) Straight shaft; (2) low heel; (3) tapering heel; (4) shaft less than 16"; (5) shaft greater than 18"; (6) shaft 16–18".

With the renewed popularity of the Frye boot in the early 1970s, a fundamental divergence occurs in the history of the fashion boot—one that persists to the present day. The Frye boot, rugged and low-heeled, was one of the earliest examples of the casual boot, a group that went on to encompass low-heeled and loose-fitting designs throughout the eighties and nineties as well as the equestrian and over-the-knee boots of today. The other grouping, sharing characteristics like high heels and more pointed toes, is the dress boots. These were very popular in the late seventies, less common during the eighties, but made a triumphant return in the years surrounding the Millennium.

A SHARPER *Edge*

Backlit by the studio lights, Debbie Harry's blonde mane is a radiant halo framing her face. Stepping up to the microphone, she fixes the camera with a sidelong look. "Listen up, you monkeys," she announces to her television audience. "This one's called 'I Am Always Touched by Your Presence, Dear." Clem Burke pounds the drums on the intro, and Blondie launches into the second single from their album *Plastic Letters* (1978). Initially Harry stands close to the mic, hands clasped behind her back, but as the song progresses she becomes more animated, stepping back from the microphone stand to pogo from one foot to the other during the song's instrumental break. She is, as ever, impeccably dressed—in contrast to her black-clad bandmates, she wears a loose, yellow wool sweater dress and matching leather over-the-knee boots, their cuffs folded down in the style of the time.[352]

Blondie's 1978 performance on the BBC music show *The Old Grey Whistle Test* came at the apogee of popularity for the thigh-length boots of the late seventies. Debbie Harry had been an earlier adopter of the style, having been photographed backstage at the Whisky a Go-Go in a black leather pair on February 9, 1977,[353] two months before Karl Lagerfeld featured similar boots in his fall collections for Chloe. The cavalier swagger of the new generation of cuissardes fitted well with the stage personas of a number of female rock stars, from disco queens like Sarah Brightman,[354] ABBA's Agnetha Fältskog, and the duo Blonde on Blonde[355] to middle-of-the-road rockers such as Cher, to punks like Siouxsie Sioux and Toyah Willcox. But these were the exceptions rather than the rule, and as the seventies drew to a close it seemed there was not much that was rock-and-roll about the fashion boot.

chapter
8

In the late seventies and early eighties, punk and New Wave singers like Blondie's Debbie Harry were quick to harness the rock-and-roll swagger of thigh-high boots. (Lynn Goldsmith/Getty Images.)

THE YEAR OF THE PUMP

The first years of the 1980s saw boot heels become more slender, while leg height dwindled. (University of Worcester.)

The first rumblings of trouble appeared in the spring of 1978, when designers showed their fall collections. "Paris styles kick long boots out of fashion," the *Atlanta Constitution* announced,[356] reviewing the impact of those collections in August of that year. For most collections, midcalf boots with very high heels had replaced the taller boots seen the previous year. But boots in general were rapidly declining in popularity. If there was a dominant style of winter footwear at the very end of the seventies, then, as far as the fashion mavens were concerned, it was the closed-toe pump.[357]

The reasons for this shift are varied, but interrelated. One was purely practical. The cost of leather soared at the end of the decade, and took the price of boots with it. The *New York Times* reported that boots had skyrocketed to $300 a pair, well over $1,000 by today's prices. "If you already have them, don't buy any more because they'll be horribly expensive," designer Geoffrey Beene was quoted as saying.[358] A similar surge in the cost of leather occurred in the late 1960s, where it was one of the factors that drove the emergence of cheaper plastic and vinyl fashion boots. Ten years later the vinyl boot was more or less extinct, and when high boots were needed, a new candidate stepped up. "For icy days," the *Times* reported in August 1979, "the answer is unanimous: rubber. Nobody says they're glamorous, but rubber boots are certainly practical and many are good looking."[359]

Another factor was a rise in hemlines. Again in the late sixties rising hemlines had taken boots along with them. But in 1979, the story was quite different. "When wearing a skirt or suit with boots," the *Times* decreed, "then heed the words of Geoffrey Beene: 'There should never be a separation between the top of the boot and the bottom of the hem. The separation is most horrendous.'"[360] But above all it was a question of proportion, a word that appeared again and again in the fashion press at this time. At least as far as most fashion journalists were concerned,[361] 1979 was "the Year of the Suit," and those suits had jackets that were shaped and skirts that were straight; as *Vogue* reported, "[T]he new silhouette close to the body is lean and makes women look slim."[362] Placing a pair of heavy, seventies-era boots at the bottom of that silhouette would disrupt the proportions.

Faced with a similar challenge in the late 1990s, designers came up with the slim-line, calf-hugging dress boot. In 1979 they changed tack completely and abandoned the excessively expensive leather boot altogether, in favor of the tailored pump, often worn with textured or patterned hosiery. As a number of writers pointed out, there was a distinctly 1950s feel to the fashions of 1979 and 1980, and the pump—an archetypical piece of fifties footwear—fit well with this. "If you follow fashion at all," Ann-Marie Schiro wrote in the *New York Times* in September 1979, "you know that as far as shoes go, this is the year of the pump, that classic closed shoe that was out of favor in recent seasons."[363] With the return of dressier styles, designers embraced the pump with enthusiasm, finding ways to add new interest by using a wider palette of colors and materials; cutting the shoe high on the instep, sometimes to the ankle; and using decorative devices such as scallops, bows, leaves, and asymmetric throats.[364]

"Boots Are Obsolete"

"Boots, you know, are obsolete," Bernadine Morris declared in April 1979,[365] but this was not entirely true. Boots could be successful—if they looked more like pumps. "The perky ankle boot is an option for this season," Elaine Louie reported in the *Times* in August.[366] "It will not only keep the feet warm, but will change and update the proportion of things already in the closet." The 1979 Gucci fall collection mixed spike-heeled pumps and ankle boots on the runway, and at Charles Jourdan the best sellers were "a leather pump with a pleated decoration on the vamp, a two-tone suede Dorsay [sic] pump and a bootie—an ankle-high cross between a shoe and a boot."

With shoes rising higher on the instep, the line between pump and boot became blurred, but—as in 1973—the ankle boot really came into its own when paired with pants. "Pants for the day," *Vogue* announced in its 1979 fall preview.[367] "The option remains open—have the same straight clean line [as the skirts] . . . and think short boots—the newest—and raciest 'accessory' for pants now." As Katherine Madden reported in the September edition, "There are beautiful short boots, around right now. Above-the-ankle or a little taller, softly crushed or strapped, moccasin like or piped. They look new, offer a real alternative to pumps and, in many ways, make a lot more sense than hot, knee high boots."[368]

The other area where the boot still reigned supreme was in western-themed fashion. For those who had money to burn, the sky was the limit for that "Urban Cowboy" look. If you were an Upper East Side matron, dropping $300 on a pair of boots in hornback lizard skin seemed like no big deal. Out in the Hamptons, "Dingo boots with a Western accent are $52.50," Andrea Aurichio reported for the *Times*, "a bargain when compared to other western-style boots being sold for several hundred dollars around town."[369] The popularity of low-heeled leather boots, particularly western-styled, provided a distinct purpose to wearing skirts. "It's a good look," said one Hamptons store owner. "You can combine Western style boots with a skirt and a sweater coat or with a blazer and you're warm, you're comfortable and you're fashionable."[370]

By 1980, changing proportions were having another effect on footwear. "The few clear trends that are evident include an unusual number of dresses with short skirts: some are minis but more have hemlines hovering around the knees," Mary Russell reported in the *Times* in March of that year.[371] "This change demands a move towards silhouettes with longer torsos and towards lower-heeled boots and shoes which bring proper balance to this shape." This was echoed in *Vogue*, which announced "shoes on lower heels to give a new proportion . . . shoes and boots with classic appeal."[372]

The year 1980 is when the number of references to boots in the press begins to climb again after the trough of 1979.[373] But it's important to note that many of these references relate to the ongoing popularity of western fashions—they're talking about cowboy boots rather than the strict definition of fashion boots that was established at the beginning of this book. So is the impressive peak in boot references seen in 1981 another reflection of this? The answer is a resounding "no." In 1981, the fashion boot really did come roaring back.

The Boot Rebounds

"Boots are back," the *New York Times* blared in September 1981.[374] And so they were. All of the major designers showed boots in their fall collections, pairing them with the season's blousy tops and calf-length skirts or culottes. And they were not just for the daytime; there were evening boots, too, in soft suede and metallic leathers. Once again, it was a matter of proportion. In 1981, there was a shift away from the slim-line silhouette of 1979–80, back to fuller, more relaxed clothes. Now shoes and stockings made legs look too thin. By contrast, as Dawn Mello, of Bloomingdale's, put it, "[B]oots act as an anchor to the big silhouette."[375] "Boots do it," Rick Goldstein, of Macy's, said in the same *Times* article. "They make the look work."

But they had also gone through a fundamental change since their 1977 heyday. "Boots give a person contemporary drama instantly," said Calvin Klein in a 1981 *Times* interview, "but it's not the old-fashioned, heavy-handed kind of drama."[376] In the same article, fashion journalist Jani Wooldridge explained that the boots of the recent past "were more like costume items than wardrobe staples, a trend that required an entire wardrobe of boots to accompany a range of ensembles." By contrast, the new generation of boots was eminently convertible, "versatile enough for almost any occasion, so that a woman does not need a closet full of them."[377] They were flat-heeled, and, although some were thigh-high, they were also soft and loose-fitting enough to be scrunched down to knee or even midcalf length. In addition to being pulled up to full height or scrunched down, they sometimes had cuffs that could be folded up or down. Made from suede or soft leather, these were no longer Cossack boots; instead, the fashion press called them "Robin Hood" boots.

And they were popular, too. Saks's best seller in the late summer of 1981 was a knee-high boot in soft leather, which could fold down to midcalf or even ankle length—it came in khaki, camel, bronze, or pearlized gray, and it had sold out completely by mid-August.[378] In contrast to the eye-watering prices of the last generation of Cossack boots, the Robin Hood boots were relatively affordable. The *Times* "Careful Shopper" column of December 6, 1981, listed a variety of styles, crushable and with tops that could be

A 1983 selection of boots from the British mail-order company Kays. Flat heels and short, straight shafts were combined with bright colors and decoration. (University of Worcester.)

folded up or down, from $74.99 to $79.99, and a tall, "dressy" boot by Etienne Aigner for $84.99.[379] In the words of Calvin Klein, "These are boots for real people, to be worn maybe 90 percent of the time with nearly everything."[380]

The resurgence in the popularity of boots continued into 1982, although this was not to the liking of everyone. Reviewing the fall collections for that year in the *Times*,

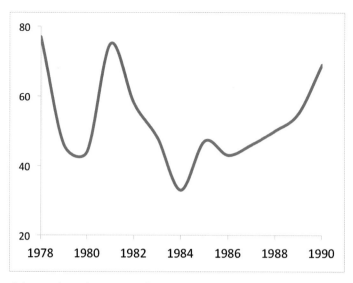

If the number of mentions of boots in the press is a measure of their popularity, the graph for the 1980s reflects a low not seen since their first emergence as a fashion item more than twenty years earlier.

John Duka expressed his great dislike for "those high-heeled, knee-high stormtrooper boots that almost everyone can live without, thank you," which had dominated the New York collections.[381] As an antidote, he hailed Vittorio Ricci's "low fitted boot reminiscent of the button up boots of the turn of the century. Mr. Ricci's are designed to lace-up or snap closed, they snugly follow the line of the leg, and the boot top is only as high as the longest hem." At Chloe, Karl Lagerfeld declared, "[M]y clothes are narrow and when they are worn with boots, as they must be, the silhouette is the same as if the woman is wearing long pants."[382] Pictured in an article for the *Times*, Lagerfeld's boots for Chloe—made for the collection by Walter Steiger—were not dissimilar to the Cossack boots of the previous decade; once again, it was the crushed look around the ankle that was remarked on by journalists.

But in 1982 the graph of popularity was falling again, down from the peak of the previous year. Some of this is a result of the sudden death of the Urban Cowboy, as reported by the *Times* in November 1982; the market for western boots had crashed, causing layoffs and factory closures as boot makers fell back on producing basic designs for their core customers. Highly decorated boots now tended to be more conventional fashion (as opposed to western) designs, as reviewed by Bernadine Morris on a 1982 visit to shoemakers in Milan. Suede boots with decorative calf inlays were selling for $200 a pair "but look well worth it."[383]

Even so, there were indications that the rest of the decade would be a struggle for the fashion boot. Summarizing the trends for the 1982 fall season, Bettina Graziani of Ungaro said that given the new emphasis on shoulders and legs; ". . . one must wear very good shoes. Boots are démodé."[384]

of the 1980s than this style of low-heeled ankle boot. Ankle boots were probably the most popular variety of boots during the eighties, and this type of slouchy shaft, which could extend to midcalf if stretched but normally sat in a series of folds around the ankle, was very typical. These boots were hugely popular and could be worn with both miniskirts and jeans (usually stonewashed denim). Even the choice of white leather cries out "eighties."

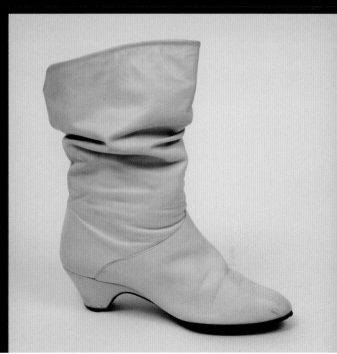

A classic pair of fashion boots from the middle years of the 1980s. The baggy fit and turned-down top were common design features. White leather, while impractical, was hugely popular during this era.

A PROBLEM OF PROPORTION

As we've already seen, there had been precipitous dips in popularity for the fashion boot in 1972–73 and 1979–80. But even by those standards, references to boots during the period from 1983 to 1988 were especially sparse. Boots had not attracted so little attention from the fashion press, for such a prolonged period of time, since their emergence as a fashion item at the beginning of the 1960s. To understand why this was, it's necessary to take a step back and look at the wider picture of fashion in the eighties.

One of the phrases most commonly used in discussion of women's fashion from this period is "power dressing." Increasingly, women were making their way in the workplace and seeking to compete on an equal footing with their male colleagues. Hence, the growth in popularity of the suit, which was given additional presence and assertiveness by jacket shoulders that were widened with pads.[385] A tapering silhouette offset the broad shoulders, with a narrow waist and short, tight skirt. Similar designs were fashionable in the late seventies, and then, just as in the mid-eighties, it weighed heavily against the wearing of boots. This sort of look called for a heeled pump or, at most, a small, high-heeled ankle boot. Anything taller or heavier unbalanced the lines of the suit.

There were times when the eighties seemed like the age of the ankle boot. (University of Worcester.)

At the same time, the eighties saw spectacular growth in the popularity of leisurewear. Fashion had changed its target audience from the young to the twenty-five-to-forty age group, a more discriminating market. In the eighties, these women were increasingly balancing career with family life.[386] Family life had become more relaxed and casual, and if you weren't one of the unlucky millions of unemployed, there was more disposable income. For those of us who remember the eighties, the term "leisurewear" usually brings to mind the ghastliness of the shell suit, but there was much more to it than this. The early eighties brought a new generation of man-made fibers, either in isolation or mixed with wool and cotton, which allowed for better fit and flexibility.[387] Clothes were layered, and there was a new emphasis on decorative legwear: patterned hosiery in a variety of colors and designs, socks, legwarmers, and a new alternative to trousers—leggings.[388]

In 1983, the boots that were around tended to fit within this casual mode of dress. The most common style, by far, was a low-heeled ankle boot, in leather or suede, with a turned-down cuff. This boot is everywhere, in fashion editorials, adverts, and the wider media. Occasionally, the taller, loose-fitting suede design known as the "Robin Hood" boot appears, and as Priscilla Tucker noted in the *New York Times* in April of that year, "English trendies this spring dress Dickensian . . . in long skirts over short, lace-up boots."[389] But in general, 1983 was a low point in the history of the fashion boot. While there was a definite trend toward shorter skirts, this was no sixties revival. Describing the fashions in the Milan shows of that year, manufacturer Aldo Pinto was blunt: "[B]oots," he declared, "have disappeared."[390]

THE ONLY WAY IS UP

From this point, there was only one way to go. Describing the fall fashions of 1983, the *Times*'s Angela Taylor reported that while the pump still reigned supreme, boots were on the rise again. Designer fashion boots "are not meant to plow through snowdrifts," she wrote, "but rather to add an Anna Karenina touch or an extra fillip to a dress or suit."[391] The boots in question were made of soft kid or suede, in a wide range of colors such as rose reds, crimson, butterscotch, forest green, and a range of blues. "Look for boots with knitted wool tops like knee socks or anklets," she advised, drawing particular attention to "Blahnik's low boot of caramel suede fastened with natural horn."

In 1984, Calvin Klein's first shoe collection featured a knee-high boot with a flat heel and a tie at the ankle.[392] Elsewhere, women were wearing long narrow skirts topped by an oversized jacket or multiple sweater layers and finished with flat-heeled boots. Other, more radical designs were making a surprising resurgence. In a January 1985 Bill Cunningham photo essay for the *Times*, the photographer snapped a woman in a watermelon-pink short coat. "Women seem to like wearing the coat with pipe-stem leg gear, such as these over-the knee boots," he noted.[393] It was indicative of a late-eighties trend toward shorter coats, with a narrow leg covering—leggings, tight pants, or very tall boots. The trousers were often paired with short boots to remove the problem of a break in the smooth pants line.

Higher-legged boots in the 1980s often mimicked those of the first half of the 1960s–loose-fitting, low-heeled, and straight-legged. These examples are from 1987. (University of Worcester.)

At Fendi, Karl Lagerfeld came up with a new, leaner shape, which he called the "tower" look—with less emphasis on the shoulders, he could place more weight at the legs—the midcalf velvet skirts and silk dresses, extravagantly patterned with butterflies and eagles, were paired with loose-fitting, high-heeled black suede boots.[394] Perry Ellis's 1985 fall/winter collection "came out strongly for miniskirts," Bernadine Morris reported in the *Times*. "They were tiny, flounced affairs, usually combined with longer tops and boots that extended to the upper thighs."[395] Meanwhile, Maud Frizon offered a riding boot in velvet for the fall of 1986: "They can be worn in a Russian way, even under a long fantasy evening dress," *Vogue* enthused, going on to discuss the new trend of combining soft satin or suede boots with long (below calf-length) skirts for evening wear.[396] Evening boots, you may recall, had been a big deal in the late '60s. Now they were back, at least for the hardened fashionista.

For the regular woman, the formula for boots pretty much conformed to the same pattern seen for much of the first half of the decade. Wide shoulders and short skirts meant ankle boots. Narrower shoulders and long, full skirts meant heavier, loose-fitting boots. This is the look seen in most of the editorial pieces of the time. Heels were more common with short skirts but not unknown with the longer ones. But by 1986, this formula was beginning to change. Hemlines continued to rise, but shoulders became a little narrower. "Setting up this season means giving some thought to legs and lengths, to shoes and heel heights," *Vogue* reported in July 1986.[397] "On the whole, you'll find two different skirt lengths dominate the season. One is shorter, to the top of the knee; the other, quite long . . . just below the calf to an inch or so above the ankle.

Suede
OVER-THE-KNEE BOOT, LATE '80s

Around the middle of the 1980s, the hard-edged fashions of the early part of the decade began to give way to a softer look. Instead of spiky ankle and calf-length boots, low-heeled suede designs began to appear. Their emergence was the result of the interplay of various factors. First, the eighties saw a reawakening of interest in loose, gypsyish, bohemian, or boho, fashions; the boho look tends to favor boots in general, and in this particular case it went well with loose-fitting, slouchy suede boots. At the same time, a different trend in eighties fashion was the development of a new breed of very short skirt—not the tailored, formal miniskirt of the early eighties, but something softer and more casual, akin to the sweater minidresses of the late seventies. Finally, there was the growing popularity of leggings as an alternative to tights or trousers.

All of these developments, singularly and in combination, opened the possibility of emphasizing the leg with a tall boot. Low-heeled and loose-fitting, it could be accessorized with decorative stitching or brocade. The pair shown here is typical of the period. The heel is almost low enough to be called flat, the leg has no shape to it, and the dark blue suede of the boot has been contrasted by a decorative pattern of leather. The boots are, strictly speaking, over-the-knee, but are so loose-fitting that they would more likely have settled between midcalf and the knee. Contemporary wearers used to overcome this by securing the top of the shaft with a decorative ribbon tied behind the knee.

With taller styles of boot, designers began to rediscover the potential of the high boot as a medium for color and decoration. This pair of suede over-the-knee boots from the second half of the eighties features decorative leather inserts.

Current thinking on length says short skirts usually take heels, most often pumps . . . with the season's renewed interest, though, in boots, both short and long—and some truly remarkable examples are turning up now—short skirts . . . often easily take to boots. With Thierry Mugler's striped wool suit, ones that are very high—with something of a heel—seem to strike just the right balance."[398]

THE ROMANTIC BOOT

So the door was opened for the return of the boot. Writing in the *New York Times* that month, Anne-Marie Schiro described boots by Maud Frizon that were reminiscent of the Russian boots of the 1920s, with trimmings of gold or soutache. "Miss Frizon believes that boots will be popular again, and the higher the better," Schiro wrote.[399] "Some of hers climb to the thighs." She went on to report that Shoe Biz at Henri Bendel was already stocking thigh-high suede boots and had sold seven pairs in two days at $450 a pair. "The boots are meant to be worn under very short skirts, so it seems as if legs will be covered this winter, even by women who don't go in for ankle-grazing skirts." Reviewing the 1986 fall shoe collections, *Vogue* identified "a new texture impact . . . not just in shoes, but in boots, in every length, every proportion, from the ankle bone to over the knee. The most extraordinary . . . are from Andrea Pfister, strong lined, classic, in licorice black crocodile. As much an investment—and a delight—as a fur, they represent the season's ultimate luxury."[400] Pfister's boots, pictured in the accompanying article, were remarkably reminiscent of Roger Vivier's boots designed for the Yves Saint Laurent collections twenty-three years earlier.

Leg coverage was the key to the popularity of over-the-knee boots in the late eighties. Calvin Klein's 1987 fall/winter collection featured hemlines no longer than fingertip or midthigh level and used stretch yarns built into the fabric to ensure that the clothes clung to the models' figures. But, as Bernadine Morris wrote in the *Times*, "nothing looked vulgar. The short skirts were worn with opaque stockings or over the-knee boots."[401] By dressing the body and legs in opaque black tights and over-the-knee boots it didn't matter where the short skirt ended, and the boots themselves also had stretch materials built in to ensure an overall smooth line. Klein wasn't the only designer to feature over-the-knee boots in

The late 1980s also saw the return of romanticism, in the form of Victorian-style lace-up ankle boots. (University of Worcester.)

Not everyone was overjoyed by the return of the thigh-length boot in the late eighties. In fact, some people were worried for their health.[403] In January 1988, a nervous reader wrote to *Vogue* that she liked over-the-knee boots but had heard that they could cause problems; was this true? The answer, according to John Waller, MD, the chief of Mount Sinai Hospital's Foot and Ankle Service, was yes. While boots are generally good for feet, gripping the instep rather than the toes, a tight-fitting over-the-knee boot could cause problems by squeezing the knees when the user sits down. This could force fluid into the tissues of the leg, causing swelling in the short term and, over longer periods, varicose veins and bruised cartilage. Wear your boots a half-size too large, Dr. Waller advised, and avoid flat heels in favor of something around 2" high.[404]

his collection that year; Donna Karan, Yves Saint Laurent, and Andrea Pfister all featured boots that went to midthigh. Pfister produced a particularly spectacular design in red leather, which included a wedge of corset elastic for fit and comfort. "Boots this fall are leg-tight to go with the shape of the body," he declared.[402]

Women worried about the state of their knees as exposed by the new hemlines. "Bony, knobby, lumpy or flabby, knees are rarely objects of beauty," Linda Wells wrote in the *New York Times* of August 23, 1987. "An even better alternative for those who want to wear short skirts, but whose legs might not be up to it, is boots. Many of the new boots extend just above the knee. When they are worn with a short skirt, only an inch or two of the leg will show."[405] The following year saw a refinement of this look. Boots got a distinctly romantic flavor. In the August 1988 edition of *UK Vogue*, an editorial titled "Guinevere" discussed the emergence of "a new heroine" emerging from "the age of chivalry . . . at the London collections there was a distinct feeling for Camelot . . . moody velvets, jewel and dull metal colours, Gothic points and drama in brave accessories—metal work, gauntlets, thigh boots, and borzois."[406]

High boots, hose, and even the occasional doublet formed part of a new sort of Shakespearean cross-dressing. High-legged suede and velvet boots decorated with brocade were intended to channel the romantic spirit of the Elizabethan era.[407] From here it was a short step to a late-'60s/early-'70s revival, typified—according to Bernadette Morra of the *Toronto Star*—by thigh-high suede boots (as shown by Byblos), ethnic prints, Italian peasant skirts, Edwardian jackets, and John Lennon glasses.[408] "Boots on runways, in top shoemakers' collections, are noteworthy, newsy, turning up in abundance," *Vogue*

Diana, Princess of Wales, was a global fashion icon during the 1980s. Like many fashionable women of this period, she was quick to embrace the potential of casual over-the-knee styles of boots, as here in 1986. (Rex.)

reported in July 1988. "Soft suede over-the-knee versions get put with shorter, swingy skirts or pulled up over the narrowest of trousers. Ankle boots . . . come as sleek and fitted as pumps, paired up with pants or long skirts to offer a clear daytime alternative."[409] The boot had come a long way from the nadir of 1983, but this newfound popularity was, for the most part, confined to the high-end fashion press. It was the coming decade that would see fashion boots return to widespread popularity.

A Footnote FROM THE '80s

If you're under the age of forty, you probably have little idea and certainly no recollection of the Iran-Contra scandal of the mid-1980s, when (to summarize briefly) the Reagan administration did a deal whereby (1) Israel would supply arms to Iran (yes, you read that right); (2) Iran would use its influence to obtain the release of American hostages in Lebanon; (3) the United States would resupply Israel with weapons; (4) Israel would pay the United States for the weapons; and (5) the United States would use the funds from the arms sales to support right-wing guerillas trying to overthrow the left-wing government of Nicaragua, something the U.S. government was prohibited by law from doing. Got it?

Well, never mind if you don't. The critical bit, from our perspective, is the subsequent inquiry held by the U.S. Senate, and in particular the testimony of Fawn Hall, secretary to the architect of the whole scheme, U.S. Marine Colonel Oliver North, a staff member of the National Security Council. Appearing before the Senate Committee on June 8, 1987, Hall made the entertaining admission that she had smuggled top-secret documents out of the NSC hidden in her boots.[410]

North had asked for Hall's assistance in shredding incriminating papers relating to the various transfers of arms, money, etc., but a few days later she discovered that she had missed several documents. What was a girl to do? "I took the copies of the altered documents, folded them, and placed them inside my boots," she testified. Then she ran into another official's office and stuffed some computer memos down her back. "I asked if he could see anything in my back," she said of Colonel North, whom she had called to insist that he come to the White House once she discovered that not all the papers had been shredded, "and he said no." Later, when she and Colonel North were in a car together, she took the papers out and gave them to him.

Without passing judgment on these nefarious activities, or on Fawn Hall (who was given immunity from prosecution on charges of conspiracy and destroying documents in exchange for her testimony), it does at least have relevance to the history of the fashion boot. Had this occurred during the Watergate scandal twelve years earlier, Hall would not have been able to fit the documents into her boots; they would have been much tighter around the legs. It was only the loose-fitting boots of the

THE YEAR
OF THE
Boot

E dward Lewis is having a bad day. His ex-wife has his Long Island house and his dog; his ex-girlfriend is moving out of their Manhattan apartment. Now he's stuck at a ghastly Beverly Hills party, far from his native New York, having to schmooze with a bunch of investors. He bails, much to the horror of his lawyer, and sets off back to the Beverly Wilshire Hotel, piloting a Lotus Esprit that he can barely drive, through a city that he doesn't know. As the camera hovers over his car, snaking its way down the canyon roads, we're serenaded by the glutinous tones of that most eighties of bands, Huey Lewis and the News.

Meanwhile, in a dingy apartment off Hollywood Boulevard, Edward's date with destiny is just waking up. Sliding out of bed, she shimmies into a tight Lycra minidress, fixes her makeup, and, after touching up a scuffed heel with a marker pen, and to the decidedly edgier sounds of Iggy Pop's "Real Wild Child," plonks a stiletto-heeled foot onto a partly open drawer and pulls up the zip-fastener (fixed with a safety pin, for a punkish touch) on a shiny black PVC thigh boot. Resplendent in a blonde Carol Channing wig, Vivian is ready for a night on the streets.

Whether *Pretty Woman*, a blockbuster hit from the summer of 1990 and one of the most successful movies of all time, was a good thing in the history of the fashion boot is open to question (see sidebar); what is unarguable is that it gave that particular pair of boots a cinematic profile to rival Dorothy's ruby slippers or Cinderella's glass ones. Even if it ensured that no fashion journalist from that date forward would be able to mention over-the-knee boots without a cautionary reference to the film, *Pretty Woman* provides

chapter
9

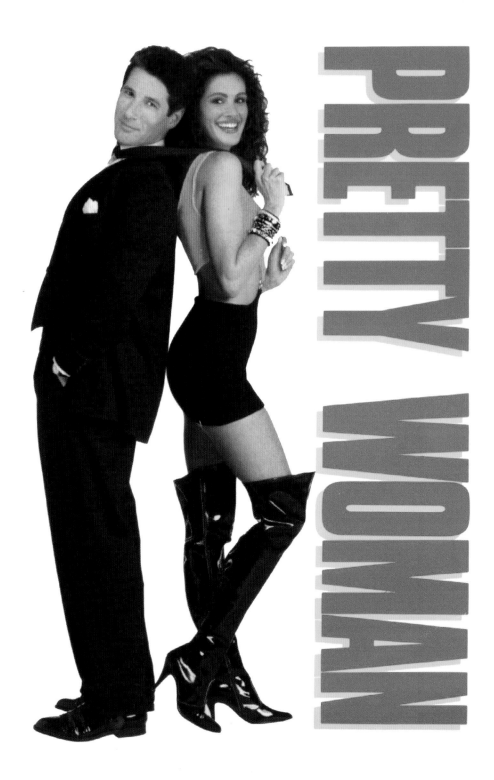

RICHARD GERE   JULIA ROBERTS

PRETTY WOMAN

In 1990 it was hard to get away from posters for the movie *Pretty Woman*, or from Julia Roberts's thigh-length PVC boots. Whether this was a good thing for the evolution of the fashion boot is open to question. (Rex.)

an early example of how fashion boots in the nineties would achieve a higher level of exposure than they had had since the end of the 1960s.

APRÈS YVES, LE DELUGE

Most of the trends in fashion boots that we see in the early nineties actually emerge in the late eighties, but, as is often the case, they don't become fully established for a few years. Regardless of where the line gets drawn, however, this is the point where the average number of citations of boots climbs above the overall average of citations for the 50-plus years from 1955 to 2010, for pretty much the first time since 1979. And once it crosses that line, in 1992, it doesn't dip back under again until up to and including the present day.[411]

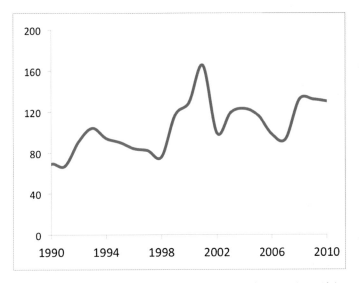

The beginning of a new decade, with its enthusiasm for the culture of the sixties, saw the fashion boot regain heights of popularity not seen since the sixties, reflected in the number of times this style of footwear was mentioned in the press.

In 1989, *Vogue* announced that the new boots for fall were "flat, stop at the ankle, come in every finish from blue leather to rugged suede."[412] For evening wear, Isaac Mizrahi was producing them in black satin. But loose, suede thigh-length boots were still a popular choice with leggings or tights, paired with an oversize sweater. Velvet and brocade boots were mentioned by *Vogue* as popular accessory choices, with short gold brocade boots becoming "decorative ornaments for a pair of black leggings and a black skirt."[413] Yves Saint Laurent's embrace of brocade boots meant that by the first fall of the nineties the stores were full of them, a combination of "sixties mod, country chic, and ethnic opulence." Quoting a fashion truism, *Vogue* declared in July 1990, "Après Yves, le deluge."[414]

By creating new proportions, "and in some cases eliminating the need for pants altogether," boots were to change the way that women dressed in the nineties. By August, the *New York Times* was declaring that boots were the ideal solution to the question of what to wear with leggings, catsuits, ski pants, or micro-miniskirts.[415] Quoting Bonnie Pressman, a vice president at Barney's New York, the paper noted that just as clothing was getting closer to the body, so footwear was hugging the ankle and the leg. Stirrup pants required the instep and ankle to be covered, matching the color of the pants to create a long, lean look. For the new, shorter styles of skirt, boots were climbing to midthigh, covering the knees and as much of the leg as possible below the hemline.[416]

The look, with ankle boots and over-the-knee styles predominating, was highly reminiscent of the sixties, something that Anne-Marie Schiro noted in the *Times*.[417] Barney's was leading the charge on sixties revivalism, with a white patent leather ankle boot, decorated with black stripes. But the most versatile boots, in Ms. Schiro's opinion, were "the soft suede styles that ascend over the knee. They can be cuffed to below the knee level, or crushed to mid-thigh." Yves Saint Laurent's black suede OTK boot, retailing for $395, had sold out at Bloomingdale's by early August 1990, but even more adventurous styles were available—a black patent pair with elastic sides by Maud Frizon ($860) and a silver pair with a rear zipper ($1,210).[418] Where late-eighties boots tended to have flat heels, by 1990 new designs were giving wearers a little more height. Although none were more than 2.5" high, their slender, curving shape made them appear taller. "A lot of women want heels," the *Times* quoted Jane Tuma of Saks as saying. "They feel more comfortable and feminine in a little heel."[419]

ROCK 'N' ROLL ROYALTY AND BIKER CHIC

But the true spectacle of 1990, as far as boots were concerned, occurred in the Paris fall couture collections. Saint Laurent may have brought the boot back into fashion, but it was its longtime champion, Karl Lagerfeld, who put it back on the map. By pairing satin cuissardes with massive, opulent ball gowns, Lagerfeld's 1990 collection for Chanel was a key moment in the history of the boot. The maestro cheekily suggested that they were an homage to Coco Chanel, who famously hated knees. He also dubbed it "Madonna meets Jayne Wrightsman," a nod to the latter's renowned collection of decorative arts of the ancien régime.[424] *Vogue* preferred to dub the whole thing "Rock 'n Royalty."[425]

By 1991, however, Lagerfeld and Chanel had moved on to an altogether different style of boots. Maybe it was the insistent, early nineties soundtrack of grunge, but while other designers like Valentino and Oscar de la Renta soldiered on with big sweaters and over-the-knee boots, Lagerfeld was digging further back into the history of the boot for inspiration. In the *New York Times* of March 21, the splendidly named Woody Hochswender described the revival of a boot that resembled nothing so much as "the old Frye biker boot, the one with the blunt toe and a ring at the ankle with three straps of leather."[426] The Chanel variant, of course, attached double-C broaches to the ring.

THE *Vivian* EFFECT

Pretty Woman was one of the biggest films of 1990; it netted over $460 million worldwide and, despite a decidedly mixed reception from critics, it still ranks as the highest-rated romantic comedy of all time, based on ticket sales. But there's a good case to be made that this is the film that single-handedly set back the mainstreaming of the over-the-knee boot, which might seem like an odd reaction to a movie whose hugely popular star, Julia Roberts, spends a good forty minutes strutting around in them.

The issue, of course, is that Roberts is playing a Hollywood Boulevard hooker. Her character, Vivian, is a small-town girl who has come to L.A. in search of her dreams and ended up a reluctant tart with a heart. In due course, an obscenely rich financial whiz, played by Richard Gere, swoops in at the wheel of a Lotus and rescues her from a life of vice. The film's message—that money can fix even the most intractable problems—is a dubious one, and, from the distance of several decades, it's hard not to feel a little queasy at the end. Strip away the hearts and flowers, and it looks very much like Vivian has swapped one kind of servitude for another.

But setting that aside, what about the boots? It is undoubtedly true that boots had a historic association with prostitution,[420] and it wasn't until the sixties that they began to gain some respectability. Even then, the acceptance wasn't universal—in 1968, 75 percent of office managers surveyed by the *New York Times* disapproved of their female staff wearing boots to work.[421] But by the seventies, boots were totally, 100 percent mainstream straight wear.

The over-the-knee boot is probably the most challenging style of fashion boot, and it took a little longer to get around the whole dominatrix angle. The shiny vinyl thigh boots of the late sixties were immediately co-opted for pinup photos,[422] and even the relatively sober designs of the late seventies, which evolved from the ubiquitous Cossack boot, had a whiff of punk and rock-and-roll brimstone about them. But by the mid-1980s, a new, softer thigh boot, low-heeled and made from suede, was beginning to gain in popularity.

Then along came *Pretty Woman*, with its iconic credits sequence of Vivian dressing for a night on the streets. As she pulls up the zipper on her shiny, spiky boots you're left in no doubt that her footwear is an integral part of her hooker persona, along with her blonde wig and her spandex microskirt. That impression is well and truly confirmed when it emerges later, during precoital negotiations with Gere, that she stashes a supply of condoms in the top of her boot.

So is there such a thing as a Vivian effect? It's hard to say, but there are certain indications that suggest there might be. The rugged, low-heeled over-the-knee boots of the early 1990s are almost indistinguishable from the very successful styles that have been around since 2009, but the nineties versions struggled to gain traction in the marketplace, and by the middle of the decade they had pretty much disappeared. Although there were sporadic attempts to relaunch thigh boots, notably around the turn of the Millennium and in the following decade, it wasn't until quite recently that they succeeded in breaking into the mainstream. Even then, it seemed that no fashion journalist could resist the urge to name-check the movie, and most articles carried a list of dos and don'ts intended to avoid the dreaded "Vivian" look—low heels, softer materials, muted colors, and no bare skin.[423]

The early years of the 1990s saw a resurgence of interest in boots of all styles, as seen here in Kays autumn/winter catalog from 1993. (University of Worcester.)

The high-fashion biker boot was responsible for one of the great iconic fashion shots of the nineties, Peter Lindbergh's black-and-white image of a Versace-clad girl gang of supermodel bikers: Cindy, Tatiana, Helena, Linda, Claudia, Naomi, Karen, and Stephanie striking tough-girl poses among the DUMBO warehouses.[427] But the new biker boot's natural territory was a long way from Brooklyn; in the *Times*, Bill Cunningham reported the startling sight of women in designer jackets and leggings striding along Fifth Avenue in heavy-duty boots.[428] With the Chanel version retailing for $1,000 a pair, it was unlikely that any fashionista was going to be wearing them on her Harley.

When Gianni Versace wasn't dressing supermodels in biker boots, he was sending them down the runway in patent leather thigh boots that were not dissimilar to those worn by Julia Roberts in the previous year's hit movie *Pretty Woman*.[429] But with all the emphasis on the ultratall versus the ultrashort, what was happening to the knee-length boot, which had been so popular barely a decade previously? The answer, of course, is that it had evolved (or mutated, perhaps) into the "riding boot," a low-heeled, straight-legged style, often with some decorative laces at the vamp to mimic the look of an equestrian field boot. This conservative boot style had been popular, without being spectacular, since the mid-1980s, but by 1992 *Vogue* was reporting some significant developments:

"tall or short, riding boots are revamped with plush leopard prints or jet beading . . . glen plaid is finished with a swirl of patent leather; zippers give smooth black leather a sharper edge."[430] The year 1992 also saw the return of that late-sixties staple, the granny boot, in everything from stretch fabric to leather or satin.

Lace-up KNEE BOOT

In contrast to the 1980s, which were a bit of a boot desert, the early nineties saw a creative explosion of different styles. One of the first to achieve widespread popularity was the lace-up knee boot. First appearing in the fashion press in 1993 (declared by *Vogue* to be "The Year of the Boot"), it was in the winter of 1994–95 that they truly came to prominence.

At first sight, they might look like a development from the previous generations of knee boots, but closer examination suggests that stylistically they were an evolution of the ankle boot. Lace-up ankle boots have a pedigree that extends far back into the nineteenth century. They were popular in the 1980s, when they were strongly associated with Goth culture. Eventually, the boots rose to calf- and then knee-length.

There were certain advantages to this type of boot. It portrayed a more rugged style, perhaps, than contemporary fashion boots. The laces also enabled the wearer to achieve a skintight fit, with the boot hugging the calf closely. But they also had one major disadvantage—tightening those laces took a long time. They were not boots to be put on in a hurry.

There was a solution: a hybrid boot that had both laces and a zip-fastener. The idea was that tightening the laces would finesse the fit, but that thereafter the boot would be taken on and off using the zipper. From there it was a quick move to purely decorative laces (as had been popular in the late '60s and early '70s). But eventually they too disappeared, and in the second half of the nineties plain, zip-fastened boots were by far the most common style.

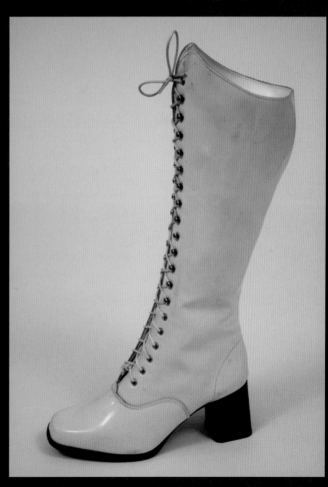

Lace-up knee boots, such as this white patent pair from the British company Dolcis, were fundamentally impractical, but fit well with the mid-nineties nostalgia for the music and fashion of the sixties.

The popularity of lace or buckled boots was not limited to retro styles. Zip-fasteners and laces allowed the boot to fit more closely to the curve of the calf, which blended well with the new, slimmer silhouettes that were becoming popular in the fall of 1992. Which is not to say that all the boots of this period were unabashedly feminine. Designers like Lagerfeld and Jean-Paul Gauthier were still favoring rugged designs based on combat boots, biker boots, or even Wellingtons. Meanwhile, Versace was producing boots accented with straps and studs, including thigh-length pairs that required the wearer to fasten nine buckles.

"THE YEAR OF THE BOOT"

The cover of the August 1993 edition of *Vogue* featured a Steven Meisel shot of Cindy Crawford. Sitting against a backdrop of the Manhattan Bridge, Crawford wore a military-themed outfit of a red brass-buttoned cardigan, white blouse, and black thigh-high leather field boots by Chanel over black leggings. This was, the cover declared, "The Year of the Boot." Building on the foundation established over the previous years, there was now "a boot for everyone," be it an engineer boot, Victorian granny boot, biker boot, thigh boot, moon boot, or riding boot.[431] To give you even more to choose from, the line between styles was blurred – U.K. shoe store Sacha sold a thigh-length biker boot, which combined the squared-off toe, heavy heel, and metal rings of the classic biker boot with an over-the-knee shaft, while Chanel stretched the field boot to skyscraping heights, as spectacularly modeled by Crawford.

In the following month's edition of the magazine, a "Last Look" piece, titled "Year of the Boot," provides probably the best synopsis of the spectacular explosion of boot styles in 1993. "This fall designers are stepping up their creative energy," *Vogue* reported, "and turning out the season's must-have accessory, the boot, in the most diverse regiment of styles ever—from fantastical eighteenth-century-inspired thigh-high boots to dainty Victorian ankle boots to sturdy military riding boots to funked-up snow boots." The accompanying piece shows forty different boot styles, from ankle- to thigh-length.[432] "Boots give clothes a fresh, modern attitude," Gianni Versace was quoted as saying, "whether they're worn with an old Balenciaga dress, a classic Chanel suit, or a modern Versace knit dress."[433] For Manolo Blahnik, "the attitude is to wear these boots all the time, morning till night—with everything from long dresses to short."[434] Hemlines were now irrelevant, while the boots themselves were both reinterpretations of old classics (the riding boot, the eighteenth-century cuissarde, or the Victorian ankle boot) or a push toward the limits of modern design (Chanel's moon boots).

One of the most interesting aspects of this selection of boots, relative to today's styles, is just how many of these boots feature either decorative or functional lacing: 15 pairs, or just over one-third, covering all heights. The short-lived popularity of tall, lace-up boots in the mid-1990s was a development from the early craze for Victorian-themed ankle boots (see sidebar); with just one or two exceptions, all the ankle boots

THIGH-LENGTH
Riding BOOT

This 1993 pair of boots from Shelley's Shoes of London is an example of the logical progression from the black suede over-the-knee boots of the late 1980s—a leather version of the same. It took a little time, but in the early years of the 1990s, fashion magazines were full of low-heeled, leather thigh boots like this, more suited to a seventeenth-century cavalier than the catwalk. In 1993, Steven Meisel photographed Cindy Crawford in Chanel thigh boots for the cover of *Vogue,* with the magazine declaring that this was "The Year of the Boot."

This self-consciously retro-baroque look had been brewing for a while. Three years earlier, Karl Lagerfeld's fall/winter haute couture collection featured thigh-length boots under long, see-through, black chiffon evening gowns, and his bride wore a floor-sweeping white satin redingote that opened in front to reveal a matching mini and white satin thigh-high boots, a startling juxtaposition of Marie Antoinette and Barbarella. Developments over the next few years ditched this rococo look in favor of something that more closely resembled a pantomime principal boy: boots were low-heeled, worn over leggings, and usually teamed with something vaguely masculine like a military tunic, cape, or newsboy cap to give the wearer some swagger. It was a self-conscious return to the swashbuckling origins of the *cuissarde*.

Only these were not cuissardes, or at least they were not the lineal descendants of the boots made popular by Bardot, Fonda, et al., during the 1960s. The pathway to the emergence of these boots runs through the low-heeled riding boots of the '80s, via their tall suede derivatives at the turn of the decade, and on to their final flourish in the 1990s. It's a case of parallel evolution—what these boots have in common is a desire to provide an aggressively masculine counterpoint to conventional ideas of feminine fashion, while still remaining avowedly feminine in nature.

Boots fit for a cavalier: a 1993 pair of women's thigh-length boots from Shelley's Shoes of London.

featured in the 1993 *Vogue* "Last Look" piece are faux-vintage.[435] The appearance of these "nouvelle granny boots" marks a transition in the history of the fashion boot during the 1990s. Thereafter, the rest of the decade was to be marked by the emergence and growth to dominance of a new, twenty-first-century take on the boots popular during the late sixties and seventies.

BACK TO THE '60S

In June 1994, *Guardian* reporter James Sherwood noted a new development on the dance floors of Britain's nightclubs. Faced with heavy coat check charges and the inconvenience of a handbag during a marathon dance session, young women had adopted a novel solution. "It's official, Sherwood announced, "thighboots are the handbags of the nineties. Call it kinky, but boots provide the perfect answer to the lipstick, lighter, cash and comb dilemma." The "handboot," as it had become known, was first used as a hiding place to evade drug searches by doormen—"hardly a bag in sight but what those girls had hidden in their boots . . . more than the average girl could fit in a bucket bag," security woman Claire Leonard said admiringly. The *Guardian* article pictured the well-filled boot tops of Columbine Strickland, a City of London secretary, who kept a Dior lipstick and Marlboro Lights in her leopard-skin thigh boots; meanwhile artist Charlotte Schepke managed to fit Lypsyl, money, and twenty cigarettes into each of her Vivienne Westwood boots and still have room for a bottle of Evian. It was, Sherwood concluded, just the latest example of "indigenous fashion ingenuity, a style movement prompted by the practicalities of nineties clubland life, which more closely resembled an endurance test than a simple evening out."[436]

Handboots notwithstanding, the years from 1994 to 1999 are not so much a trough as a dip or slump in the popularity of boots. The average number of mentions of boots in the fashion press for these years never drops below the cumulative average

By the second half of the nineties a distinctive look had emerged, based around a sixties-style mix of knee-length boots and above-the-knee skirts. (Geo Martinez/Shutterstock.)

for the period 1955–2010, but it does form a trough between the two impressive peaks of the early nineties and the Millennium.[437] In a very real way, this period is completely framed by two years that *Vogue* separately declared to be "The Year of the Boot": 1993 and 2001.[438] The boots seen in 1993 are very different from those of 2001, and the process of transition between the two begins in the middle years of the 1990s. So even if the level of media attention seems at a relatively low ebb, this is an important period for understanding the later history of the fashion boot. At the same time, it has received nothing like the attention lavished on the 1960s, in part because this is recent history and also because it seems to lack the earthshaking fashion events of that earlier decade.

But while the nineties may have lacked the sheer creativity of the sixties, it certainly looked to them for inspiration. Starting around 1994–95 there was an extraordinary rediscovery of many aspects of that culture, especially in Britain. It's most often associated with a body of guitar-oriented pop music from the years 1994 to 1996 that is commonly known as "Britpop," but the phenomenon goes much wider than this. It encompasses politics (the rise of the dynamic, Blairite Labour Party after eighteen years of increasingly moribund Conservative rule); the arts (Damien Hirst and the Young British Artists movement); literature (Irvine Welsh and Nick Hornby); film (*Four Weddings and a Funeral*; *Shallow Grave*; and *Trainspotting*); postfeminism; and the New Lad culture. Just like the sixties, it had its own cast of luminaries: media figures (Chris Evans and Jonathan Ross); comedians (Reeves

Knee-Length BOOT, 1996

This simple but elegant knee-length boot by Russell & Bromley was a contemporary take on the boots of the late sixties and early seventies.

With its curved calf, block heel, and square toe, this boot, from the British company Russell & Bromley, self-consciously mimics the designs of the late sixties. It is typical of the boots of the middle years of the nineties, which were designed to be worn with the shorter skirts of the period.

Russell & Bromley was founded in 1873. The firm relocated from Kent to London in the late 1940s, when the company's focus shifted to high-end footwear. In 1968, the owners closed about a quarter of the stores to complete this change of focus, which continues to this day.

and Mortimer, Harry Enfield, and Paul Whitehouse); musicians (the Gallagher brothers, Damon Albarn, and Justine Frischmann); actors (Ewan McGregor and Robert Carlyle); and models (Kate Moss, Honor Fraser, and Jodie Kidd).

Also just like the sixties, there were some talented British designers associated with this period, including John Galliano, Alexander McQueen, and Stella McCartney, although for the most part they were working across the Channel, in Paris. But there were others whose influence was just as important: Gianni Versace, Donna Karan, Marc Jacobs, Anna Sui, and so on. The social aspects may be easier to see in Britain, but the sixties fashion revival was a much wider phenomenon, and its influence can be seen in collections from Milan, Paris, and New York, to name just three.

Ask most people to sum up sixties fashion and they'll probably start with the miniskirt, so it's not surprising that the mid-nineties saw the triumphant return of this iconic item. Describing Marc Jacobs's fall/winter 1994 collection in the *New York Times*, Bernadine Morris reported that most of his outfits featured "a brief, flared skating skirt that is one of fashion's strongest statements this season."[439] Skirts were short, Bernadette Morra wrote in the *Toronto Star*, but tall boots and long coats kept the models covered.[440] "Even shy women will wear minis," Isabella Rossellini, modeling in one collection, was quoted as saying, "because the coats are long and the boots are high. Only about 5cm of flesh is actually showing."[441]

In the Milan collections of 1994, Anna Molinari was revamping and heating up vintage styles "a la Jackie Kennedy," wrote Bernadine Morris. Meanwhile Gianni Versace challenged the conventional view of "evolution rather than revolution" in fashion with clothes "in clear colors like taxicab yellow, fire-engine red, and bubble gum pink," Morris continued. "They gleamed with lacquered surfaces so that leather looked like plastic and silk glowed through mother-of-pearl finishes. Skirts were as short as feasible, boots covered the knees and cutouts in the middle of the dresses looked titillating but bared little. It was Andre Courréges 30 years later, updated and exaggerated for a new audience."[442] There were some critical differences, of course. Courréges had worked mostly in white, Versace in color; Courréges preferred straight edges, while Versace tended to emphasize curves. What they shared was a sense of provocation—Versace's clothes engendered as much shock in the nineties as Courréges had, at least initially, in the sixties.

THE LADY AND THE MOD

The year 1994 also saw a return to spindly heels, a reaction against the heavy, clumpy boots of the grunge years. In the *Toronto Star*, Bernadette Morra reported that grunge was on the wane; Birkenstocks and combat boots were being packed away and glamor was back, with the return of pencil-thin stilettos.[443] Also back with a vengeance was patent leather, with both Robert Clergerie and Manolo Blahnik offering knee-high boots in the shiny material. Patent boots were not limited to black—bright colors like pink, red, and yellow recalled the spectacular colored designs of the late sixties.[444] And just like the late sixties, synthetic materials—plastic, neoprene, vinyl, and rayon—were all the rage again. Dolce & Gabbana even made stiletto-heeled knee boots in clear plastic.

While some said glamor was back, for Blahnik it had never gone away. In the words of the *Times*'s Amy Spindler, his designs "are the sort of shoes that should be toying with a man's pant cuff beneath a linen tablecloth . . . his boots are the type one imagines Nancy Sinatra was singing about."[445] Discussing Blahnik's knee-high stiletto boots, *Vogue*'s director of accessories, Candy Pratts Price, decreed, "[A] pair of hotpants and these boots and you own the city."[446] Apparently, *Vogue* printed T-shirts with that edict on them. Reviewing YSL's 1994 fall/winter collection, Bernadine Morris noted (not entirely approvingly) that Saint Laurent's outfits, which paired thigh-high skirts and short, fur-trimmed coats with over-the-knee boots, were an attempt by the designer to say, "You want trendy? I can do trendy!"[447] Meanwhile Ralph Lauren was still pursuing the

BLACK *Patent* LEATHER BOOT, 1996

This boot represents a high point of the Britpop-era reverence for sixties design in nineties Britain. Their high-gloss, patent leather finish is a direct throwback to pairs of boots that were around almost thirty years earlier, an effect heightened by the decorative buckle across the instep. The only thing that marks the boot as retro rather than vintage is the height of its heel, which is more stacked than would have been the case for a genuine 1960s pair.

The boots were made by Red or Dead, a British design company founded by Wayne and Gerardine Hemingway in 1982. From 1995 through 1997, Red or Dead won the British Fashion Council's Streetstyle Designer of the Year Award each year.

Sixties nostalgia runs riot in this 1996 boot by Red or Dead, with silver buckles and black patent leather.

principal boy vision of the boot from the early part of the decade, pairing leather jerkins and tunics with over-the-knee boots.[448]

By 1995, grunge was officially dead, its obituaries written in the pages of *Vogue* and the *Times*; chic was in. Versace's Versus collection featured short go-go boots as an homage, yet again, to Courréges.[449] "Young girls don't even know who Courréges is," Donatella Versace is quoted as saying. "So we better teach them some culture in fashion." Versace's patent boots with bows were a direct lift of Courréges's early sixties designs. Courréges approved. "He's a visionary," his wife, Coqueline, said in a *Times* article from March 20 of that year. "It shows that his style has kept up for 40 years."[450] "The Sixties retro looks that the designers are throwing our way all have their roots in a nostalgia for elegance, from the polished finish of Jackie O to the edgier, glossy beat of the mod movement," the *Guardian* reported in September 1995. But what mattered in the nineties was that they serve as reminders rather than blueprints for the season, the guiding principle of this was simplicity: plain wool shift dresses, slim skirts that finish at the knee, a single-breasted princess-line coat, or a skinny tailored shirt. Accessories mattered, "if only to strike a note of levity among all this spare classicism. Glossy knee-high boots . . . add both wit and polish."[451]

"This winter, for the first time in around 30 years, long, elegant boots have been hugely fashionable," wrote Julia Thrift in the *Guardian*, "ousting Doc Martens and other heavy unisex shoes in female foot fashion. . . . Most of the women who are buying these boots—or raiding their mothers' or aunts' cupboards for seventies originals—were children last time they were fashionable and so have not worn such long boots before."[452]

In the 1990s, boots were often used as an accent to give contemporary outfits a 1960s feel. Here, model Erin Mooney wears a 3/4-length camel coat jacket with black boots from September 1997. (Trinity Mirror / Mirrorpix / Alamy Stock Photo)

More and more frequently, fashion articles were referencing go-go boots in collections. As discussed in an earlier chapter, it's not straightforward to nail down what a go-go boot actually *is*. Certainly the boots of the mid-nineties were quite different from those of the sixties; they were more of a pastiche of what people thought sixties fashion should be. Dolce & Gabbana's 1995 collection, for example, had a strong sixties theme: plasticized trench coats, Courréges-style white-dresses, belted safari suits, Jackie Onassis dresses with sashes at the waist, and white belted trench coats, with white gloves and handbags. But it also featured riding crops and tall, shiny stiletto boots—"Vixens for Nixon," as Amy Spindler wrote in the *Times*.[453] Scott Crolla for Callaghan put his models in patent leather boots with clunky low heels. "Think Emma Peel on *The Avengers*," Anne-Marie Schiro wrote.[454]

Schiro identified the defining feature of the 1995 fall/winter collections; like the god Janus, to use her analogy, fashion that year had two faces: the "Lady" and the "Mod."[455] The Mod had miniskirts, bobbed hair, thick black eyeliner, frosted pale lipstick, a hip-slung belt, and—perhaps most distinctively—shiny go-go boots with a squared toe and a chunky heel. Without the boots, the belt, and the frosting, the Mod look would fall flat. But give the boot a low, curved Sabrina heel and a pointed toe, and pair it with gloves, a designer scarf, and a skirt that hits just above the knee, and you have the Lady. The Sabrina heel was the look of the moment, the *Toronto Star* reported in October 1995.[456] Named after the late-1950s fashions created by Hubert de Givenchy for Audrey Hepburn in the movie of that name, the Sabrina heel tapered down from the sole before flaring slightly as it touched the ground. Also known as a kitten heel, it gave boots of the mid-nineties a lighter, daintier profile.

The Fiercest of Boots

The Milan shows of that year were a study in these contrasts. The Prada collection featured short patent boots with the clean lines of Courréges-inspired dresses. By contrast, the D&G collections were an *Austin Powers* riot of acid-green feathery jackets, boucle miniskirt suits, big fake furs, go-go boots, and thigh-high patent leather boots. But the crossover in boots was explicit: "the elegant woman will wear boots this fall," as Kalman Ruttenstein of Bloomingdale's said in the *Times*.[457] Across the Atlantic, Calvin Klein was showing a collection that was, in his words, "a little 60s." He continued, "We're not trying to hide that, but it's not retro. Its modern." To go with this, he had come up with a new style of boot—clunky, three-quarter length, and worn over bare legs. Constance White of the *Times* was not a fan, reporting that it "looked like a cross between go-go boots and Fryes . . . they did nothing to enhance the clothes."[458]

Klein's boots may have been loose-fitting, but this was not the way the trend was going. The calf-hugging boot was back with a vengeance. "Out of fashion for decades," the *Toronto Star* reported in September 1995, "it's now striding onto centre stage in kid-soft leather or gleaming patent, on high stacked heels or short, dagger-sharp stilettos. There haven't been so many boots in fashion since Nancy Sinatra first grabbed a microphone." The most

It wasn't just about knee-length boots. Ankle-length styles maintained their enduring popularity in the nineties, as with this pair from the British company Hobbs.

THE
Dress
BOOT
RETURNS

The nineties saw the return to fashion of the dress boot—a more feminine design characterized by a high heel, close-fitted leg, and pointed toe. The origins of the dress boot lie in the neo-Victorian ankle boots of the late 1980s and early '90s. Lengthening of the leg gave rise to the lace-up knee-length boot of the mid-nineties, where the lacing was used to ensure a glove-tight fit. Eventually the fiddly laces were abandoned in favor of zip-fasteners, and the dress boot was reborn, in both knee-length and thigh-high versions.

flattering calf- or knee-high boots fit close to the leg "to avoid that stepped-in-a-bucket look." With fuller, more fluid skirts, "plain pull-on or zippered boots are chic-er and sleeker than last year's granny-laced looks or clunky, chunky work boots."[459]

The delicate Sabrina heel didn't last; by 1996 it was gone, along with the three-quarter-length boot. In July of that year, Anne-Marie Schiro announced in the *Times* that fall boots would be either ankle-length, to wear with pants or long skirts, or knee-high, to wear with shorter skirts. Toes were squared, and heels could be any height but were always thick, not spindly.[460] So the Mod was dead, and so, too, was the Lady. New styles of skirts that flared out at the hem, or pants that were boot-cut or bell-bottomed, required a heavier shoe or boot to balance them. The new skirts were trending long and thin—from midcalf to ankle—which again called for a heavier boot.[461] And so, remarkably, the platform sole returned after twenty years in fashion purgatory, in thicknesses that ranged from barely visible to a full half-inch deep.

Leather was very much the flavor of the year, according to Suzy Menkes in a *New York Times* piece from September 1996, its "soft-hard image" being a powerful fashion force. In part, this was due to the incorporation of many uniform-based styles in that year's fall collection, but it also reflected the availability of new materials that combined leather with stretch fabrics to add new smoothness of fit to knee- and thigh-high boots, giving them, in Menkes's words, "a new kick."[462] In many ways, this mirrored developments in the late sixties, when new materials like vinyl and plastic allowed boots to be used to accentuate a sleeker silhouette. Back then, these were seen as alternatives to leather, which was suffering a surge in price, but in the nineties the new materials were worked into the leather itself.

"Worn with skirts or pants," *Vogue* reported, "tall boots with a sexy heel are following in the footsteps of fashion toward a long lean look with a curvy fit." When worn with pants, the shoe designer Richard Tyler explained, a higher boot gave a "nice long line" when sitting down. "It doesn't cut you off anywhere. . . . The tight boot is an elegant look, but not for everybody. Then again, who wants something for everybody?"[463]

If the boots of 1996 were challenging, by 1997 they had become absolutely ferocious. "Farewell to comfort," Anne-Marie Schiro declared in the *Times*. "Fashion's flirtation with square toed, chunky heeled shoes is over."[464] The state-of-the-art boot, according to Sarah Van Sicklen of *Vogue*, had a pointed toe, ice-pick heels, "and a heady dose of attitude." After several seasons of sensible, clunky heels and square toes, this was a femme fatale boot, "the accessory of the season for balancing a man-tailored jacket and trousers or a flirty suit." Marc Jacobs, who had produced a variation on the theme of an English riding boot, with a calf-hugging top and super-sharp toe, commented, "I like the sexy but tailored look of a pointy boot—the slick black leather gives them a menswear finish."[465]

So in the space of three or four years during the mid-nineties, the fashion boot had recapitulated an entire decade of history, from the loose-fitting styles of the early sixties through the shiny patent, mod years of the mid-sixties to the close-fitting knee and thigh-length styles of the late sixties. And now, it seemed, they were heading back into the decade that, in the words of the *Times*'s Amy Spindler, "won't go away."[466] Truth be told, there were more differences between the boots of the late seventies and late nineties than there were similarities, but over the next few years those differences would become blurred. The boot was about to enter its greatest period of popularity ever. As Sarah Van Sicklen wrote, "Birkenstock wearers, live in fear."[467]

INTO THE
NEW
Millennium

February 20, 2002, the Earls Court Exhibition Centre, London. The 2002 Brit Awards[468] are in full swing. Onstage, the electronic percussive notes of New Order's 1983 dance anthem "Blue Monday," familiar to generations of clubbers, grind into life. As robotic dancers twist and flex to the beat, high above the stage a hydraulic platform, shaped like a record turntable, swings slowly from horizontal to vertical, bringing with it a diminutive figure. As the music segues smoothly from New Order to her own latest hit, "Can't Get You Out of My Head," Kylie Minogue takes the stage. Minogue is dressed in a white Dolce & Gabbana corset minidress, which barely reaches the tops of her thighs, and silver, spike-heeled over-the-knee boots by Jimmy Choo. There is an unwritten rule that says that short women cannot wear thigh-length boots without looking like they've stepped into a hole. Minogue, at 5' 2", is the exception to that rule.

The Jimmy Choo boots were classic examples of a style that was extremely popular in the early years of the new Millennium: slim-fitting, with needle-sharp heels and pointed toes. Minogue had worn a black leather pair for a TV special, *An Audience With Kylie Minogue*, in 2001,[469] and for live performances at the San Remo Festival, World Music Awards, and Bambi Awards in 2002. The silver pair that debuted at the Brit Awards formed part of a cyborg-themed "Kylie Bot" or "Kyborg" outfit, reminiscent of the "sexy robot" designs of Japanese artist Hajime Sorayama,[470] which was a major feature of Minogue's Fever2002 world tour.[471] The juxtaposition of music from 1983, the low point in the last half century of the history of the fashion boot, with such an iconic image from its period of peak popularity is more than a little ironic.

chapter
10

A walking history of the fashion boot in the first decade of the Millennium: Kylie Minogue performs in Jimmy Choo over-the-knee boots at the 2002 Brit Awards. (Dave Benett/Getty Images.)

There is a good case to be made that you could chart the entire history of the fashion boot in the first decade of the twenty-first century just by documenting the footwear choices of Kylie Minogue. A quick review of published photos from this period suggests that she wore more than sixty different pairs of boots in the years 2000 and 2010, encompassing ankle, knee-length, and over-the-knee styles; lace-up and buttoned-up pairs; biker boots, riding boots, casual boots, and dress boots; in leather, suede, fur, and with sequins. Her wardrobe provides a vivid illustration of just how diverse boot styles are today.

THE KEY PIECE

The years from 1990 to the present day represent the longest sustained period of popularity of the fashion boot since the beginning of the 1960s; in 2002 that popularity reached heights that exceeded even those of the late sixties and early seventies. But at the same time, the press coverage doesn't have the level of attention or excitement that it did thirty years earlier. You certainly don't see pieces in the media about excited women rushing to the store to buy ten pairs of boots in one go.[472] Which is not to say that boots weren't seen as desirable. "I think shoes say a lot about a woman, and I want my footwear to say, 'I'm hot.' That's why I love boots," said Michelle, a thirty-three-year-old marketing executive interviewed in *Marie-Claire*. "Their sleek lines scream sex appeal. I own at least thirty pairs."[473]

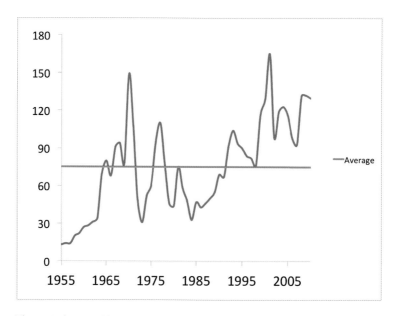

The period since 1990 represents the longest sustained run of popularity for the fashion boot since Beth Levine first began to promote it as a high-fashion item for women in the mid-1950s. For most of this period, the average number of mentions of boots in the press per year (blue line) remains above the average for 1955–2010 (red line).

What consistently emerges throughout this period is the sense of the boot as a key piece for fall wardrobes. So in 1999, *Marie Claire* declared the ballet flat to be "out," replaced by the knee-high stiletto boot. "Update your wardrobe with a pair of knee-high boots," the magazine stated, "preferably nude-colored and flat (Chanel), thick-heeled with a forward thrust (Jacobs) or Cerruti's zippered-back boots with kitten heels."[474] The reason for the renewed interest in boots was related in part to another phenomenon documented in the "key pieces for fall":[475] the replacement of the straight, ankle-length skirt by the "inverted-pleat knee-length skirt." Long skirts and pants were most definitely "out," abandoned in favor of skirts that fell to the knee, or two inches above or below. This look became popular in the workplace; "for the office, team dress boots with skirts or dresses falling to just above the knee, or mid-thigh," *Marie-Claire* instructed.

In fact, the first years of the twenty-first century saw the return of a look that hadn't been popular since the end of the seventies: an A-line dress or skirt paired with tall boots, the hem of the skirt just skimming the top of the boots. Also back from the seventies was the idea of boots as an investment item. They were often the most expensive part of the outfit. So, for example, in a *New York Post* article from 2002 titled "From Fab to Frugal," the total cost of the "frugal" outfit was $472.50, of which $185 was a pair of knee-length beige leather boots by Nine West. For the "fab" outfit, $725 of the $3,251 spent went on a pair of black leather knee boots with side button detail by Marc Jacobs.[476]

Another contributory factor in the reemergence of boots as a significant element of twenty-first-century style was the growth in popularity of "bohemian," or "boho," fashions that blended aspects of the American West with design features that were by equal parts hippie, Renaissance, and folkloric, and had the chic stamp of something that had been assembled through visits to flea markets and thrift stores. Boots tended to go well with this neo-ethnic look. It wasn't restricted to neo versions of the Frye boot, either; Charles David and Dolce & Gabbana produced brown suede stiletto knee boots with swirling embroidered or printed patterns running the length of the shaft.

An enthusiasm for boots was not confined to the glossies and daily papers. As we've seen in earlier chapters, mail-order and other catalogs often give a more accurate sense of what people were actually wearing, and here the evidence is unequivocal. The Saks Fifth Avenue catalog from the fall of 2002 showcases a seemingly endless procession of black leather stiletto-heeled knee boots. The fall Victoria's Secret catalogs from 1998 onward are crammed full of stiletto-heeled boots, while the 2002 J.Crew mail-order catalog featured another procession of stiletto-heeled boots: four knee-length, four calf-length, two ankle, all of which were resolutely pointy-toed. "Point-taken," the catalog declared, showcasing the company's stitched-sole high boot.

Das Boots

All of this makes the dominance of the stiletto knee boot look positively monolithic. In a July 1999 piece highlighting accessories for the coming season, *Marie Claire* presented a sequence of almost identical knee-high boots in black leather, ranging from $145 for Ralph Aaron to $300 for BSBG Max Azria, $665 for YSL, and $750 for Celine.[477] Price aside, it's almost impossible to tell them apart. But looks can be deceptive. Boots of the early twenty-first century were a lot more diverse than this. One example of this, and arguably the most distinctive boot to emerge from the Millennial years, is a style that at the time was known as the Prada boot, after the company that pioneered it. First featured in a number of collections in the late 1990s, the Prada boot was a nod to the iconic sixties designs of Courréges, but with its own unique, Millennial twist.[478]

The boot defied easy categorization. It was longer than calf-length, but shorter than knee-high, with a leather upper and a very distinctive molded rubber sole, which formed a wedge heel that had much in common with that of an athletic shoe or sneaker. The style of boot was extremely popular and immediately attracted cheaper mass-marketed imitators, but what exactly was it? Was it intended for dress or for leisure wear? Arguably, it marked an early emergence of the more casual styles of boot that would become increasingly popular from the middle of the next decade onward. Within a very few years, the emergence of these more rugged, low-heeled boots was clear to see—"the leather riding boot," as it was described in the 2002 fall J.Crew catalog, where it sat alongside its dressier contemporaries.

But the days of the practical boot were still some way off, and at the dawn of the twenty-first century it was all about the boot as an "excessory" as *Vogue Germany* termed it in 1999. "The shiny boot is a representative of this hot-blooded race: this winter has made—from the office to the Night Club—a worldwide stage for boots with entertainment value. They play a variety of roles: as Diva (Gucci), garden (Prada), Evening Gown (Galliano) or wild animal (Marni)."[479] "Boots are back," *Marie Claire* announced the same year, "in every possible shape and form, and sexier than ever. Either mile-high or super-low, in bright leathers and exotic pastels with unexpected details—they're virtually all you need for fall." Particularly notable were Louis Vuitton's "high-heeled and high voltage" leather knee boots ($990),[480] which proved popular with celebrities like Jennifer Lopez.

Interestingly, *Marie Claire* chose to combine its 1999 fashion editorial on boots with a health and beauty piece on how to exercise to improve your legs.[481] This was ironic, because the new breed of boots presented some significant challenges for those women who took fitness seriously. "The last time knee-high boots were this popular, in the mod 1960's and hippy-dippy 1970's, women had soft, ethereal, pliant calves," wrote Alexandra Jacobs in the *New York Observer* the following year[482]. "A couple of aerobic decades, however, have carved a new, firm, decisive calf which stubbornly defies the lean, mean cuts of the mostly Italian designers who are capitalizing on the *Charlie's Angels–Almost Famous* revival.[483] Which has left scores of women chagrined about not being able to zip up this season's boots and asking themselves, What, a new body part I have to feel insecure about?"[484]

Versace's 1995 fall ready-to-wear collection introduced a new style of boot. In many ways, it was a high-legged equivalent of the popular high-heeled pumps of this period, combining the stiletto heel and pointed toe of the pump with a glove-tight leather upper climbing to just below the knee. This was the forerunner of the ladies' dress boot, an incredibly popular style for both workplace and evening wear. The peak of its popularity occurred in the years following the turn of the Millennium, but the dress boot is still around, in one form or another, today.

This boot is not a Versace boot but represents a mass-market version of the style from the U.S. fashion chain Nine West, dating from the early years of the twenty-first century. Compared with the last time that boots were this popular, during the 1970s, there are some big differences. Take the toe box, for example, which extends out in a wicked point, far beyond the ball of the foot. This is an extreme feature that this particular boot shares with its Versace progenitor—many contemporary pairs squared off the end of the box, truncating the toe and reducing the amount of vacant space.

The heel is a very minimalist structure—the point in contact with the ground is a painfully small area of about 0.5 square centimeter. The heel sustains the tiny diameter for at least half its length, giving a completely different profile to the blocky stacked heel of the seventies boots. And no contrasting wooden heel here—the whole assembly is a uniform glossy black, matching the color of the rest of the boot.

Dress' Boot, EARLY 2000s

With its elongated toe, stiletto heel, and tightly fitted shaft, this boot by the American company Nine West is typical of the dress boots of the years immediately before and after the turn of the Millennium.

The ankle is sharply constricted and the shaft tightly curved. A large elasticized gusset provides a little legroom, but like the snug boots of the early seventies that contributed to cases of phlebitis, the new generation of dress boots attracted complaints about tightness of fit, with a distinctly twenty-

Jacobs's article is redolent with (often hilarious) detail on the lengths to which women would go to try to fit into their boots. "I found some tall boots with a medium-sized heel," said "lithe, 5-foot-8 graphic designer and yoga enthusiast" Andrea Brake. "I got it about midway up my calf. The zipper would not go any farther. I tried sort of, like, shoving my skin, pushing it in. I was smooshing the flesh, to no avail. . . . I developed a blister on my index finger from trying so hard to pull the zipper."[485] Miranda Morrison, one-half of shoe designers Sigerson Morrison, justified her company's wickedly tight boots by saying, "We made a decision . . . to cater to the shapeliest legs, just because that's how the product looks the best. I mean, you know there are companies who try and fit everybody, and the result is that, for a lot of stylish girls, their boots fit like Wellingtons! . . . You can put your leg into a smaller boot . . . you may spend a couple of days wondering where your toes are."[486]

THE NEW "YEAR OF THE BOOT"

Pain did not decrease popularity, which peaked in 2001 with what *Vogue* declared to be "The Year of the Boot." In fact, it was the second of *Vogue*'s years of the boot, the first one having taken place in 1993. The post-Millennial year was described in an article by Vicki Woods,[487] and one of its most interesting aspects was the idea that the rules for wearing boots had changed. Prior to 2001, Woods wrote, there was a clear set of dos and don'ts for women and boots. Boot length was determined by the accompanying garment: knee-length for skirts that skim the knee, calf-length for swirly skirts that dip below, ankle boots for pants, over-the-knee for miniskirts. Sturdy boots should be paired with heavy tweeds and winter woolens, while glovelike boots on slender spikes were the accessory for fine wools, crepes, and chiffons. By 2001, that rule book had been thrown away. Designers teamed beaded evening boots with a simple

In the late sixties, 75 percent of managers surveyed by the *New York Times* were uncertain that boots were suitable footwear for the office. Three decades later, the suit-and-boots combination was a common one for many working women. (Gemenacom/Shutterstock.)

black minidress (Calvin Klein), layered chiffons with flat-heeled cavalry boots (Chanel), and Audrey Hepburn cocktail sheaths with shiny black croc over-the-knee boots (Gucci).[488] In 1993, it was about the boot that was right for you. But in 2001, it was your choice of what you wore with the boot that mattered.

More often than not, that outfit was what the *New Yorker* described as ". . . the professional woman's default uniform of the moment: a smart knit dress in a dark color, worn with knee-high black leather boots."[489] Around this time, I was living and working in Manhattan; in the fall, winter, and even the spring a significant number of the women sharing my commute were wearing a similar outfit: knee-length, high-heeled black leather boots, worn with skirts that fell either just above the knee or just below, skimming their boot tops. Starting in the late nineties, boots had entered the workplace in a big way. Previous generations of working women would probably have swapped boots for shoes once they got to the office, but the latest generation of boots was designed to be worn *at* work rather than on the way there and back. The sleek, clear lines complemented skirt suits and workday dresses.[490]

These boots drew their inspiration from high fashion designs like Versace's couture knee boot of 1995, and the early versions at least shared a lot of the same fashion DNA—viciously pointed toes, spiky stilettos, and a glovetight fit. Over time, however, they were modified to

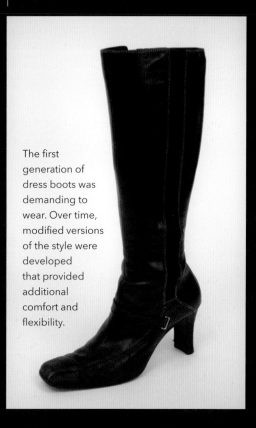

Dress Boot
MID-2000S

The first generation of dress boots was demanding to wear. Over time, modified versions of the style were developed that provided additional comfort and flexibility.

The earliest dress boots of the Millennial years were unforgiving of all but the narrowest range of leg types, so it's not surprising that the next few years saw the evolution of the style into something a little more flexible. This 2005 boot, from the American retailer Anne Klein, shows several features designed to make it a little more wearable by mere mortals. The toe is squared off, and the heel is a "compressed stack," which looks like a stiletto from the side but spreads the wearer's weight across a wider surface area. Even the various decorative inserts are actually elasticated gussets that allow the shaft of the boot to expand to accommodate calves of a variety of shapes and sizes.

place fewer demands on the wearer. The toes were often squared off, at least at the tip, to reduce wear and tear on the feet; the fit of the shaft was loosened, especially around the ankle; and stilettos made way for stack heels, which are easier to walk in. A frequent, and very distinctive, variant on this style was the "compressed stack"; viewed in profile, it looked like a stiletto, but from the rear it was apparent that the heel ran the full width of the sole and went straight to the ground without any taper. Combine these eminently practical features with the increasing use of cheaper materials, such as stretch "leather" or "pleather," which meant that it was possible to acquire a pair of knee-length boots for less than $50, and the reasons for their popularity become clear.

The Return of the OTK Boot (Part 1)

After a flurry of interest in the late eighties and early nineties, over-the-knee (OTK) boots made only sporadic appearances for the rest of the decade, either on the catwalk or in the pages of high-end fashion journals. They rarely, if ever, made it as far as the streets—a sighting of these boots in the nineties was about as likely as seeing a unicorn. But around the turn of the Millennium, things began to change. With the great popularity of knee-length dress boots at the end of the 1990s, it was almost inevitable that designers would start to experiment with over-the-knee versions of this style, just as had happened with vinyl boots in the late sixties, Cossack boots in the late seventies, and the low-heeled riding boot in the late eighties. Because the new boots were derivatives of contemporary knee-length dress boots, they had the same general characteristics: close-fitting, high-heeled, and with a pointed toe, they were quite different from the more robust styles of the early nineties.

There were a number of factors involved in the reemergence of the OTK boot. First, boots of all varieties were about as popular at the turn of the Millennium as they had ever been before or since. Second, the new styles were adopted by a number of high-profile celebrities, which guaranteed coverage not only in the fashion press but also in newspaper celebrity columns and magazines with much wider circulation, such as *Us Weekly* and *People*.[491] Celebrity stylists recognized that thigh boots have that elusive "wow" factor that makes photos of your client more likely to be pulled for publication from the mass of red-carpet shots at a big event.

The result was a flurry of press coverage, usually marked by terrible puns ("The Thigh's the Limit," "Thigh-High Style," etc.).[492] The tone of these pieces suggests that the writers were not entirely convinced this footwear was a good thing for any mere mortal to risk wearing. "It takes a savvy star like Lauren Hutton or Jessica Alba to wear this season's over-the-knee boots without evoking a dominatrix or swashbuckler," *People* cautioned in November 2003. The secret, the magazine confided, was to pair them with subtle clothing, but to tread boldly. Certainly actress Nora Zehetner was a fan. "I'm working up the courage to wear them without tights," she was quoted in the same *People* article. "They're just so fun and sexy and make you feel like such a woman!"[493]

As designers like Alexander McQueen and Roberto Cavalli, and fashion houses like Gucci, Missoni, and Fendi began to pack their fall fashion shows with ultratall boots, the trend became hard to ignore. But, as it turned out, the enthusiasm for these boots was not sustained. On the December 3, 2003, episode of the NBC morning show *Live with Regis and Kelly*, Kelly Ripa appeared in a pair of Roberto Cavalli thigh boots from two years earlier.[494] She admitted that at the time she had been desperate to own a pair, but having bought them they had never been worn, remaining "in the bag, in the box, in my closet" until she wore them for the first time that morning. Later in the show, she was forced to unzip and fold them down, because the close-fitting boots made her thighs itch. It was this basic lack of practicality that doomed the early '00s incarnation of the thigh-high boot to failure. But the look never entirely left the catwalks over the next few years, and when OTK boots returned, six years later, it was in a very different form.

The early years of the new decade saw a resurgence of interest in over-the-knee styles, as worn here by actress Nora Zehetner in October 2003. In this early version, they didn't get far beyond celebrities and the red carpet. But by the end of the decade, this style of boot had achieved mass popularity. (Paul Smith/ Featureflash/Shutterstock.)

"THE TUCK"

Another look that emerged in the early years of the twenty-first century, has—thus far—proved more enduring, although the early auguries were not encouraging. Writing for the *New York Observer* in January 2005, Anna Schneider Mayerson described a new look that was becoming increasingly popular on the streets of the city. "Across West Chelsea bars, sleek boutiques in Madison Avenue and grungy boîtes of the Lower East Side," she wrote "the women of the city can be found peg-legging their jeans and parading around with them scrunched into the legs of their boots like crumpled bed sheets. They're pulling sculpted stiletto boots up over trousers and walking around with them in plain view, like a pair of knee socks. Or they're rolling their jeans up so that they rest just where the boot ends, thus shortening the appearance of their legs by about 40 percent. And somehow they seem to think this is a good idea."[495]

"The Tuck," pairing tall boots with jeans for a casual look, first emerged in the middle years of the 1970s, before being "rediscovered" for the new Millennium. (Claudia K/Shutterstock.)

Note that little zinger at the end, because for all the enthusiasm of the women interviewed for the article, there was not universal approbation for "the Tuck." Ms. Mayerson describes it as a "frumpy-mom look that was last hot in 1982, the year of *Flashdance* and Gloria Vanderbilt perfume" and marshals a chorus of male disapproval, including such gems as "they do the jeans inside of their big white boots and try to do the 'hipster rock slut' look, but it's also like, 'I just moved here from Des Moines"; "It looks kind of medieval. It reminds me of Robin Hood and his friends, more like a costume than a stylish outfit. I don't think it's particularly flattering or subtle"; and "It makes the legs look stubbier. I think it's just so much less flattering. It's a little frame for the middle part of the body. It makes everyone look a little rounder."[496]

This only goes to prove that most guys know nothing about women's fashions. "The Tuck," as Mayerson termed it, is still going strong a decade later. Its emergence (or perhaps reemergence, given the popularity of the look in the 1970s) marks a significant shift in the history of the fashion boot, one of those periodic swings from feminine/formal to robust/casual that are a feature of the history of women's boots. The *Observer* article touched on some possible reasons for the shift, of which the most convincing was the emergence of new styles of boots, less tight-fitting and with heavy heels, that couldn't be worn under pants and required a different proportionality in outfits. But it could also be argued that this process was circular; with the growing popularity of "the Tuck," and the outfits that featured it, there was a need for new styles of boot that could more easily be pulled on over skinny jeans or leggings: straight-legged, relatively loose-fitting, and with a heavier heel to counterbalance the slim silhouette of the pants.

A Casual Affair

We've seen already how part of the attraction of the fashion boot is the subversion of the masculine by the feminine—taking what was a predominantly male form of footwear and turning it into something that women could wear. If the high-heeled dress boots of the late nineties represented the ultimate reflection of this trend, the boots of the years since 2005 represent a dramatic reversion toward masculine style. The driving force was a trend that had previously been seen in the second half of the 1970s: a shift from wide-legged trousers to tighter, leg-hugging styles—skinny jeans, leggings, and that bizarre hybrid of the two known as "jeggings."[497]

With the leg narrowed, the possibility exists to tuck the trouser leg into a high boot, giving a look that mimics that of the equestrienne. This necessitated some changes in the boots. A straighter shaft made pulling them over the trouser legs easier, while a looser fit provided more room for thick fabric like denim and reduced unsightly bunching of the pants around the top of the boot. To emphasize the rugged look, the boots were often adorned with various design accents, like straps or buckles (see sidebar), and were low-heeled.[498]

The equestrian boot has been the most popular style of women's boots for the past ten years—a casual boot that works equally well with jeans, leggings, or skirts.

In contrast to the dress boot, this was a casual boot, more likely to be worn on the weekends than at the office. Its roots lie way back in the 1970s, with the popularity of the Frye Campus boot that we looked at earlier. So it's not surprising that Frye was one of the main companies to benefit from the emergence of the Tuck.[499] The new boots also drew upon more recent styles of casual boot from the 1990s. These boots, which featured a one-piece, molded rubber sole fused with a leather upper that could be ankle-, calf-, or knee-length, were comfortable, ideal for striding around city streets or running for a bus and were an instant hit with younger consumers.

It was astonishing how quickly these equestrian boots, as they became known, caught on. In 2005, the *New York Observer* was describing the tucked-in look as a fashion aberration, yet by the end of the decade, that look was ubiquitous. College girls, suburban moms, celebrities, rich or poor— it seemed like almost every woman was determined to take the plunge. The equestrian boot wasn't always worn with pants, either. Juxtapositions can be very attractive in fashion, so the rugged, quasi-masculine boot was sometimes teamed with a floaty dress or skirt to emphasize the contrast between the two, something that was especially apparent if the boot was also worn over bare legs. This was yet another rebirth of the boho look.[500]

A MATTER OF *Decoration*

Going back to the earliest days of their history, fashion boots have always provided a canvas that allowed designers and wearers to accent their outfits. As we've already seen, the Russian boots of the 1920s often featured decorative stitching and combinations of different materials like patent leather and fur. In the 1960s, designers experimented with new materials like vinyl and Corfam to provide new textures and colors; in the early 1970s, laces and buttons were used as eye-catching features on the retro-themed boots; while in the late 1980s, brocade and decorative inserts provided the boots of the time with a Renaissance swagger.

In recent years, with the swing in popularity toward more aggressively masculine boots for women, the emphasis has changed from materials to various structural accents. These include straps and buckles, at the ankle, the top of the shaft, and pretty much anywhere in between; studs or rivets inserted into the leather; and strap-and-ring arrangements that give the appearance of a rider's stirrup or spurs. Leather is often combined with stretch fabrics, which give the comfort of a gusset while providing yet another reason for straps and buckles, to limit the expansion of the fabric panels. The resulting heavy boot is a far cry from the clean lines of the dress boots of the early Millennium.

As the pendulum swung back to more masculine styles of boots, rugged design accents like buckles, straps, and rivets were frequently added.

THE RETURN OF THE OTK BOOT (PART 2)

By the end of the first decade of the twenty-first century, the equestrian boot had reached the level of mass popularity that the dress boot had achieved ten years earlier. So it was not a surprise that various shoe designers began to experiment with taller, over-the-knee versions of this style. The surprise was that this time women began to actually wear them, and in surprising numbers. The reasons for this are not entirely clear. One possibility is that over-the-knee boots had been around for most of the decade and, while they had not achieved mass popularity, they were worn by enough high-profile celebrities that they remained in the public consciousness as at least a marginally "acceptable" style.

Then there was the growth in popularity of "the Tuck." Heavier fabrics, like denim, sometimes bunched around the top of a knee-length boot, creating an unsightly mess; in an over-the-knee boot, this bunching is concealed. Wearing tall boots over pants or leggings avoided the problem of tall boot–plus–short skirt/bare skin; the "Vivian effect" (see sidebar, Chapter 9) that bedeviled earlier versions of the thigh-length boot. The new styles were also very practical; not only were the low heels comfortable, but the higher leg actually provided additional warmth and protection on freezing-cold or wet days. Plus they looked good, the Cavalier style of the low-heeled, high-legged boots giving the wearer a sort of buccaneering swagger that was assertive while remaining feminine.

The final element was the mass press coverage, most of which was positive[501] (even if they couldn't avoid the dreadful puns[502]). A few writers made the obligatory references to Julia Roberts, but the boots themselves were a million miles away from her spike-heeled, black PVC thigh highs and, in any case, twenty years on, many of the target audience of young women had never actually seen *Pretty Woman*. But the key difference was that by the end of the decade, a lot of fashion coverage came not from the mainstream media but from bloggers, and, by and large, the bloggers *loved* over-the-knee boots.[503] Social media was flush with hundreds of images and videos from amateur fashion journalists enthusiastically singing the praises of very tall boots.

The style even had its own tough girl TV heroine, in the mold of *The Avengers*' Cathy Gale. Kalinda Sharma, played by the British actress Archie Panjabi, was a private investigator on the Emmy-winning CBS series *The Good Wife*. Sharma was very much a twenty-first-century heroine: enigmatic, bisexual, highly competent, and capable of doling out physical violence when needed. The character was also noted for her boots—high-heeled,

The end of the first decade of the new Millennium saw over-the-knee boots achieve a transition to mainstream popularity that they had never previously managed. (Studioloco/Shutterstock.)

black leather over-the-knee styles that, in the words of the *New York Times*, "telegraphed inscrutability and sexual boldness."[504] As with Cathy Gale nearly half a century earlier, the boots quickly became Sharma's signature wardrobe piece.[505] Originally, the detective wore pumps, but Panjabi thought they "grounded her in the character."[506] Reflecting on her departure from the series, she told an interviewer, "[W]hen I unzipped the boots, it felt so right. I had reached a stage of closure."[507]

As in sixties, the new generation of boots benefited from novel applications of materials. The 5050 boot, created by Stuart Weitzman and the subject of numerous imitators, combined a leather instep and front with an elasticized heel and back (see

THE
Stuart Weitzman
5050 BOOT

The 5050 has a good claim to be a modern design icon. launched in 1993, it is still in such high demand that it regularly sells out at stores worldwide every year. Much beloved of fashion editors and stylists, in the words of the company's twentieth-anniversary press release, "from the Sundance Film Festival (Elizabeth Olsen), to the set of *The Amazing Spider-Man* (Emma Stone), to the red carpet (Olivia Wilde), to the concert stage (Ke$ha), the 5050 is as versatile and well-rounded as the Hollywood celebrities who wear it."[510]

The distinctive feature of the 5050 is its mix of a micro stretch fabric back panel with a nappa leather, patent leather, or kidskin suede front and vamp. The elasticized micro helps keep the line of the boot sleek across a variety of different shapes and sizes of leg, while the robust rubber sole makes it practical in good or bad weather.

In 2013, Weitzman celebrated the twentieth anniversary of the 5050 with a twenty-piece Anniversary Collection, which included ten limited-edition styles such as zebra-hair calf, sea crystal snake calfskin, black goosebump nappa, and even a $10,000 Swarovski pave version, with 25,000 crystals hand-set in an elaborate leopard pattern.

Stuart Weitzman's 5050 boot is a design classic that has been around for more than twenty years.

sidebar), giving a very slim-line fit. Another Weitzman design, the Highland, spliced and backed its leather or suede outer layer with Lycra to provide a legging-like fit. With a 24" shaft, 3.25" heel, and a frankly challenging 14" circumference, the Highland was much beloved of a leggier breed of celebrity,[508] such as the model Gigi Hadid. "A few days ago I was at the airport," she was quoted by *People*, "and I was wearing my Highland black boots and security was like really busy so once I got through security I had to run like 70 gates to catch my flight and I ran in my Highlands and it didn't kill my feet. So I think that's a pretty good test of comfortable shoes."[509]

If over-the-knee boots had remained the purview of Gigi Hadid, Cara Delevingne, et al., then it's likely that their charms would have quickly faded. But the remarkable thing about their second coming in the late '00s is that the style seems to have been embraced by a wide variety of women. In this respect, it is very different from all the previous incarnations of the ultratall boot, from the 1960s cuissardes to the OTK boots of the Millennium. For this most challenging variety of fashion boot, it seemed that its time had finally arrived.

Nothing New under the Sun

The skintight, thigh-length boot styles shown by Dior in 2016, worn here by actress and singer Hailee Steinfeld, consciously hark back to the stocking boots of the late 1960s. (Helga Esteb/Shutterstock.)

You don't have to be a biblical scholar to recognize the fundamental truth behind Ecclesiastes 1:9: sometimes it seems that there is nothing new under the sun.[511] At times, in the second decade of the twenty-first century, it seemed that this was a particular issue with fashion. Designers have always mined the past for inspiration, but never have they done so as remorselessly as they have in the past few years.

In the winter of 2016, the continuing enthusiasm for over-the-knee boots, which was now entering its eighth year, generated a set of boots that would not have looked at all out of place in 1967–68. The selection chosen by *InStyle* magazine for its fall fashion preview that year featured some of the tallest, narrowest boots seen in decades; these were basically boots as pants, covering the leg from the ankle almost to the hips.[512] But as a shameless example of the raiding of fashion's attic, they were nothing

BOOTS *Onstage*

There's a long tradition of women wearing boots onstage to convey a masculine or heroic side to their character; the principal boy characters of British pantomime are a good example of this. So it's not surprising that in the 1960s and '70s, women rock singers started wearing boots as part of their stage outfits. What you wear onstage goes a long way toward shaping an audience's perception of you, and this goes equally for what you wear on your feet (or what you don't wear—the social anthropologist Desmond Morris argued that women who performed barefoot were subconsciously suggestive of nudity,[516] although expressing purity or vulnerability seems just as likely).

In the 1960s, the women who performed in boots were expressing the energy and youthful exuberance of the times, with a healthy dose of assertiveness; think Nancy Sinatra or the French *yé-yé* girls like Françoise Hardy, France Gall, and Sylvie Vartan. In the glam-rock era, it was all about theatricality, as typified by Agnetha Fältskog and Anni-Frid Lyngstad of ABBA. But as glam rock gave way to punk rock, boots were used to portray confidence, strength, and a certain "fuck-you" buccaneering swagger by performers like the Runaways, Debbie Harry, Siouxsie Sioux, and Toyah Willcox.

That image is still very evident in today's performers: a vast array of modern-day warrior-women like Beyoncé, Rhianna, Jennifer Lopez, Madonna, Carrie Underwood, Taylor Swift, Mary J. Blige, and Iggy Azalea, covering the whole spectrum of popular music from pop to country to R&B, who use boots to present an assertive image of themselves and their music in performance.

Taylor Swift rocks Madison Square Garden in August 2009. Going back to the 1960s, female singers have used boots to portray an assertive, confident image onstage. (Everett Collection/ Shutterstock.)

compared to Gucci's "Lillian" over-the-knee "horsebit" boots. These were, in all respects, a pair of boots lifted directly from 1968, complete with the buckle and the tongue flap on the vamp.

But it turns out that the plundering of the past doesn't stop there. If you wanted to go a little further back for inspiration, there was the "Reserve" crocodile-print patent leather boot from Stuart Weitzman, which is a dead ringer for YSL's 1963 crocodile-skin cuissarde. Meanwhile Chloé's 2015 take on the OTK boot was, like the Gucci pair, an absolute retro reproduction, this time of Chloé's own Lagerfeld-designed boots, c. 1977, and Prada produced a stack-heeled, platform-soled knee boot that would not have looked out of place in 1975. There were even calf- and knee-length lace-up styles, last seen more than twenty years previously. At the time, they were the only real alternative to the loose-fitting boots of the previous decade, and, as it turned out, their popularity lasted only as long as it took people to realize that if you used a zip-fastener, you could avoid spending hours lacing yourself up.

This increasing tendency to look backward has led some fashion industry experts, such as the trend forecaster Li Edelkoort, to claim that fashion is dead. Speaking in 2015, Edelkoort said her interest in fashion had now been replaced by an interest in clothes, since fashion had lost touch with what is going on in the world and what people want.[513] The following year, *The Atlantic* was discussing whether the whole idea of fashion shows and seasonal collections was anachronistic, with many designers looking to alternatives such as informal "presentations," videos, pop-up shops, and Instagram feeds.[514]

At the same time, there has been a mass democratization of dress.[515] Blogging and other social media platforms give anyone with an interest in clothing an opportunity to create, document, and share their own sense of style, while online retailers like Zappos can carry a much wider range of stock than any conventional store, or even the old-style mail-order catalog companies, and provide their customers with the opportunity to review products. Increasingly the old debates over whether, for example, over-the-knee boots are "in" or "out" are becoming irrelevant—if people want to wear them, they will be able to find and purchase them. With the growth in websites devoted to vintage fashions and marketplace platforms like eBay and Etsy, even the past is not out of reach. Many of the vintage pairs of boots pictured in this book, for example, were acquired online over the past five years.

FULL CIRCLE

Winters in New England are not for the fainthearted. During the past week, we've had a couple of snowstorms to contend with—now it's warming up, temporarily at least, and things are getting muddy. Out and about, I was reflecting on the number of women who were bravely scrambling over snowbanks and through the mud in a variety of fashionable boots of the knee-length (and occasionally over-the-knee) variety. A couple of thoughts struck me.

First, the modern equestrian boot is a remarkably elegant and practical piece of footwear. It is undeniably feminine and yet eminently wearable in even the worst

LAMPSHADING

"Lampshading" is a trend that combines a loose-fitting top with tall boots. This example is from the BCBG Max Azria fashion show during Mercedes-Benz Fashion Week Fall 2015 in New York City. (Fashionstock.com/Shutterstock.com.)

The year 2016 saw a new trend, in which boots played an integral role. "Lampshading" is the practice of wearing a sweater, tunic, or dress with a loose or bell-shaped hem over a pair of knee-high or over-the-knee boots, with the hem of the top hitting the top of the boot, or just a few inches above it, giving off a distinctive "lampshade" effect.[517] Originating on college campuses, the "lampshade" description was first applied to girls who wore a T-shirt that was so long and baggy it covered their shorts[518]; the boots were a later addition. Much beloved by celebrities such as Rihanna, Kendall Jenner, and Gigi Hadid, the *Daily Mail* described this style as a nod to "the mod look of '60s shift dresses and go-go boots."[519]

conditions. The shaft of the boot is straight enough that it can be easily pulled on over a pair of jeans and yet curved enough to show off the leg. The various buckles and straps used to accent the boot give it a rugged look without detracting from its stylishness.

The second, and maybe the more significant, point refers to the evolution of the boot, the theme of this book. The history of the modern fashion boot is essentially progressive—one style gives rise to, or influences, another, and so we move forward through the twentieth century to today.

But as I look at the modern equestrian boot, it occurs to me that maybe we've come full circle. The leather or suede Russian boot of the 1920s was intended as a fashionable, but also practical, twist on the riding boot. When it failed to gain traction in the changing world of the 1930s, the stylish rubber rain boot replaced it.

Over time, the utilitarian side of the rain boot came to the fore, and boots ceased to be regarded as a fashion item. Then along came Beth Levine and others, who reinvented the dowdy rain boot as high fashion footwear in the 1960s, and so it flourished and diversified until today, almost a century after the first Russian boots appeared, we've come full circle to the balance of style and practicality typified by the twenty-first-century equestrian boot. Where the fashion boot goes over the next hundred years is anyone's guess, but the chances are it will still be striding out in some form or other into the next century and beyond.

PREFACE

1. The boots in question, from the collection of Lionel Ernest Bussey, are, sadly, no longer on display, but they can be viewed online on the V&A's collection website. Their catalog number is T.320&A-1970.

CHAPTER 1: WHY BOOTS?

2. "Fashion: The Beautiful People in Boots," *Vogue* 149, no.4 (1967): 126–33.

3. Genevieve Antoine Dariaux, *Elegance* (New York: Doubleday & Company, 1964), 21.

4. "Fashion: The Beautiful People in Boots," *Vogue*, 126–33.

5. "Boot," entry in *The Compact Oxford English Dictionary*, s.v. "boot" (Oxford, U.K.: Oxford University Press, 1971).

6. Samuel Johnson, *A Dictionary of the English Language*, vol. 1 (London: J. F. Rivington, etc., 1755), 272.

7. Leon Pales, *Les gravures de la Marche: Les humains*, vol. 2 (Bordeaux, France: Imprimeries Delmas, 1969).

8. Marie-Josèphe Bossan, *The Art of the Shoe* (New York: Parkstone International, 2015), 12.

9. Ibid., 32.

10. Ibid., 37.

11. For examples, see a bronze statuette of Diana from the first century BCE of Asia Minor and a Gallo-Roman mosaic depicting Diana and Calisto from the second century CE, both in the collections of the Getty Museum. In the case of the mosaic, both Diana and Calisto wear boots rising almost to the knee.

12. Bossan, *Art of the Shoe*, 48–49

13. Ibid., 77.

14. Joan's cross-dressing was considered so critical to the charges of heresy laid against her that it was exhaustively documented in the testimony given at her trial. Some confusion exists as to whether the leather garments in question were boots or leggings. See Adrien Harmand, *Jeanne d'Arc: Ses Costumes, Son Armur* (Paris: Imprimerie Aulard, librairie Ernest Leroux, 1929), 177–85; Robert Wirth, ed., *Primary Sources and Context Concerning Joan of Arc's Male Clothing* (Minneapolis: Historical Academy [Association] for Joan of Arc Studies, 2006), 21.

15. This definition of "bootlegging," or variations thereof, crops up regularly, being variously attributed to the boot-hiding behavior of pirates, civil war soldiers, and the Russian boots of Prohibition-era flappers. The *Oxford American Dictionary* claims a late-nineteenth-century origin, from the smugglers' practice of concealing bottles in their boots, which ties in to early references associated with early Prohibition laws in the Midwest (see B. R. Porter, Probate Judge of Anderson County, Kansas, in *The Economics of Prohibition*, 1890, for an early definition). In the opinion of the *Oxford English Dictionary*, the word "booty" originates from the Old Norse word meaning barter, share, or exchange, and has nothing to do with footwear, piratical or otherwise. The concept of concealing money in the tops of boots is something that might be familiar to anyone who's paid money to a stripper.

16. Elizabeth Howe, *The First English Actresses: Women and Drama 1660–1700* (Cambridge, U.K.: Cambridge University Press, 1992).

17. Ibid.

18. Jacqueline Pearson, *The Prostituted Muse: Images of Women and Women Dramatists 1642–1737* (New York: St. Martin's Press, 1988).

19. For a prime example of this, see Emma Akbareian, "Over-the-Knee Boots Are Back in This Season (As Long As You Know the Dos and Don'ts)," *The Independent*, October 20, 2014. Ms. Akbareian manages to reference not just pirates and principal boys, but also the 1990 movie *Pretty Woman*, every fashion journalist's go-to cultural touchstone when discussing over-the-knee styles.

20. Writing erotica in the 1940s, Anaïs Nin described the prostitute and sometime artist's model Bijou, the protagonist of several short stories, as wearing tall boots with a clinging black dress. Undressing for an art class at the Grande Chaumière, "she wore high stockings and sometimes, if it was a rainy day, high leather boots, men's boots. As she struggled with the boots, she was at the mercy of anyone who approached her. . . . Sometimes she was asked to keep her boots on, the heavy boots from which expanded, like a flower, the ivory colored female body." From Anaïs Nin, "Bijou and the Basque," in *Delta of Venus* (New York, Harcourt Brace Jovanovich, 1977).

21. Comfort was actually quite dismissive of boots: "Good for dressing-up games if you like them. Not very practical for serious sex unless you keep them for non-horizontal non-bed activities. If your man likes them, try appearing suddenly in long, tight, black, shiny ones." Alex Comfort, *The Joy of Sex* (London, Mitchell Beazley, 1972).

22. Julia Thrift, "Boot Leggers: Knee-High Power Dressing for Your Feet," *Guardian*, March 3, 1995, A8.

23. Ibid.

24. See Valerie Steele, *Shoes: A Lexicon of Style* (New York: Rizzoli, 1999).

25. Thrift, "Boot Leggers," A8.

26. John Willie, *The Complete Reprint of John Willie's Bizarre* (Cologne, Germany: Taschen, 2005).

27. Thrift, "Boot Leggers," A8.

28. Helene Verin, *Beth Levine Shoes* (New York: Stewart, Tabori & Chang, 2009), 43.

29. "Short Skirts, Higher Boots," *New York Times*, April 11, 1915.

30. Rachelle Bergstein, *Women from the Ankle Down* (New York: Harper Perennial, 2012), 106–99.

31. Ibid., 115.

32. Ibid., 116.

33. Beth Levine, quoted in Marian Christy, "A Society Is Revealed by Its Women's Shoes?," *Boston Globe*, June 2, 1970, 18.

notes

34. The history of Wonder Woman's origins is described in Jill Lepore, "The Surprising Origin Story of Wonder Woman," *Smithsonian*, October 2014.

35. Costume designer Lindy Hemming confirmed that the boot heels were intended to double as weapons. "Production Notes," *The Dark Knight Rises*, directed by Christopher Nolan (Warner Bros., 2012), 14, retrieved from Deadline.com, accessed August 3, 2016.

36. Dialogue from *The Dark Knight Rises*, ibid.

37. Lepore, "Surprising Origin Story of Wonder Woman".

38. For example, see Velvet Rose, "Female Superhero Representation in Comics," *The Artifice*, August 20, 2015, http://the-artifice.com/female-superhero-representation-in-comics/, accessed September 21, 2016.

39. The complete quote is (speaking of Yara): "I have loved researching her and breathing life into the wonderful scripts—wearing her exceptionally empowering leather thigh-high boots has helped, of course!," in Bryan Cogman, David Benioff, George R. R. Martin, and D. B. Weiss, *Inside HBO's Game of Thrones: Seasons 1 & 2* (San Francisco: Chronicle Books, 2012), 125.

40. This is when she's not complaining about the need to drain the boots of water during filming. See Jennifer Vineyard, "*Game of Thrones*' Gemma Whelan on Yara's Sexuality and Freezing on Set," *Vulture*, July 6, 2016.

41. Sandbrook quotes an article by Prudence Glynn, a fashion journalist from *The Times* (London), describing her observations on her fellow travelers on the London Underground in August 1966: "[T]here wasn't a mini skirt in sight." Dominic Sandbrook, *White Heat: A History of Britain in the Swinging Sixties* (London: Abacus/Little Brown Book Group, 2006), 248.

42. "Management Views Office Fashions," *New York Times*, July 14, 1968.

43. Searches on the terms "boots" and "over-the-knee boots" were run at https://www.google.com/trends/ in October 2013.

44. Data sources are as follows: *Vogue* Archive, 1892–2014 via ProQuest.com; *New York Times*, 1851–2010 via ProQuest Historical Newspapers; *Les archives de L'Officiel De La Mode*, 1921–2013 via Jalou Galleries.

45. This is, of course, a huge assumption. Clearly the word "boot" has many different meanings. A reference to "boots" could come from the fashion pages, but equally it could be from a sports report, or from the front line of a conflict (numerous references to "boots-on-the-ground" proved to be a significant confounding factor in the '60s (Vietnam) and the '00s (Iraq and Afghanistan). I tried to get around this, as much as possible, by using various techniques—a combined search on the terms "boots" and "fashion," for example, in articles only. The end result was a little crude, but its consistency across multiple publications suggests that the pattern is real.

46. For examples, see "The Sun Between the Storms, Part II, Berlin," *TranverseAlchemy* (blog), July 20, 2014, transversealchemy.com/2014/07/the-sun-between-storms-part-ii-berlin.html, accessed August 4, 2016.

47. Nin, *Delta of Venus*.

48. Willie, *Complete Reprint of John Willie's Bizarre*.

49. Town and Country, or "ToCo" as it is affectionately known to this day by a small but dedicated coterie of fans, produced a series of magazines between 1953 and 1976. *Spick*, *Span*, and *Beautiful Britons* were the longest running and most successful of the pinup magazines to emerge in postwar Britain. Featuring cheerful girl-next-door types posing in 1950s-style underwear, often in blatantly suburban settings including G-Plan sideboards, two-bar electric fires, chintzy sofas, and extravagantly patterned wallpaper, ToCo magazines seem delightfully innocent to the modern eye.

50. This was a lot less fun than it sounds; hard though it may be to believe, there was a point when I became heartily sick of naked pneumatic women, booted or otherwise. I recorded a simple "yes" or "no" for whether the model wore boots at all in the pictorial. In some cases, this might be in candid shots that accompanied the pinup photography. It might be a single image out of many, or multiple images. Also, the boots might appear in outtakes from the photo session, which are often published on the Web these days. Regardless, they just got scored "yes." For the purposes of this analysis, I counted only fashion boots: ankle, calf-length, knee-length, or over-the-knee. I excluded cowboy boots, riding boots, rain boots, hiking boots, and fisherman's waders (and, yes, there were a couple of instances of models in waders). There are caveats, of which the biggest is that the numbers here are very small in comparison to the datasets that I was using for, say, *Vogue*. We're basically looking at a situation where an observation of 7 is a major peak. But it is interesting that the patterns over time are more or less the same even at radically different scales.

51. Linzi Drew, *Try Everything Once Except Incest and Morris Dancing* (London: Blake Publishing, 1993), 109–10.

52. For a good example of this, see Niles Eldredge's work on cornets: "Material Cultural Evolution: An Interview with Niles Eldredge," FCJ-017, *The Fibreculture Journal*, issue 3 (2004), http://three.fibreculturejournal.org, accessed June 6, 2016.

53. Well-known examples of memes include "LOLcats," Tay Zonday's "Chocolate Rain," and "Rickrolling."

54. Richard Dawkins, *The Selfish Gene*, 2nd ed. (Oxford, U.K.: Oxford University Press, 1989), 368.

55. The concise definition of "meme" is from Gordon Graham, *Genes: A Philosophical Inquiry* (New York: Routledge, 2002), 196.

CHAPTER 2:
MADAME POIRET'S BOOTS

56. Major biographical sources used include Harold Koda and Andrew Bolton, *Poiret* (New York: Metropolitan Museum of Art, 2007), and Hamish Bowles, "Fashioning the Century," *Vogue*, May 2007, 236–50.

57. Reputedly he outraged an elderly Russian princess with a kimono cloak, and the owner of the salon referred to Poiret's dresses as "dishrags." See Judith Thurman, "Cut Loose: Paul Poiret's Revolution," *The New Yorker*, May 21, 2007.

58. Poiret was not a man to hide his light under a bushel; his autobiography, from which this quote is taken, was titled *King of Fashion*. The two had undergone an acrimonious divorce two years earlier, so perhaps Poiret can be forgiven his self-congratulatory tone.

59. The account of Poiret's visit and its impact on his later designs is taken from an interview with Svetlana Amelekhina, keeper and curator of the fabrics department at the Kremlin Museums, which appeared in *Passport* in September 2011. See Aline Kalinina, "Paul Poiret: King of Fashion," *Passport*, September 2011, http://www.

passportmagazine.ru/article/2344/, accessed June 2014.

60. Figures taken from P. Hall, H. Gracey, R. Drewett, and R. Thomas, *The Containment of Urban England*, vol. I, *Urban and Metropolitan Growth Processes* (London: George Allen & Unwin, 1973).

61. Joan Perkin, *Victorian Women* (London: John Murray Ltd, 1993).

62. For an in-depth consideration of the various styles of nineteenth-century boot, see Jonathan Walford, *Sixties Fashion: From Less Is More to Youthquake* (London: Thames & Hudson, 2013).

63. Koda and Bolton, *Poiret*, 204.

64. "Short Skirts, Higher Boots," *New York Times*.

65. Walford, *Sixties Fashion*, 136.

66. Bowles, "Fashioning the Century," 236–50.

67. Judith Watt, *Fashion* (London: Dorling Kindersley, 2012), 244.

68. Ibid.

69. For a detailed account of the Russian émigré community in China, see Harriet Sergeant, *Shanghai* (London: Jonathan Cape, 1991), 30-67.

70. Caroline Cox, *Vintage Shoes* (New York: HarperCollins, 2008), 45.

71. "Russian Boots with Fur Collars," *Manchester Guardian*, September 9, 1926; "Russian Boots: New Fashions with Laced Tops," *Irish Times*, February 15, 1926.

72. "New Style Russian Boots, Lady Duff Gordon's Hymn of Praise," *Irish Times*, September 9, 1926, 7.

73. *Boots, Boots, Boots–Russian Styles for Eve*, British Pathé Archive, Media URN 21766, Film ID 992.10, 1930.

74. "Paris Fashion Turns in Favor of Boots," *Washington Post*, May 2, 1926.

75. "A Bombay Woman's Causerie: X'mas Shopping: The Missing Russian Boots," *Times of India*, December 25, 1925, 3.

76. "London Girls, Wearing Russian Boots, Arrive," *Boston Daily Globe*, December 23, 1925, A1.

77. Ibid.

78. "Manners and Modes," cartoon series, in *Punch or the London Charivari*, January 4, 1922, 7.

79. *Punch or the London Charivari*, January 27, 1926, 89.

80. *Punch or the London Charivari*, November 25, 1925, 588.

81. "While Taking Off Her Boots, Woman's Tug Breaks Thigh," *Times of India*, April 10, 1928, 10. History, sadly, does not record Miss Bradley's fate.

82. Anon., "Russian Boots Endanger the Health of English Women: Discarding High Shoes for Evening Slippers Seen as Bid for Pneumonia." *New York Herald*, Dec 9, 1925. 4.

83. This should immediately be a cause for suspicion—the journalistic equivalent of "I know this guy, and his brother says . . ."

84. "Russian Boots Trap Girl," *New York Times*, November 27, 1925, 6.

85. "Boots for Women Sign of Changes," *Los Angeles Times*, December 30, 1927, A13.

86. Cox, *Vintage Shoes*, 45.

87. *Woman Putting Flask in Her Russian Boot*, Washington D.C., photograph, Library of Congress, Prints & Photographs Division, Reproduction Number LC-USZ62-97941, January 21, 1922.

88. *A Pair of "Bootlegs" Found in the Office of Lincoln C. Andrews?,-* photograph, Library of Congress, Prints & Photographs Division, Reproduction Number LC-USZ62-97065, 1920–1932(?). The reference to "bootlegs," while probably a play on words, is interesting given the etymological confusion over the origin of that phrase (see Chapter 1).

89. "Snow, Mud, and Fog Drive London Women to Boots," *New York Herald Tribune*, November 10, 1925, 1.

90. "Russian Boots Trap Girl," *New York Times*, 6.

91. "Russian Boots," *Manchester Guardian*, November 19, 1925, 8.

92. "Russian Boots Doomed, Say London Modistes," *New York Herald Tribune*, December 13, 1925, A8.

93. "Women of Paris Spurn London's Russian Boots," *China Press*, February 4, 1926, 7.

94. "Paris Approves Boots for Street and Dancing," *New York Herald Tribune*, May 16, 1926, D6.

95. "Boots, Boots, Boots," *Austin American*, July 11, 1926, A11.

96. Especially, one suspects, in the face of jibes from the French.

97. "Russian Boots with Fur Collars, Higher and Stouter," *Manchester Guardian*, September 9, 1926, 5.

98. For a proper consideration of the life and work of this fascinating woman, see Valerie Mendes and Amy de la Haye, *Lucile Ltd: London, Paris, New York and Chicago 1890s–1930s* (London: Victoria & Albert Museum, 2009).

99. Reports of Lucile's speech in Birmingham are taken from "New Style Russian Boots, Lady Duff Gordon's Hymn of Praise," *Irish Times*, September 9, 1926, 7, and "D.M.L.," "Russian Boots," *Irish Times*, September 17, 1926, 2.

100. Survey information taken from "Look Out for the Bootleg from Russia," *Boot and Shoe Recorder*, May 6, 1922, 71–73.

101. "Russian Boots: Trade Criticism," *The Scotsman*, February 18, 1926, 9.

102. "Russian Boots: The Question of Cost," *Manchester Guardian*, February 20, 1926, 26.

103. "Russian Boots Lose Prestige," *Hartford Courant*, October 10, 1926, 17.

104. "6.5 Minutes to Lace Up Boots: Milady Will Spend Most of Time Lacing Boots," *Austin American*, September 18, 1927, 2.

105. The 1922 discovery of the tomb of the pharaoh Tutankhamen by Howard Carter and George Herbert was a major cultural phenomenon in the 1920s.

106. "6.5 Minutes to Lace Up Boots," *Austin American*, 2.

107. "Russian Boots," *Manchester Guardian*, November 19, 1925, 8.

108. See "London Modistes See Russian Boot's Doom," *Washington Post*, December 6, 1925; George Turnbull, "The London Observer," *The Spur*, November 15, 1926.

109. The Russian boot may have been gone, but it was not entirely forgotten. While working through newspapers from the 1960s, I came across a letter written to the *Daily Mail* by a Miss R. Deere of Worthing, Sussex, and published by the paper on July 27, 1963. "There's nothing new in women's fashions," Miss Deere complains. "I wore a coat similar to that shown by Iris Ashley 36 years ago, with Russian boots—also now fashionable again."

CHAPTER 3:
MRS. LEVINE'S INSPIRATION

110. Story taken from Eugenia Sheppard, "Hey, Where's Your Horse?," *Hartford Courant*, June 16, 1963, 7E.

111. Boots by André Perugia, c. 1939, Brooklyn Museum Costume Collection at the Metropolitan Museum of Art, gift of the Brooklyn Museum, 2009; gift of Millicent Huttleston Rogers, 1951; accession numbers 2009.300.3136a, b and 2009.300.4626a, b.

112. The pictures on this page come from World of Kays (www.worldofkays.com), a fascinating website hosted by the University of Worcester (U.K.), devoted to the British mail-order company Kays & Co. Ltd. It's a visual record of U.K.

fashion in the twentieth century, and it gives some fascinating insights into the evolution of the fashion boot.

113. Cox, *Vintage Shoes*, 132

114. Verin, *Beth Levine Shoes*.

115. Biographical details taken from Eric Wilson, "Beth Levine, 'First Lady of Shoe Design,' Is Dead at 91," *New York Times*, September 23, 2006, C10, and Karen Von Hahn, "A Step Ahead," *Globe and Mail*, June 3, 1999, D10.

116. Verin, *Beth Levine Shoes*, 16.

117. Biographical details taken from Anne-Marie Schiro, "Herbert Levine, 75, Manufacturer of High Fashion Women's Shoes," *New York Times*, August 10, 1991, 26.

118. Sonia Bata, in Verin, *Beth Levine Shoes*, 10.

119. Boots by Herbert Levine Inc., 1952, the Metropolitan Museum of Art, gift of Beth and Herbert Levine, 1977; accession number 1977.287.14a, b.

120. Sheppard, "Hey, Where's Your Horse?," 7E.

121. Eugenia Sheppard, "They All Laughed at Her White Boots," *Washington Post*, August 16, 1967, C3.

122. Stocking shoe by Beth Levine for Herbert Levine Inc., 1953, Brooklyn Museum Costume Collection at the Metropolitan Museum of Art, gift of the Brooklyn Museum, 2009; gift of Beth Levine in memory of her husband, Herbert, 1994; accession number 2009.300.2240a, b.

123. Boots by Herbert Levine Inc., 1959, the Metropolitan Museum of Art; gift of Beth and Herbert Levine, 1977; accession number 1977.287.23a, b.

124. Boots by Herbert Levine Inc., 1959–1963, the Metropolitan Museum of Art; gift of Beth Levine, 1976; accession number 1976.166.19a, b.

125. Evening boots by Herbert Levine Inc., 1959, the Metropolitan Museum of Art; gift of Beth and Herbert Levine, 1977; accession number 1977.287.36a, b.

126. "What it Takes to be the New Young Fashion Whiz." *Vogue*, Aug 15, 1958, 50–77; "Fashion: What's Newer and Better." *Vogue*, Oct 15, 1958, 48–56, 119; "Fashion: American Fashion Territory - News in the Shirt-and-Skirt life." *Vogue*, Oct 15, 1959, 44, 108–119.

127. Verin, *Beth Levine Shoes*, 43.

128. This earlier generation of boot is mentioned in "High-Style Boots Rise to the Knee: Fall Versions Will Be an Important Part of Many Costumes," *New York Times*, May 9, 1961, 68.

129. Ibid.

130. Boots, leather, 1961, Brooklyn Museum Costume Collection at the Metropolitan Museum of Art, gift of the Brooklyn Museum, 2009; gift of Bonnie Cashin, 1963; accession number 2009.300.7266a, b.

131. "High-Style Boots Rise to the Knee," *New York Times*, 68.

132. Rattner, Joan. "Beauty in Boots: new shapes in leather: they're jauntily high." *New York Herald Tribune*, Oct 26, 1958. SM31.

133. Biographical details for Evins taken from "Obituary: David E. Evins, 85, a Designer of Shoes for Ex-First Ladies," *New York Times*, December 29, 1991, and "The Legacy of Shoe Designer David Evins," *Today @ Colorado State University*, October 15, 2009; https://today-archive.colostate.edu/storydfa7.html?id=2394, accessed November 14, 2017.

134. He also holds the distinction of having made shoes for every first lady from Mamie Eisenhower to Nancy Reagan.

135. Raymonde Alexander, "Shoes Once Again Point to Fashion," *Atlanta Constitution*, July 30, 1960, 15.

136. "Stylish Look for Campus or Country Life Is Casual: Campus Fads This Autumn to Run from Head to Toe," *New York Times*, August 19, 1961, 11.

137. "The Boot in Fashion," *New York Times*, November 18, 1961, 16.

138. For examples of coverage, see "Fashion: Where the Square Toe Is Going," *Vogue*, September 1, 1961; "Fashion: What Difference Does Paris Fashion Make This Season?," *Vogue*, October 1, 1961; "Paris Couture Has Put Figure Back into Fashion," *New York Times*, August 3, 1961; and "The Fashion Scene Abroad," *New York Times*, August 27, 1961.

139. Marjorie Hunter, "'Typical' American Amazes Japanese: Mrs. Rusk Is Hostess at Fashion Show for Visitors, "*New York Times*, December 5, 1962, 60.

140. Searches run on the terms "boot" using the ProQuest archival platform for the *New York Times* and *Vogue*; "bottes" and "cuissardes" for *L'Officiel* at http://patrimoine.editionsjalou.com. The *Times* and *Vogue* show a steady rise in references to boots in 1962, continuing an upward trend that, for the *Times* at least, starts in previous year. *L'Officiel*, however, is still flatlining.

141. Iris Ashley, "Fini the Mini," *Daily Mail*, July 30, 1970, 4.

142. Ibid.

143. Raymonde Alexander, "Fashions Will Stand on Solid Footing as Boots Kick Off the Fall Season," *Atlanta Constitution*, July 16, 1962, 17.

144. Patricia Peterson, "Fall '62 Forecast," *New York Times*, August 26, 1962, 248.

145. "Cutout Pattern Distinguishes Varied Shoe Styles for Fall," *New York Times*, August 15, 1962, 22.

146. Olive Dickason, "Shoe Fashion in Hasty Retreat from Long Toes; Focus on Heels," *Globe and Mail*, July 25, 1962, 9.

147. Ibid.

148. "Balenciaga Is Praised by Buyers," *New York Times*, August 2, 1962, 18.

149. Iris Ashley, "Iris Ashley with Balenciaga Yesterday," *Daily Mail*, August 29, 1962, 4.

150. "Balenciaga Ends Show in Glory," *Atlanta Constitution*, August 3, 1962, 23.

151. Iris Ashley, "On the Wave of a New Rave," *Daily Mail*, October 31, 1962, 10.

152. Iris Ashley, "I'm Walking on Gold," *Daily Mail*, November 14, 1962, 10.

153. Marylin Bender, "French Buyer's Job Is to Be Choosy for the U.S.: Varied Clients Include Department Stores, Top Designers," *New York Times*, November 29, 1962, 43.

154. Charlotte Curtis, "Shoe Stylist Is Advocate of Tall Heel," *New York Times*, April 3, 1962, 34.

155. List of celebrity Levine boot clients from Verin, *Beth Levine Shoes*, 50.

156. Vivian Infantino, quoted in Verin, *Beth Levine Shoes*, 156.

157. Herbert Levine press release from 1970, quoted in Verin, *Beth Levine Shoes*, 43.

158. Beth Levine, *Easton Express*, December 3, 1971, quoted in Verin, *Beth Levine Shoes*, 133.

159. Verin, *Beth Levine Shoes*, 44.

160. Ibid., 44.

CHAPTER 4:
CHAPEAU MELON ET BOTTES DE CUIR

161. The description of this *Avengers* episode is taken from Anthony Carthew, "All Honor Honor—A Sex Kitten in Boots, Honor Blackman, Wows Britain's Males by Knocking Them Out," *New York Times*, March 1, 1964, SM73.

162. Claudia Goldin and Lawrence Katz, "The Power of the Pill: Oral

Contraceptives and Women's Career and Marriage Decisions," *Journal of Political Economy* 110, no. 4 (2002): 730-70.

163. Iris Ashley, "At Last TV Gets Fashion in Focus," *Daily Mail*, September 25, 1963, 12.

164. The three novels are *The Country Girls* (1960), *The Girl with the Green Eyes* (1962), and *Girls in Their Married Bliss* (1964).

165. Edna O'Brien, *Girls in Their Married Bliss* (London, Jonathan Cape, 1964).

166. Leonard Sloane, "Boots Make a Splash in Fashions: Women's Boots Take Big Strides," *New York Times*, May 12, 1963, F1.

167. Raymonde Alexander, "The Pressure's Off As Fall Fashions Kick Out in Style," *Atlanta Constitution*, July 29, 1963, 17.

168. Raymonde Alexander, "Foundations Begin with Silhouettes—So First Understand the Line of Fashion," *Atlanta Constitution*, November 8, 1963, 27.

169. Raymonde Alexander, "Fall Fashions Have Two Moods," *Atlanta Constitution*, July 14, 1963, 6E.

170. Patricia Peterson, "Cardin's Youthful Styles Are the Highlight of a Busy Day in Paris," *New York Times*, July 27, 1963, 18; "St. Laurent and Chanel Designs New but Familiar," *New York Times*, July 30, 1963, 16; "Balenciaga Favors the Look of Capes in His Showing, Last of the Paris Season," *New York Times*, August 2, 1963, 30; and "Paris Designers Favor Lean and Natural Look," *New York Times*, August 5, 1963, 39.

171. Jeanne Molli, "Noted in Paris: Sleek Wigs and Boots," *New York Times*, August 29, 1963, 50.

172. "Shop Adapts Style to Suit a Customer," *New York Times*, September 10, 1963, 65.

173. Peterson, "Paris Designers Favor Lean and Natural Look," 39.

174. "Boots Take Over: For Every Weather, Total Chic," *Vogue*, August 1963, 46.

175. "For Kicks—Legs," *Vogue,* August 15, 1963, 52-58.

176. "Paris: The First Full Report: Vogue's First Report on the New French Clothes and the Fresh Excitement of Paris," *Vogue*, September 1963, 164-81, 243, 245.

177. Iris Ashley, "Yves Brings on the Beat Look in Tweed!," *Daily Mail*, July 30, 1963, 3.

178. Iris Ashley, "Picking the Winter Winners from Paris," *Daily Mail*, August 27, 1963, 9.

179. Quotes from Barbara Cartland and Diana McLeod and account of Lucille Soong's visit to Hampstead taken from Charles Greville, "How London Reacted Yesterday to the Fashions Paris Had Decreed the Day Before," *Daily Mail*, August 28, 1963, 4.

180. Ibid.

181. Judy Innes, "Bootlemania," *Daily Mail*, November 22, 1963, 12.

182. Bradley Quinn, *The Boot* (London: Lawrence King Publishing, 2010).

183. It is often reported that John Sutcliffe, a fetish photographer who published the well-known fetish magazine *AtomAge*, designed Blackman's costumes. Although Sutcliffe did design some costumes for film, notably Marianne Faithfull's black leather catsuit from *The Girl on a Motorcycle* (1968), his role in *The Avengers* seems to have been limited to influence. See Will Hodgkinson, "King of Kinky," *Guardian*, September 11, 2010.

184. Iris Ashley, "At Last TV Gets Fashion in Focus," *Daily Mail*, September 25, 1963, 12.

185. Searches run on the terms "boot" using the ProQuest archival platform for *Vogue*; "bottes" and "cuissardes" for *L'Officiel* at http://patrimoine.editionsjalou.com.

186. "Shoes for Spring: Feminine, Pretty," *New York Times*, February 20, 1964, 20.

187. Angela Taylor, "Round Toes Have Appeal for All Ages," *New York Times*, December 5, 1964, 35.

188. Iris Ashley, "There's Magic in the Name Paris," *Daily Mail*, January 27, 1964, 8.

189. Dariaux, *Elegance*, 21.

190. Angela Taylor, "College Girls Vote the Conservative Ticket—in Fashion," *New York Times*, August 4, 1965, 38.

191. Searches run on the term "boot" using the ProQuest archival platform for the *New York Times*.

192. Alison Adburgham, "View of Fashion," *Guardian*, January 3, 1964, 6.

193. Wilson's speech was made at the Labour Party Conference in Scarborough on October 1, 1963. A retrospective account of the speech and its impact can be found in Matthew Francis, "Harold Wilson's 'White Heat

of Technology' Speech 50 Years On," *Guardian*, September 19, 2013.

194. Sally Ride flew on the space shuttle *Challenger* on June 18, 1983.

195. Biographical details taken from "André Courréges, Fashion Designer: Obituary," *Daily Telegraph*, January 10, 2016; Vanessa Friedman, "André Courréges, Fashion Designer Who Redefined Couture, Dies at 92," *New York Times*, January 8, 2016; Veronica Horwell, "André Courréges: Obituary," *Guardian*, Jauary 8, 2016.

196. Friedman, "André Courréges, Fashion Designer Who Redefined Couture."

197. Horwell, "André Courréges: Obituary."

198. June Wilson, "Your Own Sense Is Best Fashion Guide," *Atlanta Constitution*, January 25, 1966, 14.

199. Friedman, "André Courréges, Fashion Designer Who Redefined Couture."

200. Quote from Mary Quant is taken from Brenda Polan and Roger Tredre, *The Great Fashion Designers* (New York: Berg, 2009), 103-4.

201. Raymonde Alexander, "Rain Boots Get in a Fashion Whirl; Most Varieties a Far Cry from Galoshes," *Atlanta Constitution*, December 7, 1965, 21.

202. Opening credits of the U.S. version are described from a clip posted to YouTube, https://www.youtube.com/watch?v=frFWpzwos4I, accessed June 26, 2016.

203. According to Macnee, this was because Diana Rigg disliked wearing leather and insisted on a new line of fabric athletic wear for the fifth series. See Patrick Macnee and Dave Rogers, *The Avengers and Me* (New York: TV Books, 1997).

204. "Women's Boots Are Going Up," *Atlanta Constitution*, January 13, 1964, 24.

205. "Fashion: Ideas from the Paris Boutiques," *Vogue*, April 15, 1963, 63.

206. Angela Taylor, "Boots: In Snow or Cold or Even When It's Mild," *New York Times*, December 23, 1966, 29.

207. Alison Adburgham, "Mainly for Women: Paris Fashion Follow-up," *Guardian*, August 12, 1966, 8.

208. Raymonde Alexander, "Boots Keep the Knees Warm under Short Skirts," *Atlanta Constitution*, July 15, 1966, 31.

209. John Hart, "Rome Fashion," *Guardian*, July 22, 1966, 10.

210. Gloria Emerson, "Does New

York Outrank Paris from the Fashion Standpoint?," *Atlanta Constitution*, August 9, 1966, 14.

211. "Vogue's Eye View: Boots for a Heroine," *Vogue*, October 1, 1966, 181.

212. Angela Taylor, "Boots: In Snow or Cold," 29.

213. See Sheppard, "They All Laughed at Her White Boots," C3; Wilson, "Beth Levine, 'First Lady of Shoe Design," C10; Verin, *Beth Levine Shoes*, 50.

214. See Bergstein, *Women from the Ankle Down*, 105–12.

CHAPTER 5:
THE AGE OF THE BOOT

215. Gilles Verlant, *Gainsbourg: The Biography* (Los Angeles, TamTam Books, 2012).

216. Christy, "A Society Is Revealed by Its Women's Shoes?."

217. The Altamont Speedway Free Festival, held in December 1969, was marred by violence, accidental deaths, and the killing of a concertgoer by Hells Angels; Charles Manson and his followers committed a series of nine murders at four locations in California over a period of five weeks in the summer of 1969; the Tet Offensive, a campaign of surprise attacks by Viet Cong and the North Vietnamese Army against military and civilian commands and control centers throughout South Vietnam in January and February of 1968, is generally recognized as the point when the U.S. government and public realized that the war in Southeast Asia was unwinnable; civil rights leader Martin Luther King Jr. and Democratic presidential candidate Robert F. Kennedy were assassinated within two months of each other in 1968.

218. Phyllis Heathcote, "Paris Fashion: It's Not What You Wear It's the Way That You Wear It," *Guardian*, August 11, 1967.

219. It was also more than a little creepy.

220. Sheppard, "They All Laughed at Her White Boots."

221. Eugenia Sheppard, "Boots Become a Status Symbol," *Washington Post*, January 8, 1967.

222. Alison Adburgham, "The Shops in September," *Guardian*, August 31, 1967, 4.

223. Felicity Green, *Daily Record*, November 17, 1967.

224. Sheppard, "Boots Become a Status Symbol."

225. "Mini Dresses and Boots Take to Sky," *Washington Post*, March 24, 1967.

226. Phyllis Heathcote and Alison Adburgham, "Cardin . . . the Dangerous Divide," *Guardian*, July 29, 1967, 9.

227. *Australian Women's Weekly*, November 20, 1968, 114.

228. *Australian Women's Weekly*, March 6, 1968, 72.

229. "What People Are Wearing in Sydney—on Their Way to Work," *Australian Women's Weekly*, June 12, 1968, 96.

230. John Lennon, *Skywriting by Word of Mouth* (London: Harper and Row, 1986), 24.

231. Verlant, *Gainsbourg*.

232. *Australian Women's Weekly*, February 7, 1968, 92.

233. "Accents Shaped and Shimmering," *Washington Post*, July 1, 1968.

234. Marylin Bender, "Warm Weather or Not, Women Are Boot-Minded," *New York Times*, September 2, 1968.

235. Ibid.

236. Frances Cawthon, "Boots Go with Almost Anything Now," *Atlanta Constitution*, September 13, 1970,. 18G.

237. Enid Nemy, "The Great Boot Boom of '70: Expense, It Seems, Is No Object," *New York Times*, September 29, 1970.

238. Ibid.

239. "Mini Flou Flou," *Guardian*, January 29, 1970, 9.

240. Dale Cavanagh, "Knickers—Just Made for Boots," *Washington Post*, April 25, 1971.

241. Cawthon, "Boots Go with Almost Anything Now," 18G.

242. Angela Taylor and Bernadine Morris, "Knickers Hold Center Stage, but Shorts Are Waiting in the Wings," *New York Times*, December 26, 1970.

243. Cawthon, "Boots Go with Almost Anything Now."

244. Mary Ann Crenshaw, "Well, They Don't Have to Look Like Boots," *New York Times*, February 24, 1971.

245. Ibid.

246. "Bernadette Devlin Arriving for t he Court Case in Londonderry, Northern Ireland, December 1969," Alamy.com, Image ID B55JMM.

247. Accounts of Devlin's trial are taken from "Court Told Miss Devlin Urged Crowd to Attack," *Guardian*, December 16, 1969.

248. The comment was made by William Stratton Mills, the Unionist MP for North Belfast. See "'Castro' of

Ulster," *Guardian*, September 3, 1969.

249. Somini Sengupta, "Memories of a Proper Girl Who Was a Panther," *New York Times*, June 17, 2000.

250. See Mariann Wizard, "Warrior-Poet Marilyn Buck: No Wall Too Tall," *The Rag Blog*, May 19, 2010, Theragblog. blogspot.com, accessed July 14, 2016.

251. Margalit Fox, "Marilyn Buck," *New York Times*, August 5, 2010.

252. Dinitia Smith, "No Regrets for a Love of Explosives; in a Memoir of Sorts, a War Protestor Talks of Life with the Weathermen," *New York Times*, September 11, 2001; and Matt Bellassai, "The Dohrn Identity," *North by Northwestern*, February 29, 2012, northbynorthwestern.com, accessed September 16, 2016.

253. Bill Ayers, *Fugitive Days: Memoirs of an Anti-War Activist* (Boston: Beacon Press, 2002).

254. John Ardill, "The Girl Who Stays Out in the Cold," *Guardian*, October 30, 1969.

255. Nemy, "The Great Boot Boom of '70."

256. Raymonde Alexander, "Boots Are Going up to Meet Declining Skirts," *Atlanta Constitution*, July 9, 1970, 1B.

257. Bergstein, *Women from the Ankle Down*, 98.

258. Alexander, "Boots Are Going up to Meet Declining Skirts."

259. Sheppard, "They All Laughed at Her White Boots."

260. Alison Adburgham, "Paris Collections Autumn 1970," *Guardian*, July 28, 1970, 7.

261. Vincent Canby, "*L'Ors et la Poupée* (review)," *New York Times*, September 17, 1971.

262. Lauren Valenti, "Exclusive: Jane Fonda on the 40th Anniversary of *Klute*, Iconic Film Fashion, and Her Broken Pact with Sally Field," *Elle*, October 12, 2012, http://www.elle.com/culture/movies-tv/news/a22265/jane-fonda-klute-interview/, accessed September 21, 2016.

CHAPTER 6:
EVERYTHING OLD IS NEW AGAIN

263. Charko's reminiscences are taken from her blog. Kasia Charko, "Leicester College of Art and Leicester Market, the Vintage Clothing Addiction Begins," *Kasia Charko* (blog), November 12, 2012, https://kasiacharko.wordpress.com, accessed June 28, 2016.

264. "Fashion: The Shoe for Pants," *Vogue*, August 15, 1972, 70–71.

265. Shawn Levy, *Ready, Steady, Go! Swinging London and the Invention of Cool*

(London: Fourth Estate, 2003), 7.

266. Deirdre Clancy, *Costume Since 1945: Historical Dress from Couture to Street Style* (London: Bloomsbury Academic, 2015).

267. Ibid., 104.

268. Ibid., 105.

269. Kasia Charko, "Art and Entertainment, Leicester College of Art," *Kasia Charko* (blog), December 2, 2012, https://kasiacharko.wordpress.com, accessed June 28, 2016.

270. Details about the history of the Biba boot are taken from Barbara Hulanicki and Martin Pel, *The Biba Years, 1963–1975* (London: V&A Publishing, 2014), 138–39.

271. Cox, *Vintage Shoes*, 152.

272. Charko, "Art and Entertainment."

273. Sally Fawkes, "The Knickerbocker Glories," *Daily Mail*, July 22, 1970, 5.

274. Alison Adburgham, "Femme Chic and Tough Chick," *Guardian*, August 4, 1970, 7.

275. Ross, Nancy L., "As Midis Draw the Eyesight Downwards the Fashion Look Turns to Boots," *Washington Post*, August 22, 1970.

276. Angela Taylor, "For the Lower Hemlines, Higher Heels," *New York Times*, August 26, 1970.

277. Hart, John. "Black Masses." *The Guardian*, April 14, 1970, 9.

278. Searches run on the terms "boot" using the ProQuest archival platform for the *New York Times* and *Vogue*; "bottes" and "cuissardes" for *L'Officiel* at http://patrimoine. editionsjalou.com.

279. Alison Adburgham, "Legs and What Goes with Them," *Guardian*, February 9, 1971, 9.

280. "Fashion: The Shoe for Pants," *Vogue*, August 15, 1972, 70–71.

281. "Fashion: How to Look Marvelous and Beat the Weather," *Vogue*, October 15, 1972, 58–59.

282. "Fashion: Fashion Essentials: What You Wear with What," *Vogue*, August 1, 1973, 122–29.

283. Kasia Charko, "You're Not Going Out Like That, Are You?," *Kasia Charko* (blog), November 16, 2012, https://kasiacharko.wordpress.com, accessed June 28, 2016.

284. See Ionna Zikakou, "Killer Heels in Ancient Greece," *The Greek USA Reporter*, January 5, 2015, http://usa.greekreporter.com, accessed September 21, 2016.

285. See "Editorial: The Platform Shoe Is the Ugliest Style Conceived in the Modern History of Footwear," *Guardian*, May 3, 1973, 14; and Ruth Moss, "A Step Ahead of the Pain: Hold Your Feet High, They Don't Ache Alone . . . ," *Chicago Tribune*, May 2, 1974, 2.3. My vote for the best headline on this subject, however, is "Fashion Boots Step into Danger" (*Daily Mail*, October 25, 1973, 17), which sounds much more exciting than the actual article, a piece discussing a report on workplace hazards produced by U.K. Employment Secretary Maurice MacMillan, turned out.

286. Data sources: John Moores 1969–70; Grattan 1970–71; Freemans 1970–71; Janet Frazer 1971–72; Peter Craig 1971–72; Kays 1972–73; John Moores 1972–73; Janet Frazer 1973–74; Janet Frazer 1975–76; Littlewoods 1976–77; Grattan 1976–77; Trafford 1976–77; Grattan 1977–78; Marshall Ward 1978–79; Freemans 1979–80; Kays 1979–80. All autumn/winter editions.

287. Kasia Charko, "Kasia from Sacha, Sacha Shoe Shop Summer 1971," *Kasia Charko* (blog), February 2, 2013, https://kasiacharko.wordpress.com, accessed June 28, 2016.

288. Ibid.

289. "Devonshire wide-fitting boot in easy-care man-made material, fashionable metallic finish and top. Elasticated gusset at top, full side zip and comfortable foam lining. 3" platform, durable sole and 2–4" heel, Leg height approx. 16". Order the colour you want. Metallic-blue or metallic-brown. £10.99." *Janet Frazer Autumn/Winter 1973–74 Catalogue*, 199.

290. "Fashion boot in real leather with metallic finish. Shaped top, full-length side zip and 1½" platform. Durable sole and heel. Heel height 3", leg height 16" approx. Silver. £15.99." *Janet Frazer Autumn/Winter 1973–74 Catalogue*, 176.

291. "Fashion boot in easy-care vinyl with contrast red and yellow sections and comfortable foam lining. Full length side zip, 1" platform. Durable sole and heel. Heel height 3". Leg height 15". £8.99." *Janet Frazer Autumn/Winter 1973–74 Catalogue*, 177.

292. Charko, "Kasia from Sacha, Sacha Shoe Shop."

293. Alison Adburgham, "No Feathers in Lyon's Hat," *Guardian*, November 14, 1972, 13. The complaints about overly tight boot styles have been around for almost as long. See Alexandra Jacobs, "Das Boots: Women Beg for Torture, Wrapping Calves in Tight Leather," *New York Observer*, October 16, 2000; Claudia Connell, "Will ANY Boots Zip Up on a Normal Size Leg? How to Overcome the Challenge of Too-Tight Boots on the High Street," *Daily Mail*, October 21, 2015; and Gabrielle Dirvanauskas, "Can You Fit into Knee-High Boots from the High Street?," *Sun*, November 16, 2015.

294. Paul H. Steel, "Boot-Leg Phlebitis," *Journal of the American Medical Association* 218, no. 5: 739.

295. William A. Rossi, *The Sex Life of the Foot and Shoe* (New York: Saturday Review Press/E. P. Dutton, 1976), 166–67. Rossi (1910–2003) is a fascinating character who is revered by many podiatrists for his belief that shoes are the source of most foot ills and people would be better off without them. *The Sex Life of the Foot and Shoe* is probably his best-known work. In the words of his *Boston Globe* obituary, it "elicited laughs from laymen and knowing nods from shoe salesmen."

296. My wife, who is a petite woman, took one look and declared that there was no way she could get into them, despite their being notionally her size.

297. Charko, "Kasia from Sacha, Sacha Shoe Shop."

298. "Defying the 'Freeze'; the Boot That Never Ever Went Away, *Daily Mail*, January 7, 1974, 10.

299. Philip Norman, "The Quatro Gang," *Sunday Times* (London), April 6, 1975, 58(S).

300. Chris Hastings, "ABBA Admit They Only Wore Those Ridiculous Outfits to Avoid Tax! Forty Years after Waterloo, the Band Reveals Story of Their Success in Their Own Words and Unseen Pictures," *Daily Mail*, February 15, 2014.

301. Lyngstad was also wearing platforms, in snakeskin leather that was almost as outrageous. Sensibly, perhaps, she chose to cover them up with a floor-length skirt.

302. For data sources, see note 284 above.

303. Enid Nemy, "Boots Have Changed—Especially in Price: Droopy Look," *New York Times*, September 20, 1974, 47.

304. Ibid.

CHAPTER 7:
THE NEW EASE IN FASHION

304. Account and quotes taken from Georgia Dullea, "A Boot-in on 8th Ave.,"

New York Times, January 17, 1975, 39.

305. Ibid.

306. Nemy, "Boots Have Changed," 47.

307. Ibid.

308. The Mỹ Lai Massacre was the killing of between 350 and 500 unarmed civilians by U.S. troops in the South Vietnamese village of Mỹ Lai in March 1968.

309. In October 1973, Arab members of the Organization of Petroleum Exporting Countries (OPEC) instituted an oil embargo as a protest against U.S. support of Israel in the Yom Kippur War, which caused oil prices to rocket and had global economic effects that lasted for much of the decade; strikes by workers in a number of industries had major impacts in many countries, especially the United Kingdom; terrorism became a major global crisis, examples including sectarian killings in Northern Ireland, left-wing terrorism by groups like Germany's Baader-Meinhof gang, and the Palestinian armed struggle, of which the most notorious incident was the murder of Israeli athletes at the 1972 Munich Olympics.

310. For social history overviews of the decade from a U.K. and U.S. perspective, see Dominic Sandbrook, *Seasons in the Sun: The Battle for Britain, 1974-1979* (London: Allen Lane, 2012), and Bruce J. Schulman, *The Seventies: The Great Shift in American Culture, Society, and Politics* (New York: Free Press, 2001).

311. Brian L. Grant, *Back to the Land*, 2005, http://mcnweb2.mcn.com/backtotheland/, accessed September 21, 2016.

312. For a history of Frye, see Marc Kristal, *Frye: The Boots That Made History: 150 Years of Craftsmanship* (New York: Rizzoli, 2013).

313. Anne Roiphe, "Tweedledum and Tweedledee," *New York Times*, January 26, 1976, 256.

314. Ibid.

315. Michelle Baran, "Riding High: After More Than 140 Years of Bootmaking, Frye's Vast Archives Are Fueling a Fashion Renaissance," *FN: Footwear News* 60, no. 48 (2004): 24.

316. "Fashion: Fall Guidelines: The New Ease in Fashion," *Vogue*, July 1, 1974, 40-65.

317. Barbara Griggs, "For the Girl Who Likes a Little Loose Living," *Daily Mail*, August 19, 1974, 10.

318. "Fashion: Fall Guidelines," *Vogue*, 40-65.

319. Barbara Griggs, "Softly, Softly... the Dress Stealing the Autumn Show," *Daily Mail*, November 11, 1974, 16.

320. "Fashion: The Most Beautiful Shoes in Years!," *Vogue*, July 1, 1974, 69.

321. Kathryn Samuel, "Checklist for Autumn," *Daily Mail*, September 9, 1974, 11.

322. Nemy, "Boots Have Changed," 47.

323. Barbara Griggs, "I Predict . . . ," *Daily Mail*, January 3, 1975, 14-15.

324. Bernadine Morris, "Hemmed up," *New York Times*, May 3, 1977, 52.

325. Searches run on the terms "boot" using the ProQuest archival platform for the *New York Times* and *Vogue*; "bottes" and "cuissardes" for *L'Officiel* at http://patrimoine.editionsjalou.com.

326. Bernadine Morris, "Sweaters for the Fall: Very Thick, Very Long: The Russian Look," *New York Times*, April 8, 1974, 40.

327. Nemy, "Boots Have Changed," 47.

328. Dullea, "A Boot-in on 8th Ave.," 39.

329. "Russian Boots," *Manchester Guardian*, November 19, 1925, 8.

330. *Janet Frazer Autumn/Winter 1975-76 Catalogue*, 202.

331. Barbara Griggs, "Mystery of the Missing Baggy Boots," *Daily Mail*, November 4, 1974, 13.

332. Catalog data taken from John Moores 1969-70; Grattan 1970-71; Freemans 1970-71; Janet Frazer 1971-72; Peter Craig 1971-72; Kays 1972-73; John Moores 1972-73; Janet Frazer 1973-74; Janet Frazer 1975-76; Littlewoods 1976-77; Grattan 1976-77; Trafford 1976-77; Grattan 1977-78; Marshall Ward 1978-79; Freemans 1979-80; Kays 1979-80. All autumn/winter editions.

333. Mary Ann Crenshaw, "Lesser Boots," *New York Times*, November 2, 1975, 273.

334. Barbara Griggs, "Bootnote... Down to Earth Detail," *Daily Mail*, March 31, 1977, 15.

335. Bernadine Morris, "At Lagerfeld's Paris Show, the 18th Century Goes Modern," *New York Times*, March 29, 1977, 41.

336. Bernadine Morris, "Message Is in from Paris—Bubbly, Bloused and Billowy," *New York Times*, April 5, 1977, 24.

337. "Chloeallure: Beautiful Costumes from the Dressing-Up Box," *Vogue UK*, September 1977, 126-29.

338. Nina S. Hyde, "Paris Fashions: Casanova to Puss 'n' Boots," *Washington Post*, March 29, 1977, B3.

339. Morris, "Hemmed Up," 52.

340. "Shoe Signals," *Vogue*, July 1977, 98-103; and "Walk Right In. . . . All the Terrific New Stockings & Socks, Shoes & Boots," *Vogue*, July 1977, 142-43.

341. Barbara Griggs, "The Move to the Mini—They've Not Given Up!," *Daily Mail*, March 28, 1977, 18.

342. Barbara Griggs, "Look Closer, It's the New French Revolution . . . !," *Daily Mail*, March 31, 1977, 14.

343. "Paris/Milan: The New Soft Dressing," *Vogue*, August 1977, 128-43.

344. Ibid.

345. Shirley Morris, "Fashion in Boots: Your Choice, Short or Long," *Toronto Star*, September 14, 1978, C-8.

346. Bernadine Morris, "New Convertible Boots Rise or Fall to Any Occasion," *New York Times*, December 26, 1978, 17.

347. Angela Neustatter, "Putting the Boot On: Angela Neustatter Suggests What Well-Heeled Feet Will Be Wearing This Winter," *Guardian*, September 9, 1977, 11.

348. "New Life for Old Boots," *Toronto Star*, November 24, 1977, E-1.

349. Griggs, "Look Closer, It's the New French Revolution . . . !," 14.

350. Carol Troy and Caterine Milinaire, *Cheap Chic: Hundreds of Money Saving Hints to Create Your Own Great Look* (New York: Harmony Books, 1975).

351. "Styles in Paris Kick Long Boots Out of Fashion," *Atlanta Constitution*, August 6, 1978, 6F.

CHAPTER 8:
A SHARPER EDGE

352. Description of Blondie's performance is taken from *The Old Grey Whistle Test, Vol. 1* (BBC Video, September 16, 2003), DVD.

353. Sable Starr and Blondie singer Debbie Harry, photo by Ron Galella/WireImage (Getty Images #81898634), February 9, 1977.

354. Today she's more famous as a classical crossover singer, but Brightman started out as a dancer in Arlene Phillips's provocative troupe Hot Gossip. Her ability to more than carry a tune led to her singing the lead on the group's hit single (and shameless *Star Wars* cash-in), "I Lost My Heart to a Starship Trooper" (1978).

355. Blonde on Blonde consisted of

two former pinup models, Nina Carter and Jilly Johnson. They were probably most famous for their disco version of Led Zeppelin's "Whole Lotta Love," released in 1979. They were huge in Japan (apparently).

356. "Styles in Paris Kick Long Boots Out of Fashion," *Atlanta Constitution*, 6F.

357. Anne-Marie Schiro, "Ladylike Pumps Are Back: A 1950's Favorite Returns; Pump Found Outpacing the Rest," *New York Times*, September 15, 1979, 8.

358. Elaine Louie, "Coping with the Cost," *New York Times Magazine*, August 26, 1979, 250.

359. "Stepping Lively," *New York Times Magazine*, August 12, 1979, 42–43

360. Louie, "Coping with the Cost."

361. Anne-Marie Schiro, "For Fall, the Dressy Look Is a Well-Suited One; For This Fall: A Well-Suited Look," *New York Times*, September 16, 1979, NJ21.

362. "Vogue's Point of View, July 1979. What You're Going to Want This Fall . . . and Why," *Vogue*, July 1, 1979, 121.

363. Schiro, "Ladylike Pumps Are Back."

364. Ibid.

365. Bernadine Morris, "French Ready-to-Wear: The Ever-Changing Message," *New York Times*, April 13, 1979, A12.

366. Louie, "Coping with the Cost."

367. "Vogue's Point of View, July 1979," 121.

368. Katherine Madden, "Vogue's View," *Vogue*, September 1, 1979, 440.

369. Andrea Aurichio, "East End Look: Casual, but Elegant," *New York Times*, September 16, 1979, LI21.

370. Ibid.

371. Mary Russell, "Paris: The Forecast for Fall," *New York Times Magazine*, March 30, 1980, 75.

372. "Fashion: Differences in the New Non-Stop Appeal for Feet and Legs," *Vogue*, July 1, 1980, 170–77.

373. Searches run on the terms "boot" using the ProQuest archival platform for the *New York Times* and *Vogue*; "bottes" and "cuissardes" for *L'Officiel* at http://patrimoine.editionsjalou.com.

374. Anne-Marie Schiro, "High-Style Boots at Popular Prices," *New York Times*, September 1, 1981, A16.

375. Joni Wooldridge, "The New Boot That Balances," *New York Times Magazine*, July 10, 1981, 32.

376. Ibid.

377. Ibid.

378. Schiro, "High-Style Boots at Popular Prices."

379. Jeanne Clare Feron, "The Careful Shopper: Shoe Bazaar Offers More Than Footwear," *New York Times*, December 6, 1981.

380. Wooldridge, "The New Boot That Balances," 32.

381. John Duka, "Notes on Fashion," *New York Times*, May 4, 1982, C2.

382. Bernadine Morris, "Saint Laurent: No Fuss, Just Style," *New York Times*, April 1, 1982, C8.

383. Bernadine Morris, "Fashions Afoot in Milan," *New York Times*, October 31, 1982, A12.

384. John Duka, "Notes on Fashion," *New York Times*, March 16, 1982, B6.

385. Elizabeth Ewing and Alice Mackrell, *History of 20th Century Fashion*, 3d ed. (New York: Costume & Fashion Press, 1992).

386. Ibid.

387. Ibid.

388. Ibid.

389. Priscilla Tucker, "Fashions to Please a Lady," *New York Times*, April 10, 1983, AS54.

390. Patricia McColl, "Fall Fashion Preview," *New York Times Magazine*, March 6, 1983, SM66.

391. Angela Taylor, "Far from the Classic Pump," *New York Times*, August 30, 1983, C10.

392. John Duka, "Notes on Fashion," *New York Times*, December 11, 1984, C18.

393. Bill Cunningham, "On the Bright Side," *New York Times*, January 6, 1985, SM47.

394. Bernardine Morris, "Fall Sportswear: A Wide Range of Themes," *New York Times*, May 3, 1985, B10.

395. Ibid.

396. "Vogue's Last Word: New Shoes, New Boots—for Setting Up the Coming Season/The Best Dressing in Long or in Short Skirts . . . ," *Vogue*, July 1 1986, 230.

397. Ibid.

398. Ibid.

399. Anne-Marie Schiro, "Notes on Fashion," *New York Times*, July 8, 1986, B6.

400. "Vogue's Last Word: New Shoes, New Boots," *Vogue*, 230

401. Bernadine Morris, "Calvin Klein's American Tour de Force," *New York Times*, April 8, 1987, C1.

402. Bernadine Morris, "Saint Laurent at Top of His Form," *New York Times*, March 26, 1987, C1.

403. "Health Style: Q & A: Can Exer-cise Cause Weight Gain?/Boots: Healthy for Feet?," *Vogue*, January 1, 1988, 233.

404. Ibid.

405. Linda Wells, "A Look at Knees: Rarely Objects of Beauty, Knees Are Now the Subjects," *New York Times*, August 23, 1987, SMA182.

406. "Guinevere," *Vogue UK*, August 1, 1988, 114–21.

407. "Vogue's View—Ornamentation Reigns," *Vogue*, November 1, 1988, 105–7

408. Bernadette Morra, "History, Heritage Add Eclectic Touch," *Toronto Star*, September 1, 1988.

409. "Vogue's View—Sure Shoe-ins," *Vogue*, July 1, 1988, 130, 132.

410. Summary of Fawn Hall's congressional testimony is taken from Maureen Dowd, "The Fawn Hall Story: A Big Hit on the Hill," *New York Times*, June 9, 1987.

CHAPTER 9:

THE YEAR OF THE BOOT

411. Data sources are as follows: *Vogue Archive*, 1892–2014 via ProQuest.com; *New York Times*, 1851–2010 via ProQuest Historical Newspapers; *Les archives de L'Officiel De La Mode*, 1921–2013 via Jalou Galleries.

412. Candy Pratts Price, "Elements," *Vogue*, October 1, 1989, 166.

413. "Fashion: Couture Report," *Vogue*, October 1, 1989, 358–69.

414. Andre Leon Talley, "Fall 1990: Design Inspiration," *Vogue*, July 1, 1990,. 138–61.

415. Anne-Marie Schiro, "For Fall, Stylish Feet (and Knees) Are Covered Up," *New York Times*, August 12, 1990, 48.

416. Ibid.

417. Ibid.

418. Ibid.

419. Ibid.

420. Alex Comfort, *Joy of Sex*; see also Chapter 1, this volume.

421. "Management Views Office Fashions," *New York Times*, July 14, 1968.

422. For examples, see *Fiesta* 2, no. 1 (March 1968): cover; *Fiesta* 2, no. 2, (April 1968): 29–30; *Fiesta* 2, no. 5 (July 1969): cover, 30–31; *Mayfair* 4, no. 1 (January 1969): cover; and *Mayfair* 4, no. 2 (February 1969): 37–42.

423. For a couple of examples of this, see Claire Coleman, "Thigh-High Boots Are the Next Big Thing—but Who Will Dare to Wear Them?," *Daily Mail*, July 30, 2009; and Kristyn Schiavone, "How to Wear Over-the-Knee Boots," *Chicago Tribune*, March 10, 2011.

424. Bernadine Morris, "Paris in Perspective: Outdoors to Outrageous," *New York Times*, July 31, 1990, B6.

425. "Rock 'n Royalty," *Vogue*, October 1, 1990, 328–45.

426. Woody Hochswedder, "Reporter's Notebook: In Paris, Ghastly Music and Frye Boots," *New York Times*, March 21, 1991, C10.

427. "Wild at Heart," *Vogue*, September 1, 1991, 484.

428. Bill Cunningham, "On the Street: Boots a la Brando, Dean and Harley," *New York Times*, November 3, 1991, 59.

429. A complete set of images of Versace's 1991 fall/winter collection is available via the *Vogue* website at http://www.vogue.com/fashion-shows/fall-1991-ready-to-wear/versace, accessed September 26, 2016.

430. "Vogue's View: To Boot," *Vogue*, August 1, 1992, 262–65.

431. Dodie Kazanjian, "Getting the Boot," *Vogue*, August 1, 1993, 230–35, 310.

432. "Last Look: The Year of the Boot," *Vogue*, September 1, 1993, 600–3.

433. Kazanjian, "Getting the Boot," 230–35, 310.

434. Ibid.

435. "Last Look: The Year of the Boot," *Vogue*, 600–3.

436. James Sherwood, "These Boots Were Made for Clubbing," *Guardian*, June 30, 1994, A7.

437. Searches run on the terms "boot" using the ProQuest archival platform for the *New York Times* and *Vogue*; "bottes" and "cuissardes" for *L'Officiel* at http://patrimoine.editionsjalou.com.

438. See "Last Look: The Year of the Boot," *Vogue*, 600–3; and Vicki Woods, "Look of the Moment: Year of the Boot," *Vogue*, August 2001, 684–95.

439. Bernadine Morris, "Marc Jacobs, On His Own, Wins the Crowd," *New York Times*, April 11, 1994, B9.

440. Bernadette Morra, "High Hopes: Were These Shoes Made for Walking?," *Toronto Star*, September 24, 1994, H1.

441. "Rossellini Models Genny's Minis in Milan," *Toronto Star*, March 10, 1994, E2.

442. Bernadine Morris, "With Color and Lots of Shine, Versace Designs a la Courréges," *New York Times*, March 3, 1994, C1.

443. Morra, "High Hopes," H1.

444. Anne-Marie Schiro, "By Design: Patent Is Back," *New York Times*, July 19, 1994, B6.

445. Amy M. Spindler, "Patterns: Glamour, and the Shoe Fits," *New York Times*, August 23, 1994, B7.

446. "Fantastic Plastic . . . and Other Wild Ideas," *Vogue*, July 1, 1994, 124– 129.

447. Bernadine Morris, "Yves Saint Laurent Dreams of China," *New York Times*, July 21, 1994, C1.

448. Bernadine Morris, "Lauren Takes an English Holiday: Of Tunics and Chain Mail," *New York Times*, April 13, 1994, C12.

449. "Last Look: The Boot Is Taking a Serious Cut for Fall," *Vogue*, October 1, 1995, 382.

450. Morris, "With Color and Lots of Shine," C1.

451. "The Smart Guide to Autumn," *Guardian*, September 23, 1995, B9.

452. Thrift, "Boot Leggers," A8.

453. Amy M. Spindler, "Prada, D&G, Ferretti: Three Shades of Cool: Invoking Monica Vitti and Courréges in Milan," *New York Times*, March 10, 1995, B6.

454. Anne-Marie Schiro, "Hollywood on a Runway," *New York Times*, March 7, 1995, B8.

455. Anne-Marie Schiro, "Return of the Lady and the Mod," *New York Times*, July 25, 1995, A12.

456. Nancy Jane Hastings, "Down at the Heels," *Toronto Star*, October 5, 1995, D6.

457. Schiro, "Return of the Lady and the Mod."

458. Constance C. R. White, "For CK, a Big Step in a New Direction," *New York Times*, February 28, 1995, B6.

459. Tracy Achor Hayes, "Step into Style with the Appropriate Fall Footgear," *Toronto Star*, September 7, 1995, F6.

460. Anne-Marie Schiro, "The Shoe That Will Be on Every Woman's Foot," *New York Times*, July 25, 1996, B8.

461. Anne-Marie Schiro, "By Design: The Right Skirt Is a Long Skirt," *New York Times*, October 15, 1996, B9.

462. Suzy Menkes, "In the World of Fashion, Leather Is Indestructible," *New York Times*, September 22, 1994, 49.

463. Sarah Van Sicklen, "Last Look: Tall Boots with a Sexy Heel Are Following in the Footsteps of Fashion Toward Long, Lean with a Curvy Fit," *Vogue*, October 1, 1997, 382.

464. Anne-Marie Schiro, "By Design: As the Mercury Drops, Boots Rise," *New York Times*, November 18, 1996, B15.

465. Sarah Van Sicklen, "Last Look: Pointed Toes, Ice-Pick Heels," *Vogue*, September 1, 1997, 734.

466. Amy M. Spindler, "The Decade That Won't Go Away," *New York Times*, October 12, 1997, ST1.

467. Van Sicklen, September 1, 1997. Ibid.

CHAPTER 10:
INTO THE NEW MILLENIUM

468. The Brit Awards are the British Phonographic Industry's annual pop music awards.

469. *An Audience with Kylie Minogue*, directed by Tony Gregory, LWT/ITV, broadcast October 6, 2001.

470. Hajime Sorayama (b. 1947) is a Tokyo-based artist best known for his precisely detailed, hand-painted, and airbrushed portrayals of women and of feminine, biomechanoid robots.

471. Known as the "Silvanemesis" act, this was the show opener—an instrumental introduction of "The Sound of Music," then Minogue would rise out of the stage encased in the metallic Kyborg. This would then peel back to reveal Kylie in a silver bra and miniskirt and the matching Jimmy Choo boots.

472. Nemy, "The Great Boot Boom of '70."

473. "My Style," *Marie Claire*, September 2002, 154.

474. "Shopping: Accessories," *Marie Claire*, July 1999, 250.

475. Ibid.

476. "From Fab to Frugal," *New York Post*, December 9, 2002, 39–40.

477. "Shopping: Accessories," *Marie Claire*, 250.

478. Spindler, "Prada, D&G, Ferretti," B6; Anne-Marie Schiro, "By Design: Small Touches That Add Up," *New York Times*, March 24, 1998, B9; and Anne-Marie Schiro, "By Design: Winter (and Fall) White," *New York Times*, September 22, 1998, A28.

479. "Showteile—Mode-Entertainment auf hohem Niveau: die neuen Stiefel," *Vogue Germany*, August 1999.

480. "Fashion: Fall Style '99," *Marie Claire*, September 1999, 89.

481. "The First Step," *Marie Claire*, July 1999, 173–83

482. Jacobs, "Das Boots."

483. *Charlie's Angels* (2000) was a movie based on the 1970s TV series of the same name, starring Cameron Diaz, Drew Barrymore, and Lucy Liu. The characters' footwear featured a significant number of ankle and knee-length stiletto boots. *Almost Famous* (2000) was a semi-autobiographical movie by Cameron Crowe about life on the road with a

rock band in the early 1970s. Female characters' outfits tended toward the boho look, with a lot of boots.

484. Jacobs, "Das Boots."

485. Ibid.

486. Ibid.

487. Woods, "Look of the Moment," 684–95.

488. Ibid.

489. Rebecca Mead, "Strategy Session: The Pipeline," *The New Yorker*, January 10, 2011, www.newyorker.com, accessed September 26, 2016.

490. Jose F. Blanco, Scott Leff, Ann T. Kellogg, and Lynn W. Payne, *The Greenwood Encyclopedia of Clothing Through American History, 1900 to the Present* (Westport, CT: Greenwood Press, 2008), 242; Michelle Slatalla, "Tall Boots? Low Heels? High Drama," *New York Times*, October 13, 2005; Sarah Baker, "The Ten Best . . . Boots," *Daily Telegraph*, September 21, 2005; and Clare Coulson, "Fabulous Looks to Fall for This Autumn," *Daily Telegraph*, September 30, 2003.

491. For some examples, see Samantha McIntyre, "Style Watch: The Thigh's the Limit!," *People*, November 26, 2001, 159.

492. Ibid.

493. "Style Watch: High Notes," *People*, November 10, 2003, 158.

494. Clip accessed on YouTube, July 19, 2016. Ripa was wearing the boots in response to the (ever-so-slightly unhealthy) enthusiasm shown by co-host Regis Philbin to a piece on the popularity of fashion boots ("Bootylicious!") that they had done the previous day.

495. Anna Schneider Mayerson, "Pusses in Boots, '05," *New York Observer*, January 17, 2005.

496. Quotes taken from Schneider Mayerson,"Pusses in Boots."

497. Clare Coulson, "How to Do Skinny," *Daily Telegraph*, November 16, 2005.

498. Justine Picardie, "Boots Advantage Points," *Daily Telegraph*, January 29, 2006; "Your Fall Boot Guide," *People Style Watch*, October 2012, 202–9; and "50 Best Winter Boots for 2012," *Daily Telegraph*, October 26, 2012.

499. Michelle Baran, "Riding High: After More Than 140 Years of Bootmaking, Frye's Vast Archives Are Fueling a Fashion Renaissance," *FN: Footwear News* 60, no. 48: 24.

500. Neina Hodzic Poplata, "How to Achieve the Boho Chic Look: 6 Staple Pieces," *Club Fashionista*, September 2013, clubfashionista.blogspot.com, accessed September 26, 2016.

501. For some examples, see Olivia Bergin, "Trend Alert: Over-the-Knee Boots," *Daily Telegraph*, July 10, 2009; "Over-the-Knee Boots Have Sky-High Style," *Detroit Free Press*, December 19, 2010; and "Winter 2010's Recurring Trend: Over The Knee Boots," *Times of the Internet*, November 9, 2010, http://www.timesoftheinternet.com, accessed November 22, 2010.

502. "Reach for the Thighs," *Marie Claire*, October 2009, 26.

503. For examples, see Danielle Datu, "These Boots Were Made for Strutting," MyStyle.com, January 7, 2008, accessed July 10, 2010; "Fall 2009 Trend Report: Over-the-Knee Please," Coutorture.com, March 30, 2009, accessed July 10, 2010; and Sharon Haver, "How to Wear Over-the-Knee Boots," FocusOnStyle.com, December 19, 2008, accessed July 10, 2010.

504. Kathryn Shattuck, "Goodbye 'Good Wife.' Hello Spy Life," *New York Times*, September 11, 2016, AR2.

505. Frazier Moore, "Archie Panjabi Heats Up CBS Drama 'The Good Wife,'" Boston.com, November 11, 2011, accessed October 5, 2016; and Amy Raphael, "Archie Panjabi: 'I Love Roles Which Transform Me,'" *Guardian*, September 4, 2010.

506. Daniel Lawson, "Stylewatch with Daniel Lawson," *CBS Blog—The Good Wife* (blog), April 15, 2011, archived at web.archive.org, accessed October 5, 2016.

507. Shattuck, "Goodbye 'Good Wife.'"

508. Kristen Henning, "Celebrity Shoe Trend: Stuart Weitzman Highland Boots," Footwearnews.com, December 9, 2015, accessed December 30, 2015; and Alison Payer, "The Boots Every Celebrity Has Worn Lately," WhoWhatWear.com, November 6, 2015, accessed December 30, 2015.

509. Brittany Talarico, "Boots All the Victoria's Secret Angels Are Wearing (Pre-Runway Stilettos and Wings, Obvs)," *People*, November 10, 2015.

510. "Stuart Weitzman Celebrates 20th Anniversary of the Iconic 5050 Boot with the Launch of a Digital Pop-up Shop on Gilt.com," *PR Newswire*, October 17, 2013, accessed August 2, 2016.

511. "What has been will be again,

what has been done will be done again; there is nothing new under the sun," Ecclesiastes 1:9.

512. "Shop It! Fall Boot Guide," *InStyle*, September 2015, 404–10.

513. Marcus Fairs, "It's the End of Fashion as We Know It" Says Li Edelkoort," *DeZeen*, March 1, 2015, dezeen.com, accessed August 2, 2016.

514. Kimberley Chrisman-Campbell, "Is This the End for Fashion Week?," *The Atlantic*, February 11, 2016.

515. Alyson Walsh, "Don't Dress Your Age—Modern Women Know It's about Style Not Fashion Rules for Over Forties," *Daily Telegraph*, October 26, 2016, www.telegraph.co.uk, accessed October 27, 2016.

516. Desmond Morris, *Manwatching: A Field Guide to Human Behavior* (New York: H. N. Abrams, 1977).

517. Samantha Sutton, "Solve 2016's Outfit Dilemmas before They Happen with These 45 Fashion Hacks: #22—Give Lampshading a Go," *Pop Sugar*, December 31, 2015, www.popsugar.com, accessed September 26, 2016; Laura Jane Turner, "Kardashians Lead the Pack with 'Lampshading' Trend," *The Look*, December 7, 2015, www.look.co.uk, accessed September 26, 2016; and Meghan Blalock, "Lampshading, the New Celeb Style Trend You Need to Know About," *WhoWhatWear*, December 2, 2015, www.whowhatwear.com, accessed September 26, 2016.

518. "Trends You Can Only Find at College," *The Odyssey*, March 26, 2015, www.theodyssey.com, accessed September 23, 2016.

519. Carly Stern, "Here's a Bright Fashion Idea: The Unlikeliest New Trend Sees Stars Like Kendall Jenner, Gigi Hadid, and Rihanna Taking Style Inspiration from LAMPSHADES," *Daily Mail*, December 28, 2015, www.dailymail.com, accessed September 23, 2016. Personally, I think the *Daily Mail* ought to learn more about what the "mod" look actually means. Their version sounds more like Austin Powers.

Bergstein, Rachelle. *Women from the Ankle Down*. New York: Harper Perennial, 2012.

Bossan, Marie-Josèphe. *The Art of the Shoe*. New York: Parkstone International, 2015.

Clancy, Deirdre. *Costume Since 1945: Historical Dress from Couture to Street Style*. London: Bloomsbury Academic, 2015.

Cox, Caroline. *Vintage Shoes*. New York: HarperCollins, 2008.

Ewing, Elizabeth, and Alice Mackrell. *History of 20th Century Fashion*, 3d ed. New York: Costume & Fashion Press, 1992.

Hennessey, Kathryn, ed. *Fashion: The Definitive History of Costume and Style*. London: Dorling Kindersley, 2012.

Howell, Georgina. *In Vogue: 60 Years of Celebrities and Fashion from British Vogue*. London: Penguin Books, 1978.

Hulanicki, Barbara, and Martin Pel. *The Biba Years: 1963–1975*. London: Victoria and Albert Museum, 2014.

Koda, Harold, and Andrew Bolton. *Poiret*. New York: Metropolitan Museum of Art, 2007.

Mouzat, Virginie, and Colombe Pringle. *Roger Vivier*. New York: Rizzoli, 2013.

Pattison, Angela, and Nigel Cawthorne. *A Century of Shoes*. New York: Chartwell Books, 1997.

Quinn, Bradley. *The Boot*. London: Lawrence King Publishing, 2010.

Rossi, William A. *The Sex Life of the Foot and Shoe*. New York: Saturday Review Press/E. P. Dutton, 1976.

Steele, Valerie. *Shoes: A Lexicon of Style*. New York: Rizzoli, 1999.

Verin, Helene. *Beth Levine Shoes*. New York: Stewart, Tabori & Chang, 2009.

Walford, Jonathan. *The Seductive Shoe*. New York: Stewart, Tabori, & Chang, 2007.

Walford, Jonathan. *Sixties Fashion: From Less Is More to Youthquake*. London: Thames & Hudson, 2013.

Whitley, Lauren. *Hippie Chic*. Boston: MFA Publications, 2013.

bibliog-raphy

index